David Austin, Jonathan Edwards, Joseph Bellamy

The Millennium

Or the thousand years of prosperity, promised to the Church of God, in the Old Testament and in the New, shortly to commence, and to be carried on to perfection, under the auspices of Him, who in the vision, was presented to St. John

David Austin, Jonathan Edwards, Joseph Bellamy

The Millennium
Or the thousand years of prosperity, promised to the Church of God, in the Old Testament and in the New, shortly to commence, and to be carried on to perfection, under the auspices of Him, who in the vision, was presented to St. John

ISBN/EAN: 9783337425906

Printed in Europe, USA, Canada, Australia, Japan

Cover: Foto ©Lupo / pixelio.de

More available books at **www.hansebooks.com**

THE MILLENNIUM;

OR, THE

THOUSAND YEARS OF PROSPERITY;

PROMISED TO THE

CHURCH OF GOD;

IN THE OLD TESTAMENT AND IN THE NEW;

SHORTLY TO

COMMENCE,

AND TO BE CARRIED ON TO

PERFECTION,

UNDER THE AUSPICES OF *HIM*,

WHO, IN THE *VISION*, WAS PRESENTED TO St. *JOHN*.

AND I SAW, AND, BEHOLD, A WHITE HORSE; AND HE THAT SAT ON HIM HAD A BOW; AND A CROWN WAS GIVEN UNTO HIM: AND HE WENT FORTH CONQUERING AND TO CONQUER.

We are journeying unto the place, of which the Lord said, I will give it you: come thou with us, and we will do thee good, for the Lord hath spoken good concerning Israel. MOSES.

ELIZABETH TOWN:
PRINTED BY SHEPARD KOLLOCK—1794.

PREFACE.

IF the prophetic parts of the oracles of God, from what may be stiled "a sacred Calendar;" or, "an Almanac of Prophecy," it is with the greatest propriety, that the Watchmen of Zion are disposed, now and then, to consult this sacred calendar, in view of determining the watch of the night, and, of consequence, how long before the arrival of the long-wished-for promised day. From promises which the sacred scriptures afford, calculations may, with a good degree of precision, be made, respecting the time of the accomplishments of the prophecies which relate to the future prosperity of the Zion of God. The redemption of the church of God from the bondage of Papal Babylon, as well as from the general dominion of the Powers of Darkness, is a glorious and animating subject of prophecy. The Lord hath spoken, and the decree shall be fulfilled.—If, in ancient time, the people of God believed what the Lord had spoken respecting the redemption of his people; if, from the sacred calendar, they discovered the time of the promised redemption—prayed for, and actually saw the fulfilment of the object of their hopes, in temporal and in spiritual deliverance, what forbids that, in this day *of general captivity, the prophets of the Lord should look with the same faith and prayer for the fulfilment of those promises which respect the spiritual deliverance of the Christian Church, both from the bondage of Babylon, and from the thraldom of Satan?*—And more especially, as we evidently see marks of the divine progress in this work, in his present judgments among the nations of the earth, and particularly on mystical Babylon; which all allow, are but a little to precede the glorious redemption and prosperity of the Church in the Millennial-day. —" One circumstance, saith Dr. Hallifax,* ought not to be passed by unnoticed— namely, the menaces of certain vengeance to be hereafter inflicted on the enemies of the true religion, intimated by the destruction of the body of the fourth beast; and *subsequent to that* the promise of the universal establishment of the reign of Christ, when *the stone cut out of the mountain without hands,* shall strike and *break to pieces the image on its feet; and become a great mountain, and fill the whole earth.* This part of the prophecies is yet unfulfilled; nor is it for us to ascertain

NOTE.

* Hallifax's Sermon, preached at Bishop Warburton's Lecture, Lincoln's-Inn Chapel, London, page 96, published 1776.

the manner in which so important a revolution, in the religious world, will be effected: The use intended by the observation here is, from the symptoms of decline which are now discernible in the system of the Papal power, to point out to you the presumption that arises in favor of the truth of the prophetical denunciations, and from the concussions which have already shook the tottering throne of superstition, to learn to expect, in God's good time, *its full and final demolition."*

And if this celebrated Author, in his day, thought there was ground to use the following language, in view of prophecies already fulfilled, and events then existing, with how much more reason may we confidently adopt it now, and say, that, " under the auspices of such a guide we may hope to advance, securely, in our projected work; and to have the pleasure of those, who, after long travelling in a dreary night, perceive, at last, the darkness to diminish, and the reddening streaks of the morning, betokening to them, that the day is at hand?"—

The object in publishing Dr. Bellamy's discourse is to establish the doctrine of the Millennium as to matter of fact: and by publishing President Edwards's " Humble Attempt to promote explicit Agreement and visible Union in Prayer;" *it is hoped attention will be excited to the use of those means which God hath ordained to be used in view of a gracious fulfilment of every promise made to his Church and to his People.* Thus saith the Lord, I will yet for this be enquired of by the house of Israel, to do it for them.

The design of the third and last discourse is to support the objects of the two former, by an appeal to existing facts, to the demonstration of present events. By these it appears, that what Dr. Hallifax termed " the reddening streaks of the morning," *have become entitled to the stile of the* dawn, *if not to the* morning of the day.—*How does our faith grow—our confidence increase, and our joyful hearts exult at the sight, or rather at the sound of the stately steppings of our God in the present revolutions of his providence, fulfilling the purposes of his great decree!—From what we observe to have, already, taken place, may we not confidently anticipate all that is to come?*—The testimony of Jesus, *faith the angel to St. John,* is a spirit of prophecy.—*If, in a spirit of prophecy, the Great Head of the Church hath spoken of things to come, to strengthen the faith, and to cheer the hope of his followers, it can-*

PREFACE.

not be denied, but our time and talents are well employed, whilst, in study, with meekness and prayer, we labor to understand and to possess the blessings he hath so graciously prepared, and so abundantly promised to his Church.

If, in the day in which President Edwards lived, it was thought time for the Zion of God to go into labor, in view of the approach of the time of promised redemption to Israel, with how much more courage and confidence may the Church of God now proceed in the arduous, yet noble and interesting work?

The arguments which his invaluable tract suggests for explicit Agreement and visible Union of God's People in extraordinary Prayer, for the Revival of Religion, and the Advancement of Christ's Kingdom on Earth, pursuant to Scripture-promises and Prophecies, concerning the LAST TIME, are as applicable to the state of the Church, and of the world, now, as they were then, and the encouragement, from present circumstances, much more animating.

If any individual Christian, any society of Christian People, or any Minister, or association of Ministers, should be so far impressed with the propriety of a present compliance with what President Edwards labored to bring about in his day, as to desire that measures should be taken for the accomplishment of the object of his work, and express a willingness to aid in laying a foundation for a general and united exertion in prayer throughout all the Christian Churches in our land; the Editor pledges his whole heart in aid to any such proposal, and would think himself highly favored by any communications, from any quarter, on the sublime and animating subject.

That the Great Head of the Church would graciously take this humble attempt to the honor of his name, and for the interests of his Zion, under his holy protection, and prosper, and do his own blessed will in all things which it strives to accomplish, is the fervent prayer of one, who knows no higher object of present or future ambition, than to approve himself, and to be approved of his Lord and Master, as an industrious hewer of wood, and drawer of water for the church of God.

DAVID AUSTIN.

Elizabeth Town,
May 1, 1794.

THE MILLENNIUM.

BY

JOSEPH BELLAMY, A. M.
MINISTER OF THE GOSPEL AT BETHLEM.

[*First published at Boston in 1758.*]

REVELATION xx. 1, 2, 3.
And I saw an angel come down from heaven, having the key of the bottomless pit, and a great chain in his hand. And he laid hold on the dragon, that old serpent, which is the Devil and Satan, and bound him a thousand years. And cast him into the bottomless pit, and shut him up, and set a seal upon him, that he should deceive the nations no more, till the thousand years should be fulfilled.

IN a great variety of respects the Bible is the most remarkable book in the world. In it we have God's moral character clearly exhibited to view, by a history of his conduct, as moral governor of the world, from the beginning; and the nature of fallen man painted to the life, by a history of their behaviour for four thousand years. In it we have opened the glorious and astonishing method that has been entered upon to disappoint all

Satan's defigns, by the interpofition of the Son of God; and are informed of his birth, life, death, refurrection, afcenfion and exaltation; and of the glorious defigns he has in view. And the whole is fo contrived as to be admirably fuited to all the circumftances and needs of a good man, that, as it was defigned to be the good man's book, in a peculiar fenfe, fo it is perfectly fuited to his cafe. *It is profitable for doctrine, for reproof, for correction, for inftruction in righteoufnefs, that the man of God may be perfect, thoroughly furnifhed to all good works.*

That fincere concern for the caufe of truth and virtue, for the honor of God and intereft of true religion, which is peculiar to a good man, whofe character it is to love Chrift above father and mother, wife and children, houfes and lands, yea, better than his own life, muft naturally fubject him to a peculiar kind of folicitude; even as a child, of a truly filial fpirit, is pained when it goes ill with his father's family, to whofe intereft he is clofely attached, and has a whole fyftem of inward fenfations that a ftranger intermeddles not with. The Bible, the good man's book, is, therefore, wifely adapted to eafe the good man's pained heart, and afford confolation in this interefting and moft important point, as it gives the ftrongeft affurances that the caufe of virtue fhall finally prevail.

How infupportable muft the grief of the pious Jews have been, fitting on the fides of the rivers of Babylon? *There we fat down,* fay they, *yea, we wept when we remembered Zion.* And on the willows they hung their harps, nor could any thing divert their minds. *If I forget thee, O Jerufalem, let my right hand forget her cunning! If I do not remember thee, let my tongue cleave to the roof of my mouth!* —How infupportable, I fay, muft their grief have been, while their glorious holy temple, and their holy city, the place of all their facred folemnities, were lying defolate, and God's people in captivity, had it not been for that promife, fo often repeated, that after feventy years God would vifit them, and caufe them to return to their own land. God knew before-hand the anguifh which would be apt to fill their hearts, the finking difcouragements, and all the train of dark and gloomy thoughts they would be incident to, and before-hand provided a remedy. Yea, no fooner had he denounced their doom in the xxxixth chapter of Ifaiah, but immediately in the next chapter, and for ten or twenty chapters together, does he provide for their support. *Comfort ye, comfort ye, my people; speak comfortably to Jerusalem,* &c. &c.

So, how infupportable would have been the grief of the church of Chrift, through the long, dark, cruel reign of myftical Babylon, while they beheld error and wickednefs univerfally prevail, Satan getting his will in almoft every thing, and, to appearance, no figns of better times, but all things wearing a dreadful afpect before their eyes:—How great their grief? How finking their difcouragements? How almoft infuperable their temptations to apoftatize, and forfake a caufe that heaven feemed to forfake, had not the day of deliverance been exprefsly foretold, and the glory that fhould follow opened to view by the fpirit of prophefy? But in a firm belief that the caufe they were engaged in, and for which they fpilt their blood, would finally prevail, and prevail in this world, where they then beheld Satan reigning and triumphing; I fay, in a firm belief of this, the whole army of martyrs could march on to battle courageoufly, willing to facrifice their lives in the caufe, not doubting of final victory, although they themfelves muft fall in the field.

Indeed, were the salvation of his own soul the only thing the good man had in view, he would naturally be quite easy upon a full assurance that this was secured. So, had Moses cared for nothing but the welfare of himself and of his posterity, he might have been satisfied, while the whole congregation of Israel were destroyed, if he might become a great nation, and that without any solicitude for the honor of the great name of the God of Israel; yea, although the idolatrous nations round about were fully established in the belief of the divinity of their idols, and brought to look upon the God of the Hebrews with ever so great contempt by the means. But, attached as he was to the honor of the God of Israel, nothing could give him satisfaction, but a prospect that that would be secured. The welfare of himself and of his family was of no importance in his esteem, compared with this. *See Exod.* xxxii.

It must, therefore, be remembered, that, as the Son of God left his father's bosom, and the realms of light and glory, and expired on the cross in the utmost visible contempt, that he might spoil principalities and powers, bruise the serpent's head, destroy the works of the Devil, so his true disciples have imbibed a meafure of the fame fpirit, and, as volunteers enlifted under his banner, have the fame thing in view; they long for the deftruction of Satan's kingdom, and thefe petitions are the genuine language of their hearts; " Our Father which art in heaven, " hallowed be thy name, thy kingdom come, " thy will be done on earth as it is in hea- " ven." Nor can the falvation of their own fouls, although ever fo fafely fecured, fatisfy their minds, without a clear view and fair profpect of Chrift's final victory over all his enemies: " But if our great GENERAL, who " has facrificed his life in the caufe, may but " at laft obtain a complete victory, notwith- " ftanding all the prefent dark appearances, " this is enough," fays the Chriftian Soldier; " I am willing to rifque all in his fervice, and " die in the battle too. But if Satan were " always to carry the day, Oh, who could " live under the thought!"

This having been the temper of good men, more or lefs, even from the early ages of the world, and through all fucceffive genera- tions to this day, they have evidently want- ed a peculiar fupport, which the reft of man- kind ftood in no need of, to carry them comfortably through fuch a long fcene of darknefs; wickednefs prevailing, God difhonored, Satan triumping, the world perifhing, the true church of God more generally in fackcloth. And accordingly the final victory of the caufe of truth and virtue was intimated in the very firft promife made to fallen man; and, from time to time, God repeated this comfortable prediction to his church and people; and finally made it the chief fubject of the laft book of holy Scripture he ordered to be wrote for the ufe of his church.

Now let us take a brief view of the whole feries of thefe divine predictions, from the beginning of the world, even down to this in our text, contained in one of the laft chapters in the Bible, that we may fee what full evidence there is of this truth, and fo what abundant caufe for confolation to all the people of God.

1. Immediately after the fall, when the ferpent, even the Old Serpent the Devil, had juft feduced mankind to revolt from God; and had, to all appearance, laid this whole world in perpetual ruin, even in the depths of this midnight darknefs, a ray of light

shone down from heaven—*The seed of the woman shall bruise the serpent's head.* As if God had said, " I see the scheme that Satan "has laid to ruin the world, and establish his "impious, malicious cause: I see it, and "am determined to defeat it. The feebler "woman he has over-matched, but her al- "mighty seed shall conquer him, and as ef- "fectually subdue him, and prevent all fu- "ture mischief by him, as a serpent is sub- "dued and incapacitated for further mis- "chief when his head is crushed to pieces, "under the indignant heel of one determin- "ed on his death." This was a complete doom, indeed, denounced against Satan, at the head of the kingdom of darkness. And it fully implied, that the cause of light, truth and righteousness, should finally obtain a complete victory.

2. After this gracious and glorious promise had been the chief foundation of all the hopes of God's people for two thousand years, God was pleased to point out the particular family from whence this mighty deliverer should spring, and to intimate what a universal blessing he should be to all the nations of the earth. *And in thy* SEED *shall* ALL *the families of the earth be blessed,* said

God to Abraham; which again plainly fuppofed, that the caufe of truth and righteoufnefs, notwithftanding the dark ftate the world then was in, all finking faft into idolatry, and would for many ages be in, buried in heathenifh darknefs, fhould yet, in due time, univerfally prevail over the whole earth. For *in thy* SEED *fhall* ALL *the families of the earth be bleffed.* This fame promife was repeated again and again to Abraham, and afterwards to Ifaac and to Jacob.

3. Hitherto God had fupported his peoples' hopes chiefly with promifes, with verbal predictions; but from the days of Mofes to the days of Solomon king of Ifrael, to affift his peoples' faith, God did, befides repeated promifes of the fame thing, by a great variety of wonderful works, fhadow forth the glorious day; and, at the fame time, fhew that he had fufficient wifdom and power to accomplifh the greateft defigns. That his people might be convinced that he could eafily bring to pafs, for the good of his church, whatfoever feemed good in his fight.

Ifrael, in the Egyptian bondage, were a defigned type of a fallen world, under the dominion and tyranny of Satan; nor was

Pharaoh more loth to let Israel go, than Satan is to have his subjects desert him, and his kingdom go to ruin; but notwithstanding all the seeming impossibilities in the way of Israel's deliverance, infinite wisdom knew how to accomplish the divine designs. God could even cause a member of Pharaoh's family to educate one to be an instrument of this designed deliverance. And, in due time, behold all the armies of Israel march forth from the land of Egypt, out of the house of bondage; and Pharaoh, and his chariots, and all his host, lie buried in the Red Sea! So easily can God bring forth his people, even out of the anti-christian kingdom, which is spiritually called Sodom and Egypt; and, if he pleases, raise up the instruments of this glorious work, even in the court of Rome.

And when the name of the true God was almost forgotten through all the earth, and the Devil worshipped in his room, in idols of various names, through all the nations, God knew how to make his name known, and to cause his fame to spread abroad, and fill the whole earth with his glory, by wonders wrought in the land of Ham; by descending on Mount Sinai; by leading the armies of Israel forty years in the wilderness, in a pillar of cloud by day, and of fire by night, giving them bread from heaven and water out of the flinty rock; dividing Jordan; delivering up one and thirty idolatrous kings to the sword of Joshua; raising up judges, one after another, in a miraculous manner, to deliver his people, until the days of David and Solomon, types of Christ.—Of David who, Messiah-like, subdued the enemies of Israel all around; of Solomon, who built the Holy Temple, and filled Jerusalem with riches and glory.—He who hath done all these things, can easily accomplish all the designs of his heart, preserve his church, raise up deliverance, break to pieces the kingdoms of the earth for her sake, make truth victorious, and set up the New-Jerusalem in all her spiritual glory, build up his church as a glorious Holy Temple, and set the Son of David upon the Throne; by whose hands Satan, and all the powers of darkness, shall be subdued, chained, sealed up in the bottomless pit, as much afraid, and as much unable, to attempt any mischief, as the subdued nations around Israel were in the very height of David's power.

But when shall the Son of David reign,

and the church have reſt? When ſhall the cauſe of truth and righteouſneſs thus prevail? Perhaps the very time was deſigned to be ſhadowed forth in the law of Moſes, in the inſtitution of their holy days. The *ſeventh day*, ſaid God, who always had this glorious ſeaſon of reſt in view—" *The ſeventh day ſhall be a Sabbath of Reſt, the ſeventh month ſhall be full of holy days, the ſeventh year ſhall be a year of reſt.*"—So, perhaps, after ſix thouſand years are ſpent in labour and ſorrow by the church of God, the ſeven thouſandth ſhall be a ſeaſon of ſpiritual reſt and joy, an holy ſabbath to the Lord.—And as God the Creator was ſix days in forming a confuſed chaos into a beautiful world, and reſted the ſeventh; ſo God the Redeemer, after ſix thouſand years labour in the work of the new creation, may reſt on the ſeventh, and then proclaim a general liberty to an enſlaved world, and grant a general pardon to a guilty race; as in the year of jubilee, among the Jews, every enſlaved Jew was ſet at liberty, and the debts of all the indebted were cancelled.

4. Theſe things, thus ſhadowed forth in types, were alſo expreſly declared by the mouths of the ancient prophets, from the

days of David and forward, to the end of that dispensation; and the same things are hinted here and there in the New-Testament, and largely opened to view in the Revelation of St. John. So that both the Old and New Testaments join to raise in us, who live in these ages, the highest assurance that it is God's design to *give his Son the Heathen for his inheritance, and the uttermost parts of the earth for his possession. For all kings shall bow down before him, and all nations shall serve him. And the mountain of the Lord's house shall be established in the top of the mountains, and shall be exalted above the hills, and all nations shall flow unto it. They shall beat their swords into plough-shears and their spears into pruning-hooks, and learn war no more. For the earth shall be full of the knowledge of the Lord as the waters cover the sea. A nation shall be born in a day. All thy people shall be righteous. They shall all know the Lord, from the least to the greatest. And holiness to the Lord shall be written on every thing. Kings shall become nursing fathers, and queens nursing mothers; and there shall be nothing to hurt or offend. The inhabitants shall not* [*so much as*] *say I am sick. And this kingdom shall fill the whole*

22   THE MILLENNIUM.

*earth. And all nations and languages shall serve him. And the kingdom and dominion, and the greatness of the kingdom under the whole heaven shall be given to the people of the saints of the Most High God; and the Jews shall be called in, and the fulness of the Gentiles. For the Gospel shall be preached to every nation, and kindred, and tongue, and people. And Satan shall be bound, and Christ shall reign on earth a thousand years.*** And as surely as the Jews were delivered out of the Babylonish captivity, and Babylon itself destroyed, even so surely shall all these things be accomplished in their time; and mysti-

NOTE.

* *Satan shall be bound,* &c. "The church of Christ shall enjoy purity of religion in peace, without any disturbance from those old enemies of mankind, working in the children of disobedience." *Daubuz on the Place.*

"And this seems to imply, that all shall be converted—However, if there be any that remain unconverted, they will, during the imprisonment of Satan, be in so small a number, and so feeble in comparison of the true Christians, that they shall neither dare, nor be able to disturb the peace of Christ's kingdom." *Lowman on the Place.*

A spirit of strict piety shall rise so high, and so universally prevail, that it shall be as though all the martyrs of former ages were risen from the dead, and appeared upon the stage all at once. This seems to be the sense of those words in *Rev.* xx. 4. The martyrs are said to rise from the dead and reign with Christ a thousand years, much in the same sense as *John* the *Baptist* is called *Elias*, viz. because he was a man so nearly resembling that celebrated prophet. *See Lowman on the Place.*

The MILLENNIUM.

cal Babylon shall *sink as a millstone into the sea, and shall be found no more at all.*

5. But when shall these things be? I answer, in the first place, it is plain, as yet they have not been; these great things have not been accomplished. They were not accomplished when the Jews were brought out of their Babylonish captivity; for, from thence to the coming of Christ, they never were in so flourishing a state as they had been before. They were not accomplished in the apostolic age; for St. John, when most, if not all, of the other apostles were dead, spake of these things, in the Revelation, as yet to come to pass. They were not accomplished in the three first centuries, for that was almost one continued scene of blood. They were not accomplished in the days of Constantine the Great; for it is since then that *the Man of Sin has been revealed.* Nor are they accomplished to this day; for Satan is still walking to and fro through the earth, and going up and down therein: Babylon is not fallen; the Jews are not called, nor is the fulness of the Gentiles come in, but the greatest part of the earth, to this day, sit in heathenish darkness.

When then shall they be accomplished? Not till *the holy city has been trodden under foot forty and two months.* Not till *the witnesses have prophesied a thousand two hundred and threescore days, cloathed in sackcloth.* And not till *the woman has been in the wilderness a time, and times, and half a time.* Now a time, and times, and half a time, *i. e.* three years and a half is equal to forty-two months, which is equal to one thousand two hundred and sixty days, which doubtless means one thousand two hundred and sixty years, a day for a year; as the event has proved, was the case in the prophecy of Daniel, who declared it to be seventy weeks, from the going forth of the commandment to build Jerusalem to the death of Christ; for it proved to be four hundred and ninety years, which is seven times seventy, a day for a year. *Dan.* ix. 24.

So that there is no difficulty in determining the downfall of Antichrist, but what arises from the uncertainty we are at when to date the beginning of his rise and reign.— The Bishops of Rome were some hundred years rising gradually from the honest character of a scripture-bishop to the grand title of UNIVERSAL POPE, which was obtained,

The Millennium.

A. D. six hundred and six. And it was a long time from this before they got to the height of their grandeur, and the Pope was constituted a TEMPORAL PRINCE, which was not till A. D. seven hundred and fifty-six.* And perhaps he may fall as gradually as he rose. And as now he has been falling two hundred and forty years, even ever since the beginning of the REFORMATION, so we may rationally expect he will continue to fall till BABYLON sinks AS A MILLSTONE INTO THE SEA. And then *the mountains and the hills shall break forth into singing, and all the trees of the field shall clap their hands.* And all the hosts of heaven, as loud as thunder, shall say, *Hallelujah! For the Lord God omnipotent reigneth. Let us be glad and rejoice, and give honor to him; for the marriage of the Lamb is come, and his wife hath made herself ready.*

And thus we have taken a brief view of the scripture-evidence, that the cause of truth and righteousness will finally become gloriously victorious.

6. Nor is there the least reason to doubt the accomplishment of these things; for God

---

NOTE.
See Bower's History of the Popes.

in all times paſt has been faithful to his word, and is evidently ſufficiently engaged in this affair—knows how, and can eaſily accompliſh it, and it will be much to the honor of his great name to do it.

God has been faithful to his promiſes to his church from the beginning of the world. To all human appearance, it was a very unlikely thing that the Hebrews, enſlaved in Egypt, under Pharaoh, a very powerful monarch, and ſunk down into idolatry, and very low-ſpirited, ſhould ariſe and go forth with all their flocks and herds, and march through the wilderneſs, and conquer the ſeven nations of Canaan, and poſſeſs their land. And ſo it was, to all human appearance, equally unlikely, that the Jews in Babylon ſhould ever return to their own land.—But God had promiſed in both caſes, and God performed. And an event more ſurpriſing than either of theſe, yea, the moſt aſtoniſhing that could have happened, has alſo come to paſs, juſt as God had ſaid.—The promiſed SEED has been born, and the ſerpent has *bruiſed his heel;* and methinks now not only God's faithfulneſs, but even the nature of the caſe itſelf, ſhould lead us to believe, that *the* SEED *ſhall bruiſe his heel.*

For after God has appeared to be so *infinitely engaged* to destroy the works of the Devil, as to give his only begotten Son, it can surely never once be imagined that he wants sufficient resolution to carry him thro' what yet remains to be done.

And he who could send Pharaoh's daughter to take up Moses, when an infant, out of his basket of bulrushes, and educate him in Pharaoh's court, that he might be skilled in all the arts of government; and when he had spent forty years in this situation banish him into the land of Midian, that in the solitary life of a shepherd for another forty years, he might attain to the meekest man on earth, that he might, by both, be thoroughly qualified for the work designed him; and he, who could take David from feeding his father's sheep, and, after a course of trials, so exceeding necessary to prepare frail man for high honors and great usefulness, exalt him to the throne of Israel, so thoroughly furnished to head their armies and subdue their foes, advance their external grandeur, and put great honor upon their religion; and he, who could take Daniel, one of the Jewish captives in Babylon, and raise him to such high honor and great authority, to be a father to his people thro' their seventy years captivity, and by his means, perhaps, influence Cyrus so generously to release them, and assist them in their return;* and finally, he, who could take a number of poor illiterate fishermen, and the persecuting Saul, and by them lay the foundation of the Christian church, in spite of the united opposition of earth and hell; and after their death cause the Christian church to live through, yea, at last to triumph over the ten bloody persecutions, and even conquer the Roman empire; and that which is still more wonderful, to subsist to this day, notwithstanding all the subtle and cruel methods which have, for so many hundred years, been taken by Antichrist to

NOTE.

* As Daniel understood the prophecies of Jeremiah, which had determined the time of the captivity to be seventy years, *Dan.* ix. 2. and had his heart so much in the affair of their return, as to *set his face to seek the Lord by fasting and prayer*, verse 3; and being the chief man in the kingdom, must have free access to Cyrus, *Dan.* vi. so nothing could be more natural than to shew him an ancient Jewish prophecy, wherein he was mentioned by name, near two hundred years ago, and pointed out as the person who was to let go the Jewish captives, build Jerusalem, and lay the foundation of the temple. *Isaiah* xliv. 28. and chap. xlv. 1—3. To which Cyrus no doubt refers in his proclamation. *Ezra* i. 2, 3, 4. *Thus saith Cyrus king of Persia, The Lord God of heaven hath given me all the kingdoms of the earth, and he hath* CHARGED *me to build him an house at Jerusalem, which is in Judah. Who is there among you,* &c.

extirpate Christianity out of the world; I say, he who could do these things, cannot be at a loss for means, or want power to effect the glorious things foretold, which yet remain to be accomplished.

And what if mankind are ever so estranged from God? And what if they are ever so averse to a reconciliation? And what if Satan reigns in the courts of princes, in the councils of the clergy, as well as in the cottages of the poor? And what if even the whole world in a manner lies in wickedness? So that a general conflagration might rather be expected, as it is so eminently deserved—are these things any bar in the way?

What if mankind have abused divine grace from the beginning of the world? What if they have murdered his prophets, his Son, and his apostles? What if they have resisted and grieved the Holy Spirit, and perverted the doctrines, and gone counter to the precepts of his holy word? Yea, what if it appears that mankind are really on Satan's side? And this, after all the kind methods God has taken to reclaim a guilty world, so that even the best man on earth, or the kindest angel in heaven might be discouraged, totally and finally discouraged, and think it never worth while to take any more pains with such a perverse race, but that it were more suitable to the rules of good government to resign them to destruction!—Are any, or all these things together, a sufficient bar to the accomplishment of God's designs, whose goodness is absolutely infinite? Can they be so, after the Son of God has been offered as a sacrifice of atonement, to secure the honour of the divine government, and open a way for the honourable exercise of his grace?—What! after the Messiah has been exalted to be a Prince and a Saviour, to give repentance and remission of sins?— And after all power and authority in heaven and earth is given into his hands, on purpose to destroy the kingdom of Satan, and bring every nation, kindred and tongue, to bow the knee to God! Yea, when the infinitely wise Governor of the world has before determined to permit the wickedness of mankind to come out and stand in so glaring a light, and to suffer Satan so long to practise and prosper, to this very purpose, that his power, wisdom and grace, might be the more effectually and the more gloriously displayed, in the accomplishment of all his glorious designs?

The MILLENIUM. 31

Inftead of being difcouraged, from a view of the paft, or the prefent ftate of the world, as without the light of divine revelation we fhould naturally have been, methinks now, viewing all things in the light of holy fcripture, it muft be perfectly rational to conclude, that all thefe things are only preparatory, as an introduction to the glorious day: even, as all the cruel bondage of Ifrael in Egypt, and all the haughty conduct of Pharaoh, were but preparatory as an introduction to the glorious event that God had then in his eye. And what unfpeakable honour will redound to God moft High, if after all the vile conduct of this apoftate world, and notwithftanding all their ill-defert; and after all the fubtle methods Satan has taken to make his kingdom ftrong; I fay, what unfpeakable honour will redound to God moft High, if, after all this, he fhould accomplifh his glorious defigns? And when things have been ripening thefe five or fix thoufand years, and are now fo nearly every way prepared for God, to get himfelf a great name in the total deftruction of Satan's kingdom, can we once imagine, that God will let the opportunity flip? Or rather, ought we not firmly to believe, that when every thing is quite ripe, then God will arise, make bare his arm, and fill the whole world with his glory?

Especially, considering that, as things stand, the honour of all his glorious perfections lies at stake; for ever since the Almighty gave out the word, that *the* SEED *of the woman should bruise the serpent's head,* even from that very day, that Old Serpent, with all his subtilty, has employed his whole power to defeat the divine designs, maintain his kingdom in the world, and escape the dreadful blow. He stirred up Cain to kill his brother, and never ceased till the whole earth was filled with violence, which brought on the general deluge; and after the flood, he was industrious to divert mankind from the knowledge and worship of the true God, and to establish idolatry and the worship of the Devil, in all the kingdoms of the earth; and since Christianity appeared, he has turned himself into every shape to defeat the gracious designs of the gospel, and has prevailed and reigned above a thousand years, at the head of the grand antichristian apostacy; and should the Almighty suffer him to go on and prosper, and finally prevail, what would become of his own great name? and how great would be their triumph in the infernal regions, to think that in spite of God and of his Son, from the beginning to the end of the world, they have held out in a constant war, kept the field, and at last come off victorious?—Wherefore, as when God repeats the wonderful works which he had done for Israel in the days of old, in the xxth chapter of Ezekiel, he constantly says, *I wrought for mine own great name.* So here, in this case, will he do it again, and that in the most eminent manner; as it is written, *The zeal of the Lord of Hosts will perform this.*

So that, in a word, if almighty power and infinite wisdom, at the head of the universe, infinitely engaged, are a sufficient match for the guilty, impotent powers of darkness, then we may depend upon it, Satan will meet with an overthrow, as notable as did Pharaoh and his host in the Red Sea;—and as proud Babylon, once the mistress of kingdoms, is now no more, so mystical Babylon shall sink as a millstone in the sea, and rise no more for ever. And,

D

§ 7. Whatever mistakes the Jewish Rabbies might fall into, in their interpretation of Daniel's seventy weeks, and in their attempts to fix the precise time of the Messiah's coming; and whatever mistaken notions any of them had about the nature of his kingdom, as though it was to be of this world, and he to appear in all earthly grandeur; and although his coming, to some, might seem to be so long delayed, that they began to give up all hopes of it, and to contrive some other meaning to all the ancient prophecies, or even to call in question the inspiration of the prophets; yet neither the mistakes of some, nor the infidelity of others, at all altered the case. Days, and months, and years hastened along, and one revolution among the kingdoms of the earth followed upon another, *till the fulness of time was come*, till all things were ripe, and then, behold, the Messiah was born. Even so it shall be now.

Whatever mistakes Christian Divines may fall into, in their interpretation of six hundred and sixty-six, the number of the beast; or in their endeavours to fix the precise time when the one thousand two hundred and sixty years of Antichrist's reign

THE MILLENNIUM. 35

shall begin and end; or whatever wrong notions some have had, or may have about the nature of the Millennium, as though Christ was to reign personally on earth; and if some, mean while, begin to think, that all things will go on as they have done, and to conclude, that the expectation of these glorious days, which has prevailed in the Christian Church from the beginning, is merely a groundless fancy: Yet none of these things will at all alter the case. Days, and months, and years will hasten along, and one revolution, among the kingdoms of the earth, follow upon another, until the fulness of time is come—till all things are ripe for the event; and then the ministers of Christ will accomplish in reality, what St. John saw in his visions:—*I saw an angel fly in the midst of heaven, having the everlasting gospel to preach unto them that dwell on the earth, and to every nation, and kindred, and tongue and people.* And then shall it come to pass that the veil of ignorance, which hath so long spread over all nations, shall be destroyed: and knowledge shall so greatly increase, that it shall be as though the *light of the moon* were *as the light of the sun, and the light of the sun sevenfold;* until *the knowledge of the Lord cover the earth as the waters do the sea;* and then there *shall be nothing to hurt or offend in all God's holy mountain;* for Babylon shall fall, Satan be bound, and Christ will reign, and truth and righteousness universally prevail a thousand years.

REMARKS AND INFERENCES.

1. When, therefore, our Saviour, in the days of his flesh, denominated his followers *a little flock,* from the smallness of their number, he had no design to teach us that this would always be the case; for although it was very true, that his flock was at that time *a little flock,* yet the day was coming, when that *little leaven* should *leaven the whole lump,* and *the stone cut out without hands* should become *a great mountain, and fill the whole earth.* So, although it was a saying very applicable, not only to our Saviour's day, but to most other periods of the church, that *many are called, and few are chosen;* yet it does not hence follow, that this will be the case, when *a nation shall be born in a day,* and *all the people shall be righteous.*—And although it has commonly been so, that of the MANY who have sought *to enter in at*

the strait gate, but FEW *have been able,* and the GENERALITY have, from age to age, gone *in the broad way, which leads down to destruction;* yet it shall be quite otherwise, when *Satan is bound, that he may deceive the nations no more;* and when *all shall know the Lord, from the least to the greatest,* when *the kingdom, and the greatness of the kingdom, under the whole heavens, shall be given to the people of the saints of the Most High.* For it is very plain, that these, and such like expressions used by our Saviour, which were applicable to the then times, and to most other periods, when the number of true converts hath been comparatively very small, were never designed to be applicable to that glorious period yet to come, which is to be the grand harvest time, when *the Jews,* who are, to this day, for that very purpose, no doubt, by divine Providence, preserved a distinct people, and *the fulness of the Gentiles shall come in.* Nor can it be right to interpret such expressions in such a sense, as to render them inconsistent with what the scriptures so plainly teach shall be the case in the latter days: Therefore,

2. Notwithstanding hitherto but few have

been saved, there is no evidence but that yet the greater part of mankind may be saved. Nothing can be argued against this from such expressions as have been just mentioned, for the reason already suggested. Nor can any thing be argued from any other passages of scripture; for the scripture no where teaches, that the greatest part of the whole human race will finally perish. I am sensible, many seem to take this for granted, and they are greatly strengthened in this belief from a view of the awful state mankind have been in from the beginning of the world to this day. But if we should even grant, that hitherto not one in ten thousand have been saved, yet it may come to pass, (there may be time enough for it, and men enough yet born;) I say, it may yet come to pass, that by far the greatest part of mankind may be saved.

For as the scriptures constantly teach that, in these glorious days, universal peace shall prevail, and instead of war the nations shall employ their time in useful labour, *shall beat their swords into plowshares, and their spears into pruning hooks;* so it will naturally come to pass, that mankind, who are now in vast multitudes destroyed in the wars from one generation to another, will be greatly increased in numbers, and plentifully provided for. Only remove wars, famines, and all those desolating judgments, which the sins of mankind have, from age to age, brought down on a guilty world, and let that universal peace and prosperity take place, which indeed will naturally result from the sincere practice of pure Christianity, and mankind will naturally increase and spread, and fill all the earth. And while every one improves his time well, and is diligent in his calling, according to the rules of our holy religion, and all luxury, intemperance and extravagance are banished from the nations of the earth, it is certain that this globe will be able to sustain with food and raiment a number of inhabitants, immensely greater than ever yet dwelt on it at a time. And now if *all* these shall *know the Lord from the least to the greatest,* as the scripture asserts, so that *the knowledge of the Lord shall fill the earth as the waters cover the sea,* for a thousand years together, it may easily, yea, it will naturally come to pass, that there will be more saved in these thousand years, than ever before dwelt upon the face of the earth, from the foundation of the world.

Some indeed underſtand the thouſand years in the Revelation, agreeable to other prophetical numbers in that book, a day for a year; ſo *the time, and times, and half a time,* i. e. three years and an half, and the *forty two months,* and the *one thouſand two hundred and ſixty days* are no doubt to be reckoned; and if the dark period is to be reckoned by this rule, it ſhould ſeem that the light period ſhould likewiſe; for otherwiſe the dark period, which in that book is repreſented to be the ſhorteſt, will indeed be the longeſt—the one thouſand two hundred and ſixty days longer than the thouſand years; and if the thouſand years is reckoned a day for a year, as the ſcripture-year contains three hundred and ſixty days, ſo the one thouſand years will amount to three hundred and ſixty thouſand years; in which there might be millions ſaved to one that has been loſt. But not to inſiſt upon this, if this glorious period is to laſt only a thouſand years literally, there may be many more ſaved than loſt.

If it be granted, that it is difficult to compute with any exactneſs in ſuch a caſe as this, yet it is eaſy to make ſuch a computation as may ſatisfy us in the point before us;

THE MILLENNIUM. 41

for in Egypt the Hebrews doubled at the rate of about once in fourteen years; in New-England the inhabitants double in less than twenty-five years; it will be moderate, therefore, to suppose mankind, in the Millennium, when all the earth is full of peace and prosperity, will double every fifty years. But at this rate, there will be time enough in a thousand years to double twenty times, which would produce such a multitude of people, as that although we should suppose all who live before the Millennium begins to be lost, yet if all these should be saved, there would be above seventeen thousand saved to one that would be lost; as may appear from the table below.

E

1 — — — 2	12 — — 4,096
2 — — — 4	13 — — 8,192
3 — — — 8	14 — — 16,384
4 — — — 16	15 — — 32,768
5 — — — 32	16 — — 65,536
6 — — — 64	17 — — 131,072
7 — — — 128	18 — — 262,144
8 — — — 258	19 — — 524,288
9 — — — 512	20 — — 1,048,576
10 — — — 1,024	
11 — — — 2,048	Sum total 2,097,150

In the first column, we have the twenty periods, which one thousand years will make at fifty years to a period. In the second column, we see in what proportion mankind will increase, if they are supposed to double in every fifty years. At the end of the first fifty years there will be two for one, and so on. At the end of the twentieth period there will be above a million for one. Now sup-

3. The periods past, that have been so dark, ought to be considered as introductory to this bright and glorious scene, and in various respects as preparatory thereto.

An apostate race, who had joined with the fallen angels in a course of rebellion against the Governor of the Universe, might justly have been forsaken of God, and given up to a state of perfect darkness and wo, from generation to generation, entirely un-

pose the world to stand six thousand years before the Millennium, and suppose it in every age to be as full of inhabitants as it will be when the Millennium begins. And suppose, through all the six thousand years, all the inhabitants of the earth to have died off, and new ones come in their room, at the rate of once in fifty years, six thousand years, at fifty years to a period, will be one hundred and twenty periods—one hundred and twenty worlds full, all lost; suppose, yet by the table we see, that the seventh period alone, which is one hundred and twenty-eight, would more than counter-balance the whole—

Suppose all before the Millennium lost = 120
Suppose all in the Millennuim saved = 2,097,150
Then $120 : 2,097,150 :: 1 : 17,456 \frac{40}{120}$ Q. E. D.

That is, above seventeen thousand would be saved to one lost, which was the point to be proved; therefore nothing hinders but that the greatest part of mankind may yet be saved if God so pleases. There is time enough for it, and may be men enough yet born; and if these calculations may serve to clear up this, they answer the proposed end. What proportion of mankind will finally be saved, and what lost, no one can tell—it is no where revealed; God was not obliged to save one out of all this guilty lost world. Hitherto the generality may have perished, and the Lord is righteous; but who can tell to what a degree God may yet glorify his grace? The holy scriptures encourage us to look for things exceeding great and glorious; even for such events as may put a new face on all God's past dispensations.

der the power of the Prince of Darkness.—What has happened in dark ages paſt, may help us a little to realize what might juſtly always have been the woful ſtate of a fallen world. We have had a ſpecimen of the dreadful nature and tendency of Satan's government in all the idolatry, wickedneſs and wo which have filled the world; and we have ſeen a little what is in the heart of fallen man, who have ſlain the Lord's prophets, crucified his Son, and ſhed the blood of thouſands, yea, of millions of his ſervants. And what has happened may help us to realize a little what muſt have been the ſtate of a fallen world, if grace had never interpoſed. At the ſame time it hath appeared, after the beſt contrived experiments have been ſufficiently tried, that it is not in the heart of fallen man to repent, nor can he be brought to it by any external means whatſoever, whereby the abſolute neceſſity of the interpoſition of ſupernatural grace hath been ſet in the moſt glaring light. And now, if after all, God ſhould effectually interpoſe, deſtroy the influence of Satan, ſcatter the darkneſs which fills the world, recover mankind to God, and cauſe truth and righteouſneſs at laſt to prevail, it would appear to be altogether of God, of his own mere self-moving goodness and sovereign grace. And after so long and sore a bondage mankind will be the more sensible of the greatness of the deliverance. Nor can it ever be said by a proud and haughty world, " We did not need the influences of divine " grace to bring us right;" whereas all other methods had been sufficiently tried, and tried in vain. But God may justly say, " What " could have been done more to reclaim " mankind that I have not done? And to " what purpose would it have been to have " taken one step further? I tried them e- " nough—there was no hope—their heart " was a heart of stone; therefore, behold I, " even I, will take away the heart of stone, " and give an heart of flesh; and an apostate " world shall be ashamed and confounded, " and shall never open their mouth when I " shall do all these things for them."

We are apt to wonder why these glorious days should be so long delayed, if God, indeed, intends such mercy to men; but God, infinitely wise, knows what is best—knows how to conduct the affairs of the universe— knows when is the fittest time to introduce this glorious state of things—knows when matters will be all ripened, and every thing in the moral world prepared, so that this glorious day may be ushered in to the best advantage, in a manner most suited to honor God and his Son, to humble a haughty world, and to disappoint Satan most grievously, after all his wily schemes, great success, and high expectations; I say, God knows when this will be; and this is the very time he has fixed upon for this glorious work.

4. It therefore becomes all the followers of Christ, in their several spheres, under firm belief of these things, to be of good courage, and exert themselves to the utmost, in the use of all proper means, to suppress error and vice of every kind, and promote the cause of truth and righteousness in the world, and so be workers together with God.

If one stood at the head of this glorious army, which has been in the wars above these five thousand years, and has lived thro' many a dreadful campaign, and were allowed to make a speech to these veteran troops upon this glorious theme, he might lift up his voice, and say—" Hail, noble heroes!
" Brave followers of the Lamb! Your Ge-
" neral has sacrificed his life in this glorious

"cause, and spoiled principalities and pow-
"ers on the cross, and now he lives and
"reigns! He reigns on high, with all power
"in heaven and earth in his hands! Your
"predecessors, the prophets, apostles and
"martyrs, with undaunted courage, have
"marched into the field of battle, and con-
"quered dying, and now reign in heaven!
"Behold, ye are risen up in their room, are
"engaged in the same cause, and the time
"of the last general battle draws on, when
"a glorious victory is to be won. And al-
"though many a valiant soldier may be slain
"in the field, yet the army shall drive all
"before them at last; and Satan being con-
"quered, and all the powers of darkness
"driven out of the field, and confined to
"the bottomless pit, ye shall reign with Christ
"a thousand years—reign in love and peace,
"while truth and righteousness ride triumph-
"ant through the earth; wherefore lay aside
"every weight, and, with your hearts whol-
"ly intent on this grand affair, gird up your
"loins, and with all the spiritual weapons of
"faith, prayer, meditation, watchfulness, &c.
"with redoubled zeal and courage, fall on
"your spiritual enemies: Slay every lust that
"yet lurks within, as knowing your domes-

"tic foes are the moſt dangerous; and with
"gentleneſs, meekneſs and wiſdom, by your
"holy conduct, your pious examples, your
"kind inſtructions, your friendly admoni-
"tions, ſpread the favour of divine know-
"ledge all around you, as ye are ſcattered
"here and there through a benighted world,
"labouring to win ſouls to Chriſt, to induce
"the deluded followers of Satan to deſert
"his camp, and enliſt as volunteers under
"your prince MESSIAH. And if the pow-
"ers of darkneſs ſhould rally all their for-
"ces, and a general battle, through all the
"Chriſtian world, come on, O love not your
"lives to the death! Sacrifice every earthly
"comfort in the glorious cauſe! Sing the
"triumphs of your victorious General, in
"priſons and at the ſtake, and die courage-
"ouſly, firmly believing the cauſe of truth
"and righteouſneſs will finally prevail."

Surely it is infinitely unbecoming the followers of him who is *King of Kings and
Lord of Lords*, to turn aſide to earthly pur-
ſuits, or to ſink down in unmanly diſcou-
ragements, or to give way to ſloth and effe-
minacy, when there is ſo much to be done,
and the glorious day is coming on. How
ſhould thoſe who handle the pen of the wri-

ter, exert themselves to explain and vindicate divine truths, and paint the Christian Religion in all its native glories! How should the pulpit be animated, from Sabbath to Sabbath, with sermons full of knowledge and light, full of spirit and life, full of zeal for God and love to men, and tender pity to infatuated sinners! Christ loves to have his ministers faithful, whether the wicked will hear or not.—And let pious parents be unwearied in their prayers for, and instructions of their children, and never faint under any discouragements; as knowing, that Christ is exalted to give repentance and remission of sins, and can do it for whom he will. Bring your children and friends, with all their spiritual diseases, and lay them at his feet; as once they did their sick, when this kind Saviour dwelt upon earth.—Let pious persons of every age, and in every capacity, awake from sleep, and arise from the dead, and live and act worthy their glorious character and high expectations; and in their several stations exert themselves to the utmost to promote the Redeemer's glorious cause.—Let this age do their share, as David, although the temple was not to be built in his day, yet exerted himself to lay up materials for that magnificent edifice, on which his heart was intently set; as knowing that, in his son's day, it would be set up in all its glory.—So let us rise up, and with the greatest alacrity, contribute our utmost towards this building, this living temple, this temple all made of lively stones, of stones alive, in which God is to dwell, and which will infinitely exceed in glory the Temple of Solomon, that was built of dead timber and lifeless stones.—And let this be our daily prayer, an answer to which we may be assured of, whatever other requests are denied us, *Our Father which art in Heaven*, &c.—*for thine is the kingdom, the power, and the glory, for ever.* AMEN.

AN HUMBLE ATTEMPT

TO PROMOTE

EXPLICIT AGREEMENT

AND

VISIBLE UNION OF GOD's PEOPLE

IN

EXTRAORDINARY PRAYER,

FOR THE

REVIVAL OF RELIGION

AND THE

ADVANCEMENT OF CHRIST's KINGDOM

ON

EARTH,

PURSUANT TO

SCRIPTURE-PROMISES AND PROPHECIES

CONCERNING THE

LAST TIME.

By *JONATHAN EDWARDS*, A. M.
Minister of the Gospel at Northampton.

WITH A PREFACE BY SEVERAL MINISTERS.

Printed at Boston, in New-England, 1747. *Reprinted at North-ampton, in Old England,* 1789.

ELIZABETH TOWN:
Printed by SHEPARD KOLLOCK, Printer and Bookseller. 1794.

OLNEY, May 4, 1789.

IF *any enquire why the enſuing work is republiſhed, I would beg leave to lay before them the following intelligence:*

At an aſſociation of the miniſters and meſſengers of the Baptiſt churches in the counties of Northampton, Leiceſter, &c. held at Nottingham, in the year 1784, a reſolution was formed to eſtabliſh, through the aſſociation, a meeting of prayer for the GENERAL revival and ſpread of religion. *This was to be obſerved the firſt Monday evening in every calendar month, by all the churches.* It ſtill continues.—In 1786, another Baptiſt aſſociation, commonly called the Midland, *held that year at Aulceſter, in the county of Warwick,* entered into the ſame reſolution. Many other churches, particularly in Yorkſhire, have adopted, and now follow the above practice.—

We have the pleasure also to find, that several Pædo-Baptist churches statedly meet on those evenings, for the same purpose.

The re-publication of the following work, is with the avowed design of promoting the above agreement and practice. Those concerned in its first institution, never intended it should be confined to any peculiar connection, or particular denomination. Rather they ardently wished it might become general among the real friends of truth and holiness. The advocates of error are indefatigable in their endeavours to overthrow the distinguishing and interesting doctrines of Christianity; those doctrines which are the grounds of our hope, and sources of our joy. Surely it becomes the followers of Christ, to use every effort, in order to strengthen the things which remain.

By re-publishing the following work, I do not consider myself as becoming answerable for every sentiment it contains. An author and an editor are very distinct characters. Should any entertain different views respecting some of the prophecies in the inspired page, from those that are here advanced, yet such may, and I hope will, approve of the general design.

In the present imperfect state, we may reasonably expect a diversity of sentiments upon religious matters. Each ought to think for himself; and every one has a right, on proper occasions, to shew his opinion. Yet all should remember, that there are but two parties in the world, each engaged in opposite causes; the cause of God and of Satan; of holiness and of sin; of heaven and hell. The advancement of the one, and the downfall of the other, must appear exceedingly desirable to every real friend of God and man. If such, in some respects entertain different sentiments, and practise distinguishing modes of worship, surely they may unite in the above business. O for thousands upon thousands, divided into small bands in their respective cities, towns, villages and neighbourhood, all met at the same time, and in pursuit of one end, offering up their united prayers, like so many ascending clouds of incense before the Most High! May he shower down blessings on all the scattered tribes of Zion! Grace, great grace be with all them that love the Lord Jesus Christ in sincerity! AMEN!

JOHN SUTCLIFF.

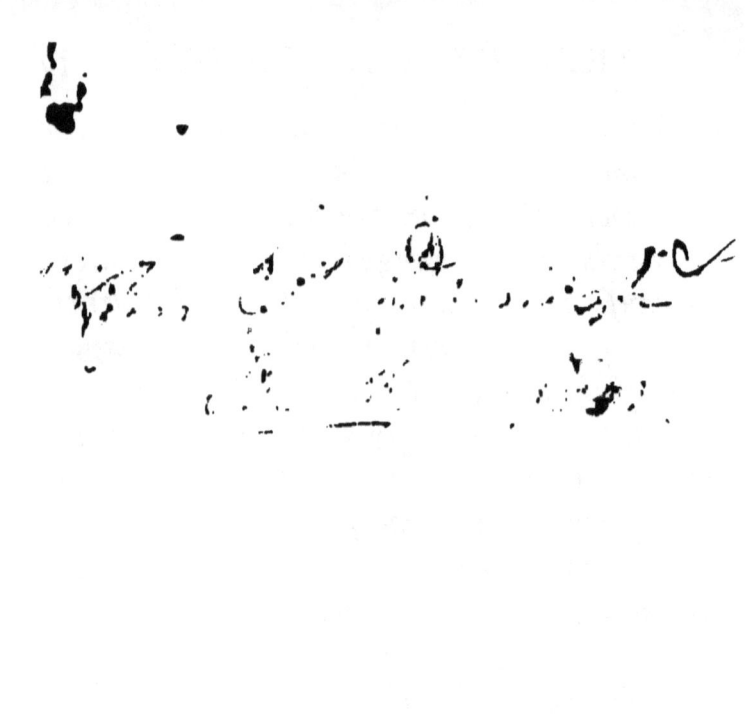

THE

PREFACE.

THE ruin of Satan's miserable kingdom, and the advancement of the universal and happy reign of Christ on the earth, were included and hinted in the sentence denounced on the serpent, that the *seed of the woman should bruise his head.* What was a terrible threatening to Satan, in the surprized ears of our first guilty parents, implied a joyful prophecy, to keep them from despair, and enliven their hopes for themselves and their descendants, of obtaining by this seed of her's an eternal triumph over him who had so sadly foiled them. And it is likely, their hopes and faith immediately arose, laid hold on the reviving prophecy, earnestly desired its happy accomplishment, and transmitted it to their posterity.

But though this prophecy was at first only delivered in the form of a threatening to Satan; it was afterwards directly given in the form of a promise to Abraham, though still in general terms, that *in his seed should all the nations of the earth be bleſſed.* Yet this general promiſe was more clearly by degrees explained in the following ages, to mean a Divine King, no other than the Son of God aſſuming human nature of the feed of Abraham, Iſaac, Jacob and David; that ſhould be born of a virgin in Bethlehem of Judah; and at firſt deſpiſed, abuſed, rejected, and put to death; but ſhould riſe to immortal life, aſcend to heaven, and thence extend his bleſſed kingdom over all nations; not by outward force, but inward overcoming influence, by his word and ſpirit, making them *his willing people in the day of his power;* and reigning in glorious light and holineſs, and love and peace for ever; and the advancement of this univerſal and happy reign has been the earneſt deſire and prayer of the ſaints in all ages to the preſent day.

But how great the honour and how lively the encouragement given in ſcripture to thoſe their prayers; by repreſenting them as offered by Chriſt himſelf with the fragrant incenſe of his own merits and interceſſion, on the *golden altar before the throne,* and aſcending together in one grateful perfume to God! And how cheering to every ſaint is that promise of his—*From the rising of the sun, even to the going down of the same, my name shall be great among the Gentiles, and in every place incense shall be offered unto my name, and a pure offering!* How pleasing to God and the heavenly hosts to see, as the sun goes round the globe, this grateful incense rising from every part on high! and the more extensive and incessant are these prayers, ascending from the circle of the earth, the more does this blessed promise go into its desired fulfilment, and the holy God is more pleased and glorified.

To promote the increase, concurrency, and constancy of these acceptable prayers, is the great intention both of the pious memorial of our reverend and dear brethren in Scotland, and of the worthy author of this exciting essay. And this design we cannot but recommend to all who desire the coming of this blisful kingdom in its promised extent and glory, in this wretched world.

As to the author's ingenious observations on the prophecies, we entirely leave them to the reader's judgment: with only observing, though it is the apprehension of many learned men, that there is to be a very general slaughter of the witnesses of Christ about the time of their finishing their testimony to the pure worship and truths of the gospel, about three or four years before the seventh angel sounds his trumpet for the ruin of Antichrist;—yet we cannot see that this is any just objection against our joint and earnest prayers for the glorious age succeeding, or for the hastening of it.

For if such a terrible time is coming in Europe, which we in depending America are likely to share in; the more need we have of joining in earnest and constant prayers for extraordinary suffering graces for ourselves and others. And that such a time is coming on the members of Christ, is no more an objection against their prayers for the hastening of the following glory, than it was before the incarnation of him their head, that his most bitter sufferings were to precede the spreading of this joyous kingdom among the nations. And the nearer the day approaches, the more need we have to be awakened to continual watchfulness and prayer.

May God pour out on all his people abundantly, the spirit of grace and supplication, and prepare them for the amazing changes haftening on the earth, both for previous trials and for following glories!

Jofeph Sewall,
Thomas Prince,
John Webb, } Minifters in Bofton.
Thomas Foxcroft,
Jofhua Gee.

Boston, N. E. *January* 12, 1747-8.

An HUMBLE ATTEMPT *to promote an explicit* AGREEMENT *and visible* UNION *of God's People through the World, in* EXTRAORDINARY PRAYER, *for the* REVIVAL *of* RELIGION, *and the Advancement of* CHRIST'S KINGDOM *on Earth, pursuant to Scripture-Promises and Prophecies concerning the* LAST TIME.

OCCASIONED

By a late Memorial published by a Number of Ministers in Scotland, and sent over to America, giving an Account of a certain Concert for Prayer, which has already been come into by many Ministers and others in Great Britain and some other Parts, and in which they desire the general Concurrence of their Christian Brethren every where.

CONTAINING

A Copy of the said Memorial, with a more particular View of the Affair it relates to: a Variety of Arguments and Persuasives to comply with the Motion therein made, for united and extraordinary Prayer; and Answers to some Objections.

TOGETHER WITH

Seasonable Considerations on the Aspects of Providence in many late wonderful Dispensations, and the present State of Things in the Church and moral World; pointing out the Fulfilling of the Scriptures, and the Voice of God to his People, in these Events.

BY *JONATHAN EDWARDS*, A. M.
Minister of the Gospel in Northampton, N. E.

PART I.

The text opened, and an account given of the affair proposed in the memorial from Scotland.

ZECHARIAH viii. 20, 21, 22.

Thus saith the Lord of Hosts—It shall yet come to pass, that there shall come people, and the inhabitants of many cities; and the inhabitants of one city shall go unto another, saying—Let us go speedily to pray before the Lord, and to seek the Lord of Hosts. I will go also. Yea, many people and strong nations shall come to seek the Lord of Hosts in Jerusalem, and to pray before the Lord.

IN this chapter we have a prophecy of a future glorious advancement of the church of God; wherein it is evident, something further is intended than ever was fulfilled to the nation of the Jews under the Old Testament. For here are plain prophecies of such things as never were fulfilled before the coming of the Messiah; particularly what is said in the two last verses in the chapter, of *many people and strong nations worshipping and seeking the true God,* and of so great an accession of Gentile nations to the church of God, that by far the greater part of the visible worshippers of God should consist of this new accession, so that they should be to the other as *ten to one*—a certain number for an uncertain. There never happened any thing, from the time of the prophet Zechariah to the coming of Chrift, to anfwer this prophecy; and it can have no fulfilment but either in the calling of the Gentiles, in and after the days of the apoftles, or in the future glorious enlargement of the church of God in the latter ages of the world, fo often foretold by the prophets of the Old Teftament, and by the prophet Zechariah in particular, in the latter part of his prophecy. It is moft probable, that what the fpirit of God has chief refpect to, is that laft and greateft enlargement and moft glorious advancement of the church of God on earth, in the benefits of which efpecially the Jewifh nation were to have a fhare, and a very eminent and diftinguifhing fhare. There is a great agreement between what is here faid and other prophecies, that muft manifeftly have refpect to the church's latter-day-glory; as that in Ifaiah lx. 2, 3, 4. *The Lord fhall arife upon thee, and his glory fhall be feen upon thee; and the Gentiles fhall come to thy light, and kings to the brightnefs of thy rifing. Lift up thine eyes round about, and fee; all they gather themfelves together, they come to thee.* That whole chapter, beyond all difpute, has refpect to the moft glorious ftate of the church of God on earth. So chap. lxvi. 8. *Shall the earth be made to bring forth in one day? Shall a nation be born at once?*—verfe 10. *Rejoice ye with Jerufalem, and be glad with her, all ye that love her.*—verfe 12. *I will extend peace to her like a river, and the glory of the Gentiles like a flowing ftream.*—Mich. iv. at the beginning: *but in the laft day it fhall come to pafs, that the mountain of the houfe of the Lord fhall be eftablifhed in the top of the mountain, and it fhall be exalted above the hills, and people fhall flow unto it; and many nations fhall come and fay, come, and let us go up unto the mountain of the Lord, and to the houfe of the God of Jacob. And he fhall judge among many people, and rebuke ftrong nations afar off: and they fhall beat their fwords into plowfhares, and their fpears into pruning-hooks; nation fhall not lift up fword againft nation, neither fhall they learn war any more.*—See alfo, Ifaiah ii. at the beginning. There has been nothing yet brought to pafs in any meafure to anfwer thefe prophecies. And as the prophecy in my text and the following verfe does agree with them, fo there is reason to think it has a respect to the same times. And indeed there is a remarkable agreement in the description given throughout the chapter, with the representations made of those times elsewhere in the prophets, as may be seen by comparing ver. 3. with *Isaiah* lx. 14.—ver. 4. with *Isaiah* lxv. 20, 22. and xxxiii. 24.—ver. 6, 7, 8. with *Ezek.* xxxvii. 2, 11, 12, 21.—ver. 7. with *Isaiah* xliii. 5, 6. and xlix. 12. and lix. 19. —ver. 12, 13. with *Hosea* ii. 21, 22. and *Ezek.* xxxiv. 22—29.—ver. 8, 12, 13. with *Ezek.* xxxvi. 28—30.—ver. 13. with *Zeph.* iii. 20. and *Isaiah* xix. 24.—ver. 19. with *Isaiah* lxi. 3. and *Jer.* xxxi. 12, 13, 14.

So that however the prophet, in some things that are said in this chapter, may have respect to future smiles of heaven on the nation of the Jews, lately returned from the Babylonish captivity, and resettled in the land of Canaan, in a great increase of their numbers and wealth, and the return of more captives from Chaldea and other countries, &c. yet the spirit of God has doubtless respect to things far greater than these, and of which these were but faint resemblances.— We find it common in the prophecies of the Old Testament, that when the prophets are speaking of the favours and blessings of God on the Jews, attending or following their return from the Babylonish captivity, the spirit of God takes occasion from thence to speak of the incomparably greater blessings on the church, that shall attend and follow her deliverance from the spiritual or mystical Babylon, of which those were a type; and is, as it were, led away to speak almost wholly of these latter, and vastly greater things, so as to seem to forget the former.

And whereas the prophet, in this chapter, speaks of God's *bringing his people again from the east and west to Jerusalem*, (ver. 7, 8.) *And multitudes of all nations taking hold of the skirts of the Jews;* so far as we may suppose that this means literally that nation of the posterity of Jacob, it cannot have chief respect to any return of the Jews from Babylon and other countries in those ancient times before Christ, for no such things as are here spoken of, attended any such return; but it must have respect to the great calling and gathering of the Jews into the fold of Christ, and their being received to the blessings of his kingdom, after the fall of Antichrist, or the destruction of mystical Babylon.

In the text we have an account how this future glorious advancement of the church of God should be brought on, or introduced, viz. By great multitudes in different towns and countries taking up a joint resolution, and coming into an express and visible agreement, that they will, by united and extraordinary prayer, seek to God that he would come and manifest himself, and grant the tokens and fruits of his gracious presence.—Particularly we may observe,

1. The duty, with the attendance on which the glorious event foretold shall be brought on, viz. The duty of prayer.—Prayer, some suppose, is here to be taken synechdochically, for the whole of the worship of God—prayer being a principal part of the worship of the church of God in the days of the gospel, when sacrifices are abolished; and so, that this is to be understood only as a prophecy of a great revival of religion, and of the true worship of God among his visible people, the accession of others to the church, and turning of multitudes from idolatry to the worship of the true God. But it appears to me reasonable, to suppose, that something more special is intended, with regard to the duty of prayer; considering that prayer is

here expressly and repeatedly mentioned; and also considering how parallel this place is with many other prophecies, that speak of an extraordinary spirit of prayer, as preceding and introducing that glorious day of revival of religion, and advancement of the church's peace and prosperity, so often foretold, (which I shall have occasion to mention hereafter) and particularly the agreeableness of what is here said, with what is said afterwards by the same prophet, of the *pouring out of a spirit of grace and supplications*, as that with which this great revival of religion shall begin, chap. xii. 10.

2. The good, that shall be sought by prayer; which is God himself.—It is said once and again, *They shall go to pray before the Lord, and to seek the Lord of Hosts.* This is the good they ask for and seek by prayer, *The Lord of Hosts* himself.—To seek God, as the expression may, perhaps, be sometimes used in scripture, may signify no more than seeking the favour or mercy of God. And if it be taken so here, *praying before the Lord,* and *seeking the Lord of Hosts,* must be looked upon as synonymous expressions. And it must be confessed to be a common thing in scripture, to signify the same thing re-

peatedly, by various expressions of the same import, for the greater emphasis.—But certainly that expression of *seeking the Lord*, is very commonly used to signify something more than merely, in general, to seek some mercy of God: It implies that God himself is the great good desired and sought after; that the blessings pursued are God's gracious presence, the blessed manifestations of him, union and intercourse with him; or, in short, God's manifestations and communications of himself by his Holy Spirit. Thus the psalmist desired God, thirsted after him, and sought him. *O God, thou art my God; early will I seek thee. My flesh longeth for thee, in a dry and thirsty land, were no water is, to see thy power and thy glory, so as I have seen thee in the sanctuary.—My soul followeth hard after thee.—Whom have I in heaven but thee? And there is none upon earth that I desire besides thee.* The psalmist earnestly pursued after God, *his soul thirsted after him, he stretched forth his hands unto him*, &c. And therefore it is in scripture the peculiar character of the saints, that they are *those that seek God. This is the generation of them that seek him. Your heart shall live that seek God.* And in many other places. If the expresfion in the text be underſtood agreeably to this ſenſe, then by ſeeking the Lord of Hoſts, we muſt underſtand a ſeeking that God, who had withdrawn, or as it were hid himſelf, for a long time, would return to his church, and grant the tokens and fruits of his gracious preſence, and thoſe bleſſed communications of his ſpirit to his people, and to mankind on the earth, which he had often promiſed, and which his church had long waited for.

And it ſeems reaſonable to underſtand the phraſe, *ſeeking the Lord of Hoſts*, in this ſenſe here, and not as merely ſignifying the ſame thing with praying to God; not only becauſe the expreſſion is repeatedly added to praying before the Lord, in the text, as ſignifying ſomething more; but alſo becauſe the phraſe, taken in this ſenſe, is exactly agreeable to other parallel prophetic repreſentations. Thus God's people's ſeeking, by earneſt prayer, the promiſed reſtoration of the church of God, after the Babyloniſh captivity, and the great apoſtacy that occaſioned it, is called their *ſeeking God, and ſearching for him;* and God's granting this promiſed revival and reſtoration is called his being *found of them*. For thus ſaith the Lord, *that after seventy years be accomplished at Babylon, I will visit you, and perform my good word towards you, in causing you to return to this place. For I know the thoughts that I think towards you, saith the Lord, thoughts of peace, and not of evil, to give you an expected end. Then shall ye go and call upon me, and I will hearken unto you; and ye shall seek me and find me, when ye shall search for me with all your heart; and I will be found of you, saith the Lord, and I will turn away your captivity.* And the prophets, from time to time, represent God, in a low and afflicted state of his church, as being withdrawn, and hiding himself. *Verily thou art a God that hidest thyself, O God of Israel, the Saviour. I hid me, and was wroth.* And they represent God's people, while his church is in such a state, before God delivers and restores the same, as seeking him, looking for him, searching and waiting for him, and calling after him. *I will go and return unto my place, 'till they acknowledge their offence, and seek my face from the house of Jacob, and I will look for him.* And when God, in answer to their prayers and succeeding their endeavors, delivers, restores, and advances his church, according to his promise, then he is said to answer, and come, and say, here am I, and to shew himself; and they are said to find him, and see him plainly. *Then shalt thou cry, and he shall say,* HERE I AM. *But Israel shall be saved in the Lord, with an everlasting salvation. I said not unto the seed of Jacob, Seek ye me in vain. The Lord will wipe away the tears from off all faces, and the rebuke of his people shall he take away from off the earth. And it shall be said in that day, Lo, this is our God, we have waited for him, and he will save us: This is the Lord, we have waited for him; we will be glad, and rejoice in his salvation. We have waited for thee: The desire of our soul is to thy name, and to the remembrance of thee. With my soul have I desired thee in the night; yea, with my spirit within me will I seek thee early. For when thy judgments are in the earth, the inhabitants of the world will learn righteousness. Therefore my people shall know my name; therefore they shall know in that day, that I am he that doth speak: behold,* IT IS I. *How beautiful upon the mountains are the feet of him that bringeth good tidings, that publisheth peace, that bringeth good tidings of good, that publisheth salvation, that saith unto Zion—Thy*

God reigneth! Thy watchmen shall lift up the voice, together shall they sing; for they shall see eye to eye, when the Lord shall bring again Zion.

3. We may observe who they are, that shall be united in thus seeking the Lord of Hosts; *the inhabitants of many cities,* and of many countries, *yea, many people and strong nations*; great multitudes in different parts of the world shall conspire in this business. From the representation made in the prophecy, it appears rational to suppose, that it will be fulfilled something after this manner—First, that there shall be given much of a spirit of prayer to God's people, in many places, disposing them to come into an express agreement, unitedly to pray to God in an extraordinary manner, that he would appear for the help of his church, and in mercy to mankind, and pour out his Spirit, revive his work, and advance his spiritual kingdom in the world, as he has promised; and that this disposition to such prayer, and union in it, will gradually spread more and more, and increase to greater degrees; with which at length will gradually be introduced a revival of religion, and a disposition to greater engagedness in the worship and ser-

vice of God, amongſt his profeſſing people; that this being obſerved will be the means of awakening others, making them ſenſible of the wants of their ſouls, and exciting in them a great concern for their ſpiritual and everlaſting good, and putting them upon earneſtly crying to God for ſpiritual mercies, and diſpoſing them to join with God's people in that extraordinary ſeeking and ſerving of God, which they ſhall ſee them engaged in; and that in this manner religion ſhall be propagated, until the awakening reaches thoſe that are in the higheſt ſtations, and until whole nations be awakened, and there be at length an acceſſion of many of the chief nations of the world to the church of God. Thus after the inhabitants of many cities of Iſrael, or of God's profeſſing people, have taken up, and purſued a joint reſolution, to go and pray before the Lord, and ſeek the Lord of Hoſts, others ſhall be drawn to worſhip and ſerve him with them; till at length many people and ſtrong nations ſhall join themſelves to them; and there ſhall, in proceſs of time, be a vaſt acceſſion to the church, ſo that it ſhall be ten times as large as it was before; yea, at length all nations ſhall be converted unto God.—

Thus ten men shall take hold, out of all languages of the nations, of the skirt of him that is a Jew, (in the sense of the Apostle) saying, " We will go with you, for we have " heard that God is with you." And thus that shall be fulfilled, *O thou that hearest prayer, unto thee shall all flesh come.*

4. We may observe the mode of their union in this duty. It is a visible union, an union by explicit agreement, a joint resolution declared by one to another, come into by being first proposed by some, and readily and expressly fallen in with by others.— The inhabitants of one city shall apply themselves to the inhabitants of another, saying, *let us go,* &c. Those to whom the motion is made, shall comply with it, the proposal shall take with many, it shall be a prevailing, spreading thing; one shall follow another's example, one and another shall say, *I will go also.* Some suppose, that those words— *I will go also*—are to be taken as the words of him that makes the proposal; as much as to say, I do not propose that to you, which I am not willing to do myself, I desire you to go, and I am ready to go with you. But this is to suppose no more to be expressed in these latter words, than was expressed be-

fore in the proposal itself; for these words, *let us go,* signify as much, as that I am willing to go, and desire you to go with me. It seems to me much more natural, to understand these latter words as importing the consent of those to whom the proposal is made, or the reply of one and another that falls in it. This is much more agreeable to the plain design of the text, which is to represent the concurrence of great numbers in this affair, and more agreeable to the representation made in the next verse, of one following another, many taking hold of the skirt of him that is a Jew. And though if the words are thus understood, we must suppose an ellipsis in the text, something understood that is not expressed, as if it had been said—Those of other cities shall say—I will go also;—yet this is not difficult to be supposed, such ellipsis are very common in scripture. We have one exactly parallel with it in Jer. iii. 22. *Return, ye backsliding children, and I will heal your backslidings: behold, we come unto thee, for thou art the Lord our God,* i. e. the backsliding children shall say—" Behold we come unto thee," &c. And in Cant. iv. *Let my beloved come into his garden, and eat his pleasant fruits.—*

I am come into my garden, my sister, my spouse, i. e. her beloved shall say—" I am come into my garden." We have the like throughout that song. So Psal. l. 6, 7. *The heavens shall declare his righteousness, for God is judge himself. Hear, O my people, and I will speak,* i. e. the Judge shall say—" Hear, O my people," &c. The psalms and prophets abound with such figures of speech.

5. We may observe the manner of prayer agreed on, or the manner in which they agree, to engage in and perform the duty. Let us go speedily to pray; or as it in the margin, let us go continually. The words literally translated are, *let us go in going.* Such an ingemination or doubling of words, is very common in the Hebrew language, when it is intended that a thing shall be very strongly expressed; it generally implies the superlative degree of a thing; as the holy of holies signifies the most holy; but it commonly denotes, not only the utmost degree of a thing, but also the utmost certainty; as when God said to *Abraham, in multiplying, I will multiply thy seed.* It implies both that God would certainly multiply his seed, and also multiply it exceedingly. So when God said to *Adam, in the day that thou eatest thereof, in*

dying thou shalt die (as the words are in the original) it implies, both that he should surely die, and also that he should die most terribly, should utterly perish, and be destroyed to the utmost degree. Yea, sometimes it seems to imply something else still; and, in short, as this ingemination of words in the Hebrew, in general, denotes the strength of expression, so it is used to signify almost all those things that are wont to be signified by the various forms of strong speech in other languages: sometimes it signifies the utmost degree of a thing; sometimes certainty; sometimes peremptoriness and terribleness of a threatening, or the greatness and positiveness of a promise, the strictness of a command, and the earnestness of a request.— When God says to *Adam, dying thou shalt die,* it is equivalent to such strong expressions in English, as, thou shalt die indeed, or, thou shalt die with a witness. So when it is said in the text, *let us go in going, and pray before the Lord,* the strength of the expression represents the earnestness of those that make the proposal, their great engagedness in the affair; and with respect to the duty proposed, it may be understood to signify that they should be speedy, fervent, and constant in it; or, in one word, that it should be thoroughly performed.

6. We may learn from the tenor of this prophecy, together with the context, that this union in such prayer is foretold as a becoming and happy thing, and that which would be acceptable to God, and attended with glorious success.

From the whole we may infer, that it is a very suitable thing, and well pleasing to God, for many people, in different parts of the world, by express agreement, to come into a visible union, in extraordinary, speedy, fervent, and constant prayer, for those great effusions of the Holy Spirit, which shall bring on that advancement of Christ's church and kingdom, that God has so often promised shall be in the latter ages of the world.

And so from hence I would infer the duty of God's people, with regard to the memorial lately sent over into America, from Scotland, by a number of ministers there, proposing a method for such an union as has been spoken of, in extraordinary prayer for this great mercy.

And it being the special design of this discourse, to persuade such as are friends to the interests of Christ's kingdom, to a compliance with the proposal and request made in that memorial, I shall first give a short historical account of the affair it relates to, from letters, papers, and pamphlets, that have come over from Scotland; to which I shall annex the memorial itself; and then I shall offer some arguments and motives, tending to induce the friends of religion to fall in with what is proposed; and lastly, make answer to some objections that may possibly be made against it.

As to the first of these things, viz. an historical account of the concert, which the memorial relates to, the following observations may give a sufficient view of that affair.

In October. A. D. 1744, a number of ministers in Scotland, taking into consideration the state of God's church, and of the world of mankind, judged that the providence of God, at such a day, did loudly call such as were concerned for the welfare of Zion, to united extraordinary applications to the God of all grace, suitably acknowledging Him as the fountain of all the spiritual benefits and blessings of his church, and earnestly praying to him, that he would appear in his glory, and favour Zion, and manifest his compassion to the world of mankind, by an abundant effusion of his Holy Spirit on all the churches, and the whole habitable earth, to revive true religion in all parts of Christendom, and to deliver all nations from their great and manifold spiritual calamities and miseries, and bless them with the unspeakable benefits of the kingdom of our glorious Redeemer, and fill the whole earth with his glory. And consulting one another on the subject, they looked on themselves, for their own part, obliged to engage in this duty; and, as far as in them lay, to persuade others to the same; and to endeavour to find out, and fix on some method, that should most effectually tend to promote, and uphold such extraordinary application to heaven among God's people. And after seeking to God by prayer for direction, they determined on the following method, as what they would conform to in their own practice, and propose to be practised by others, for the two years next following, viz. To set apart some time on Saturday evening, and Sabbath morning, every week, for the purpose aforesaid, as other duties would allow to every one respectively; and more solemnly, the first Tuesday of each quarter, (beginning with the first Tuesday of November, then next ensuing) either the whole day, or part of the day, as persons find themselves disposed, or think their circumstances will allow; the time to be spent either in private praying societies, or in public meetings, or alone in secret, as shall be found most practicable, or judged most convenient, by such as are willing, in some way or other, to join in this affair; but not that any should make any promises, or be looked upon as under strict bonds in any respect, constantly and without fail to observe every one of these days, whatever their circumstances should be, or however other duties and necessary affairs might interfere; or that persons should look upon themselves bound with regard to these days in any wise as tho' the time were holy, or the setting them apart for religious purposes were established by sacred authority; but yet, as a proper guard against negligence and unsteadiness, and a prudent preservative, from yielding to a disposition, which persons might be liable to, through the prevalence of indolence and liftleffnefs, to excufe themfelves on trivial occafions, it was propofed, that thofe who unite in this affair fhould refolve with themfelves, that if, by urgent bufinefs, or otherwife, they are hindered from joining with others, on the very day agreed on, yet they would not wholly neglect bearing their part in the duty propofed, but would take the firft convenient day following, for that purpofe.

The reafon why Saturday evening and Lord's-day morning were judged moft convenient for the weekly feafons, was, that thefe times being fo near the time of difpenfing gofpel ordinances through the Chriftian world, which are the great means, in the ufe of which God is wont to grant his Spirit to mankind, and the principal means that the Spirit of God makes ufe of to carry on his work of grace, it may be well fuppofed, that the minds of Chriftians, in general, will, at thefe feafons, be efpecially difengaged from fecular affairs, and difpofed to pious meditations and the duties of devotion, and more naturally led to feek communications of the Holy Spirit, and fuccefs of the means of grace. And as to the quarterly times, it was thought helpful to memory, that they should be on one or other of the first days of each quarter; Tuesday was preferred to Monday, because in some places people might have public prayers and sermon on the stated day, which might not be so convenient on Monday, as on some day at a greater distance from the Sabbath.

It was reckoned a chief use of such an agreement and method as this, that it would be a good expedient for the maintaining and keeping up, amongst the people of God, that great Christian duty of prayerfulness for the coming of Christ's kingdom, in general, which Christ has directed his followers to be so much in, that it may not be out of mind, and in a great measure sunk. Things, that we are too little inclined to, through sloth, carnality, or a fulness of our own worldly and private concerns, and that are to be attended at some seasons or other, but have no special seasons stated for them, are apt to be forgotten, or put off from time to time, and, as it were, adjourned without day; and so, if not wholly neglected, yet too little attended. But when we fix certain seasons, which we resolve, unless extraordinarily hindered, to devote to the duty, it tends to prevent forgetfulnefs, and a fettled negligence of it. The certain returns of the feafon will naturally refresh the memory, will tend to put us in mind of the precept of Chrift, and the obligations that lie on all his followers, to abound in fuch a duty, and renewedly engage us to the confideration of the importance, neceffity and unfpeakable value of the mercy fought; and fo, by frequent renovation, to keep alive the confideration, and fenfe of thefe things at all times. Thus the firft promoters of this agreement judged that it would be fubfervient to more abundant prayerfulnefs for effufions of the Holy Spirit at all times through the year, both in fecret and focial worfhip; particularly as to this laft, in congregations, families, and other praying focieties. And then they alfo judged, that fuch an agreed union would tend to animate and encourage God's people in the duty propofed; and that particular perfons and focieties, knowing that great multitudes of their fellow-Chriftians, in fo many diftant places, were, at the fame time, (as a token of the union of their hearts with them in this affair) by agreement, engaged in the fame holy exercife, would naturally be enlivened in the duty by fuch a confideration.

It was not thought beſt to propoſe at firſt a longer time for the continuance of this preciſe method than two years; it being conſidered, that it is not poſſible, before any trial, ſo well to judge of the expedience of a particular method and certain circumſtances of the managing and ordering ſuch an affair, as after ſome time of experience. And it was not known, but that, after long conſideration, and ſome trial, it might be thought beſt to alter ſome circumſtance; or whether others that had not yet been conſulted, might not propoſe a better method. The time firſt agreed on, though but ſhort, was thought ſufficient to give opportunity for judgment and experience, and for ſuch as were diſpoſed to union in an affair of ſuch a nature, in diſtant places, mutually to communicate their ſentiments on the ſubject.

The way, which thoſe that firſt projected and came into this agreement, thought beſt for the giving notice of it and propoſing it to others, was not by any thing publiſhed from the preſs, but by perſonal converſation with ſuch as they could conveniently have immediate acceſs to, and by private correſpondence with others at a diſtance. At firſt it was intended, that ſome formal paper, proposing the matter, should be sent about for proper amendments and improvements, and then concurrence; but on more mature deliberation, it was considered how this might give a handle to objections, (which they tho't it best, to the utmost, to avoid in the infancy of the affair) and how practicable it was, without any such formality, to spread the substance of the proposal by private letters, together with a request to their correspondents, mutually to communicate their tho'ts. Therefore this was fixed on, as the method that was preferable at the beginning. Accordingly, they proposed and endeavoured to promote the affair in this way, and with such success, that great numbers in Scotland and England fell in with the proposal, and some in North America. As to Scotland, it was complied with by numbers, in the four chief towns, Edinburgh, Glasgow, Aberdeen, and Dundee, and many country towns and congregations in various parts of the land. One of the ministers, that was primarily concerned in this affair, in a letter to one of his correspondents, speaks of an explicit declaration of the concurrence of the praying societies in Edinburgh, which they had made in a letter. The number of the praying focieties in that city is very confiderable. Mr. Robe, of Kilfyth, (in a letter to Mr. Prince, of Bofton, dated November 3, 1743,) fays—There were then above thirty focieties of young people there, newly erected, fome of which confifted of upwards of thirty members.—As to Glafgow, this union was unanimoufly agreed to by about forty-five praying focieties there, as an eminent minifter in that city informs, in a letter.

The two years, firft agreed on, ended laft November. A little before this time expired, a number of minifters in Scotland agreed on a memorial, to be printed and fent abroad to their brethren in various parts, propofing to them, and requefting of them, to join with them in the continuance of this method of united prayer, and in endeavours to promote it. Copies of which memorial have lately been fent over into New-England, to the number of near five hundred, directed to be diftributed in almoft every county in this province of the Maffachufetts-Bay, and alfo in feveral parts of Connecticut, New-Hampfhire, Rhode-Ifland, New-York, New-Jerfey, Pennfylvania, Maryland, Virginia, Carolina, and Georgia. The moft, I fuppcfe, of thefe were fent to one of the congregational minifters in Bofton, with a letter fubfcribed by twelve minifters in Scotland, about the affair; many of them to another of the faid minifters of Bofton, and fome to a minifter in Connecticut. It being fhort, I fhall here infert a copy of it at length —It is as follows:

A MEMORIAL *from feveral Minifters in Scotland, to their Brethren in different places, for continuing a* CONCERT *for* PRAYER, *firft entered into in the Year* 1744.

WHEREAS it was the chief fcope of this concert, to promote more abundant application to a duty that is perpetually binding, *prayer that our Lord's kingdom may come,* joined with *praifes;* and it contained fome circumftantial expedients, apprehended to be very fubfervient to that defign, relating to ftated times for fuch exercifes, fo far as this would not interfere with other duties; particularly a part of Saturday evening and Sabbath morning, every week; and more folemnly of fome one of the firft days of each of the four great divifions of the year, that is, of each quarter; as the firft Tuefday, or firft convenient day after;* and the concert, as to this circumstance, was extended only to two years; it being intended that, before these expired, persons engaged in the concert should reciprocally communicate their sentiments and inclinations, as to the prolonging of the time, with or without alteration, as to the circumstance mentioned; and it was intended by the first promoters, that others at a distance should propose such circumstantial amendments or improvements, as they should find proper; it is hereby earnestly intreated, that such would communicate their sentiments accordingly, now that the time first proposed is near expiring.

2. To induce those already engaged to adhere, and others to accede to this concert, it seems of importance to observe, that declarations of concurrence, the communicating and spreading of which are so evidently useful, are to be understood in such a latitude, as to keep at the greatest distance from entangling mens' minds: not as binding men to set apart any stated days from secular affairs, or even to fix on any part of

NOTE.

* The meaning is the first Tuesdays of February, May, August and November, or the first convenient days after these.

such and such precise days, whether it be convenient or not; nor as absolute promises in any respect, but as friendly, harmonious resolutions, with liberty to alter circumstances as shall be found expedient. On account of all which latitude, and that the circumstantial part extends only to a few years, it is apprehended, the concert cannot be liable to the objections against periodical religious times of human appointment.

3. It is also humbly offered to the consideration of ministers, and others furnished with gifts for the most public instructions, whether it might not be of great use, by the blessing of God, if short and nervous scripture persuasives and directions to the duty in view, were composed and published, (either by particular authors, or several joining together, which last way might sometimes have peculiar advantages) and that, from time to time, without too great intervals, the better to keep alive on mens' minds a just sense of the obligations to a duty so important in itself, and in which many may be in danger to faint and turn remiss, without such repeated incitements; and whether it would not also be of great use, if ministers would be pleased to preach frequently on the im-

portance and neceſſity of prayer for the coming of our Lord's kingdom, particularly near the quarterly days, or on theſe days themſelves, where there is public worſhip at that time.

4. They who have found it incumbent on them to publiſh this Memorial at this time, having peculiar advantages for ſpreading it, do intreat that the deſire of concurrence and aſſiſtance, contained in it, may, by no means, be underſtood as reſtricted to any particular denomination or party, or to thoſe who are of ſuch or ſuch opinions about any former inſtances of remarkable religious concern; but to be extended to all who ſhall vouchſafe any attention to this paper, and have at heart the intereſt of vital chriſtianity, and the power of godlineſs; and who, however differing about other things, are convinced of the importance of fervent prayer, to promote that common intereſt, and of ſcripture perſuaſives to promote ſuch prayer.

5. As the firſt printed account of this concert was not a propoſal of it, as a thing then to begin, but a narration of it, as a deſign already ſet on foot, which had been brought about with much harmony, by means of private letters, ſo the farther countinuance, and,

it is hoped, the farther fpreading of it feems in a promifing way of being promoted by the fame means, as importunate defires of the renewing the concert have been tranfmitted already from a very diftant corner abroad, where the regard to it has of late increafed; but, notwithftanding of what may be done by private letters, it is humbly expected, that a memorial fpread in this manner may, by God's bleffing, farther promote the good ends in view, as it may be ufefully referred to in letters, and may reach where they will not.

6. Whereas in a valuable letter, from the corner juft now mentioned, as a place where regard to the concert has lately increafed, it is propofed, that it fhould be continued for feven years, or at leaft for a much longer time than what was fpecified in the firft agreement; thofe concerned in this memorial, who would wifh rather to receive and fpread directions and propofals on this head, than to be the firft authors of any, apprehend no inconvenience, for their part, in agreeing to the feven years, with the latitude above defcribed, which referves liberty to make fuch circumftantial alterations, as may be hereafter found expedient; on the con-

trary, it seems of importance, that the labour of spreading a concert, which has already extended to so distant parts, and may, it is hoped, extend farther, may not need to be renewed sooner, at least much sooner, as it is uncertain but that may endanger the dropping of it, and it seems probable, there will be less zeal in spreading of it, if the time proposed for its continuance be too inconsiderable. Mean time, declarations of concurrence for a less number of years may greatly promote the good ends in view, tho' it seems very expedient, that it should exceed what was first agreed on, seeing it is found on trial, that that time, instead of being too long, was much too short.

7. If persons who formerly agreed to this concert, should now discontinue it, would it not look too like that fainting in prayer, against which we are so expressly warned in scripture? And would not this be the more unsuitable at this time, in any within the British dominions, when they have the united calls of such public chastisements and deliverances, to more concern than ever about public reformation, and consequently about that which is the source of all thorough reformation, the regenerating and

sanctifying influence of the almighty Spirit of God?

August 26, 1746.

The minister in Boston afore-mentioned, (to whom most of the copies of this memorial were sent) who, I suppose, has had later and more full intelligence than I have had, says, concerning the proposal, in a letter—" The motion seems to come from above, " and to be wonderfully spreading in Scot-" land, England, Wales, Ireland and North " America.

PART II.

Motives to a Compliance with what is proposed in the Memorial.

I NOW proceed to the second thing intended in this discourse, viz. to offer to consideration some things, which may tend to induce the people of God to comply with the proposal and request made to them in the Memorial.

And I desire that the following things may be considered:

1. It is evident, from the scripture, that there is yet remaining a great advancement of the interest of religion, and the kingdom of Christ, in this world, by an abundant outpouring of the Spirit of God, far greater and more extensive than ever yet has been. It is certain, that many things, which are spoken concerning a glorious time of the church's enlargement and prosperity, in the latter days, have never yet been fulfilled. There has never yet been any propagation and prevailing of religion, in any wise, of that extent and universality, which the prophecies

represent. It is often foretold and signified, in a great variety of strong expressions, that there should a time come, when all nations, through the whole habitable world, should embrace the true religion, and be brought into the church of God. It was often promised to the patriarchs, that *in their seed all the nations,* or, (as it is sometimes expressed) *all the families of the earth should be blessed.* Agreeably to this, it is said of the Messiah, That *all nations shall serve him, and men shall be blessed in him, and all nations shall call him blessed.* And it is said, that *all nations shall flow unto the mountain of the house of the Lord.* And, that *all nations shall be gathered unto the name of the Lord to Jerusalem, and shall walk no more after the imagination of their evil heart.* So it is said, that *all flesh shall come and worship before the Lord.* And that *all flesh should see the glory of God together.* And that *all flesh should come to him that hears prayer.* Christ compares the kingdom of heaven, in this world, to leaven, *which a woman took and hid in three measures of meal, till the whole was leavened.* It is natural and reasonable to suppose, that the whole world should finally be given to Christ, as one whose right it is to reign, as the proper heir of him who is originally the king of all nations, and the poffeffor of heaven and earth; and the fcripture teaches us, that God the Father had conftituted his Son, as God-Man, and in his kingdom of grace, or media'orial kingdom, to be the *heir of the world*, that he might in this kingdom have *the heathen for his inheritance, and the utmoft ends of the earth for his poffeffion.* Thus Abraham is faid to be *the heir of the world,* not in himfelf, but in *his feed,* which is Chrift. And how was this to be fulfilled to Abraham, but by God's fulfilling that great promife. that *in his feed all the nations of the earth fhould be bleffed?* For that promife is what the apoftle is fpeaking of; which fhews, that God has appointed Chrift to be the heir of the world in his kingdom of grace, and to poffefs and reign over all nations, through the propagation of his gofpel, and the power of his Spirit communicating the bleffings of it. God had appointed him to this univerfal dominion by a moft folemn oath: *I have fworn by myfelf, the word is gone out of my mouth in righteoufnefs, and fhall not return, that unto me every knee fhall bow, every tongue fhall fwear.* Though this folemn oath of God the Father is to be underftood in fo comprehenfive a sense, as to extend to what shall be accomplished at the day of judgment, yet it is evident by the foregoing and following verses, that the thing most directly intended, is what shall be fulfilled by the spreading of the gospel of his salvation, and power of the Spirit of grace, bringing *all the ends of the earth to look to him that they may be saved,* and come to him for *righteousness and strength* that, *in him they might be justified, and might glory.* God has suffered many earthly princes to extend their conquests over a great part of the face of the earth, and to possess a dominion of a vast extent, and one monarchy to conquer and succeed another, the latter being still the greater; it is reasonable to suppose that a much greater glory in this respect should be reserved for Christ, God's own son and rightful heir, who has purchased the dominion by so great and hard a service; it is reasonable to suppose, that his dominion should be far the largest, and his conquests vastly the greatest and most extensive. And thus the scriptures represent the matter, in Nebuchadnezzar's vision, and the prophet's interpretation, Dan. ii. There the four great monarchies of the earth, one succeeding another, are represented by *the great image of gold, silver, brass, iron and clay;* but at last *a stone, cut out of the mountains without hands, smites the image upon his feet, which breaks the iron, clay, brass, silver and gold in pieces, that all becomes as the chaff of the summer threshing floors, and the wind carries them away, that no place is found for them; but the stone waxes great, becomes a great mountain, and* FILLS THE WHOLE EARTH; signifying the kingdom which the Lord God of heaven should set up in the world, last of all, which should break in pieces and consume all other kingdoms. Surely this representation leads us to suppose, that this last kingdom shall be of vastly greater extent than any of the preceding. The like representation is made in the viith chapter of Daniel; there the four monarchies are represented by four great beasts that arose successively, one conquering and subduing another; the fourth and last of these is said to be *dreadful* and *terrible,* and *strong exceedingly,* and *to have great iron teeth,* and *to devour and break in pieces, and stamp the residue with his feet;* yea, it is said, verse 23, that the kingdom represented by this beast shall *devour the whole earth;* but last of all, *one like the Son of Man* appears, *coming to the Ancient of*

Days, and being brought near before him, and receiving of him a dominion, and glory, and a kingdom, THAT ALL PEOPLE, NATIONS AND LANGUAGES *should serve him.* This last circumstance, of the vast extent and universality of his dominion, is manifestly spoken of as one thing greatly distinguishing this holy kingdom from all the preceding monarchies; although of one of the former it was said, that it should *devour the whole earth,* yet we are naturally led, both by the much greater emphasis and strength of the expressions, as well as by the whole connexion and tenor of the prophecy, to understand the universality here expressed in a much more extensive and absolute sense; and terms used in the interpretation of this vision are such, that scarcely any can be devised more strong, to signify an absolute universality of dominion over the inhabitants of the face of the earth; ver. 27. *And the kingdom, and dominion, and* GREATNESS OF THE KINGDOM UNDER THE WHOLE HEAVEN, *shall be given to the people of the most high God.* Agreeably to this, the gospel is represented as *preached unto them that dwell on the earth, and to every nation, and tongue, and kindred, and people.* The universality of the prevalance of true religion in the latter days, is sometimes expressed by its reaching to *the utmost ends of the earth. To all the ends of the earth, and of the world. All the ends of the earth with those that are far off upon the sea. From the rising of the sun to the going down of the same. The outgoings of the morning and of the evening.* It seems that all the most strong expressions, that were in use among the Jews to signify the habitable world in its utmost extent, are made use of to signify the extent of the church of God in the latter days, and in many places a variety of these expressions are used, and there is an accumulation of them, expressed with great force.

It would be unreasonable to say, these are only bold figures, used after the manner of the eastern nations, to express the great extent of the Christian church, at and after the days of Constantine; to say so, would be in effect to say, that it would have been impossible for God, if he had desired it, plainly to have foretold any thing that should absolutely have extended to all nations of the earth. I question whether it be possible to find out a more strong expression, to signify an absolute universality of the knowledge of the true religion through the habitable world, than that in Isai. xi. 9. *The earth shall be full of the knowledge of the Lord*, AS THE WATERS COVER THE SEAS. Which is as much as to say, as there is no place in the vast ocean where there is not water, so there shall be no part of the world of mankind where there is not the knowledge of the Lord; as there is no part of the wide bed or cavity possessed by the sea, but what is covered with water, so there shall be no part of the habitable world, that shall not be covered by the light of the gospel, and possessed by the true religion. Waters are often in prophecy put for nations and multitudes of people; so the waters of the main ocean seem sometimes to be put for the inhabitants of the earth in general; as in Ezekiel's vision of the waters of the sanctuary which flowed from the sanctuary, and ran east, till they came to the ocean, and were at first a small stream, but continually encreased till they became a great river; and when they came to the sea, the water even of the vast ocean was healed, representing the conversion of the world to the true religion in the latter days.—It seems evident, that the time will come, when there will not be one nation remaining in the world, which shall not embrace the true religion, in that God has expressly revealed, that no one such nation shall be left standing on the earth; *The nation and kingdom that will not serve thee shall perish; yea, those nations shall be utterly wasted.*—God has declared that heathen idolatry and all the worship of false gods shall be wholly abolished, in the most universal manner, so that it shall be continued in no place under the heavens, or upon the face of the earth; *the gods that have not made the heavens and the earth, even they shall perish from the earth, and from under these heavens. They are vanity, and the work of errors, in the time of their visitation they shall perish.* This must be understood as what shall be brought to pass while this earth and these heavens remain, *i. e.* before the end of the world. Agreeable to this is that in Isaiah. *Sing, O barren, and thou that didst not bear;—for more are the children of the desolate than the children of the married wife, saith the Lord. Enlarge the place of thy tent, and let them stretch forth the curtains of thy habitation; spare not; lengthen thy cords, strengthen thy stakes. For thy maker is thy husband; the Lord of Hosts is his name; and thy Redeemer the Holy One of Israel;* THE GOD OF THE WHOLE EARTH SHALL HE BE CALLED.

The prophecies of the New Testament do no less evidently shew, that a time will come when the gospel shall universally prevail, and the kingdom of Christ be extended over the whole habitable earth, in the most proper sense. Christ says, *I, if I be lifted up from the earth, will draw all men unto me.* It is fit, that when the Son of God becomes man, he should have dominion over all mankind: it is fit, that since he became an inhabitant of the earth, and shed his blood on the earth, he should possess the whole earth: it is fit, seeing here he became a servant, and was subject to men, and was arraigned before them, and judged, condemned and executed by them, and suffered ignominy and death in a most public manner, before Jews and Gentiles, being lifted up to view on the cross upon an hill, near that populous city Jerusalem, at a most public time, when there were many hundred thousand spectators, from all parts, that he should be rewarded with an universal dominion over mankind; and it is here declared he shall be. The apostle, in the xith of Romans, teaches us to look on that great outpouring of the Spirit and in-gathering of souls into Christ's kingdom, that was in those days, first of the Jews, and then of the Gentiles, to be but as the first-fruits of the intended harvest, both with regard to Jews and Gentiles; and to look on the in-gathering of those first fruits as a sign that all the remainder both of Jews and Gentiles shall in due time be gathered in. *For if the first-fruit be holy, the lump is also holy: and if the root be holy, so are the branches.* And in that context, the apostle speaks of the FULNESS of both Jews and Gentiles, as what shall hereafter be brought in, as distinct from that in-gathering from among both, which was in those primitive ages of Christianity; we read of the fulness of the Jews, and of the fulness of the Gentiles; and the apostle teaches us to look upon that infidelity and darkness, which first prevailed over all Gentile nations, before Christ came, and then over the Jews after Christ came, as what was wisely permitted of God, as a preparation for the manifestation of the glory of God's mercy, in due time, on the whole world, constituted of Jews and Gentiles. God hath concluded them all in unbelief, that he might have mercy upon all. These things plainly shew, that the time is coming when the whole world of mankind shall be brought into the church of Christ; and not only a part of the Jews, and a part of the Gentile world, as the first-fruits, as it was in the first ages of the Christian church; but the fulness of both, the whole lump, all the nation of the Jews, and all the world of Gentiles.

In the last great conflict between the church of Christ and her enemies, before the commencement of the glorious time of the church's peace and rest, the kings of the earth, and the *whole world,* are represented as gathered together, and then the seventh angel pours out his vial into the air, which limits that kingdom that Satan has, as god of this world, in its utmost extent;—and that kingdom is represented as utterly overthrown. In another description of that great battle, Christ is represented as riding forth, having on his head many crowns, and on his vesture and on his thigh a name written, KING OF KINGS AND LORD OF LORDS. Which we may well suppose signifies, that he is now going to that conquest, whereby he shall set up a kingdom, in which he shall be king of kings, in a far more extensive manner than either the Babylonish, Persian, Grecian, or Roman monarchs were. And an angel appears standing in the sun, that overlooks the whole world, calling on all the fowls that fly in the midst of heaven, to come and eat the flesh of kings, &c. And in consequence of the great victory Christ gains at that time, *an angel comes down from heaven, having the key of the bottomless pit, and a great chain in his hand, and lays hold on the devil, and binds him, and casts him into the bottomless pit, and shuts him up, and sets a seal upon him, that he should deceive the nations no more.* Satan's being dispossessed of that highest monarchy on earth, the Roman empire, and cast out, in the time of Constantine, is represented by his being cast down from heaven to the earth; but now there is something far beyond that; he is cast out of the earth, and is shut up in hell, and confined to that alone, so that he has no place left him in this world of mankind, high or low.

Now will any be so unreasonable as to say, that all these things do not signify more than that one third part of the world should be brought into the church of Christ, beyond which it cannot be pretended that the Christian religion has ever yet reached, in its greatest extent? Those countries, which belonged to the Roman empire, that were brought to the profession of Christianity, after the reign of Constantine, are but a small part of what the habitable world now is; as to extent of ground, they altogether bear, I suppose, no greater proportion to it, than the land of Canaan did to the Roman empire.—And our Redeemer, in his kingdom of grace, has hitherto possessed but a little part of the world, in its most flourishing state, since arts are arisen to their greatest height, and a very great part of the world is but lately discovered, and much remains undiscovered to this day.

These things make it very evident, that the main fulfilment of those prophecies that speak of the glorious advancement of Christ's kingdom on earth, is still to come.

And as there has been nothing as yet, with regard to the flourishing of religion, and the advancement of Christ's kingdom, of such extent as to answer the prophecies, so neither has there been any thing of that duration that is foretold. The prophecies speak of Jerusalem's being made *the joy of the whole earth,* and also the *joy of many generations.* That *God's people should long enjoy the work of their hands.* That they should *reign with Christ a thousand years;* by which we must at least understand a very long time. But it would be endless to mention all the places, which signify that the time of the church's great peace and prosperity should be of long continuance: almost all the prophecies that speak of her latter-day glory, imply it; and it is implied in very many of them, that when once this day of the church's advancement and peace is begun, it shall never end, till the world ends; or, at least, that there shall be no more a return of her troubles and adversity for any considerable continuance; that then *the days of her mourning shall be ended;* that her tribulations *should then be as the waters of Noah unto God; that as he has sworn that the waters of Noah should no more pass over the earth, so he will swear that he will no more be wroth with his people, or rebuke them;* that *God's people should no more walk after the imagination of their evil heart;* that *God would hide himself no more from the house of Israel, because he has poured out his Spirit upon them;* that *their sun should no more go down, nor the moon withdraw itself;*

that *the light should not be clear and dark;* (i. e. there should be no more an interchange of light and darkness, as used to be) but that it *should be all one continued day; not day and night,* (for so the words are in the original in Zech. xiv. 7.) alternately, *but it shall come to pass, that at evening-time* (i. e. at the time that night and darkness used to be) *it shall be light;* and that *the nations should beat their swords into plow-shares, and their spears into pruning-hooks; and that nation shall not lift up sword against nation, nor learn war any more;* but that there *should be abundance of peace so long as the moon endureth.* And innumerable things of this nature are declared.

But the church of Christ has never yet enjoyed a state of peace and prosperity for any long time; on the contrary, the times of her rest, and of the flourishing state of religion, have ever been very short. Hitherto the church may say, *Return, for thy servants' sake, the tribes of thine inheritance; the people of thy holiness have possessed it but a little while.* The quietness that the church of God enjoyed after the beginning of Constantine's reign was very short; the peace the empire enjoyed, in freedom from war, was not more than twenty years; no longer nor greater than it had enjoyed under some of the heathen emperors. After this the empire was rent in pieces by inteſtine wars, and waſted almoſt every where by the invaſions and incurſions of barbarous nations, and the Chriſtian world was ſoon all in contention and confuſion, by hereſies and diviſions in matters of religion. And the church of Chriſt has never as yet been for any long time, free from perſecution; eſpecially when truth has prevailed, and true religion flouriſhed. It is manifeſt, that hitherto the people of God have been kept under, and Zion has been in a low afflicted ſtate, and her enemies have had the chief ſway.

And another thing that makes it exceeding manifeſt, that that day of the church's greateſt advancement on earth, which is foretold in ſcripture, has never yet come, is that, it is ſo plainly and expreſsly revealed that this day ſhould ſucceed the laſt of the four monarchies, even the Roman, in its laſt ſtate, wherein it is divided into ten kingdoms, and after the deſtruction of Antichriſt, ſignified by the little horn, whoſe reign is contemporary with the reign of the ten kings. Theſe things are very plain in the second and seventh chapters of Daniel, and also in the Revelation of St. John. And it is also plain by the ninth chapter of Romans, that it shall be after the national conversion of the Jews, which shall be as life from the dead to the Gentiles, and the fulness of both Jews and Gentiles should be come in, and all the nation of the Jews, and all other nations, shall obtain mercy, and there shall be that general in-gathering of the harvest of the whole earth, of which all that had been converted before, either of Jews or Gentiles, were but the first fruits. And many other evidences of this point might be mentioned, which for brevity's sake I omit.

And thus it is meet, that the last kingdom which shall take place on earth, should be the kingdom of God's own Son and heir, whose right it is to rule and reign; and that whatever revolutions and confusions there may be in the world, for a long time, the cause of truth, the righteous cause, should finally prevail, and God's holy people should at last inherit the earth, and reign on earth; and that the world should continue in tumults, and great revolutions, following one another, from age to age, the world being, as it were, in travail, till truth and holinefs are brought forth; that all things fhould be fhaken, till that comes which is true and right, and agreeable to the mind of God, which cannot be fhaken; and that the wifdom of the ruler of the world fhould be manifefted in the bringing all things ultimately to fo good an iffue. The world is made for the Son of God; his kingdom is the end of all changes that come to pafs in the ftate of the world of mankind; all are only to prepare the way for this; it is fit therefore that the laft kingdom on earth fhould be his.— It is wifely and mercifully ordered of God that it fhould be fo, on this account, as well as many others, viz. that the church of God, under all preceding changes, fhould have this confideration to encourage her, and maintain her hope, and animate her faith and prayers, from generation to generation, that God has promifed, her caufe fhould finally be maintained and prevail in this world.

Let it now be confidered,

2. The future promifed advancement of the kingdom of Chrift is an event unfpeakably happy and glorious. The fcriptures fpeak of that time, as a time wherein God and his Son Jefus Chrift will be moft emi-

nently glorified on earth; a time, wherein God, who till then had dwelt between the cherubims, and concealed himself in the holy of holies, in the secret of his tabernacle, behind the veil, in the thick darkness, should openly shine forth, and all flesh should see his glory, and God's people in general have as great a privilege as the high priest alone had once a year, or as Moses had in the mount; a time, wherein *the temple of God in heaven should be opened, and there should be seen the ark of his testament;* a time, wherein both God will be greatly glorified, and his saints made unspeakably happy in the view of his glory; a time, wherein God's people should not only once see the light of God's glory, as Moses, or see it once a year with the high priest, but should dwell and walk continually in it, and it should be their constant daily light, instead of the light of the sun, which light should be so much more glorious than the light of the sun or moon, that *the moon shall be confounded, and the sun ashamed, when the Lord of Hosts should reign in Mount Zion, and in Jerusalem, before his ancients gloriously.*

It is represented as a time of vast increase of knowledge and understanding, especially in divine things; a time, wherein God would *destroy the face of the covering cast over all people, and the veil spread over all nations;* wherein *the light of the moon shall be as the light of the sun, and the light of the sun seven-fold. And the eyes of them that see shall not be dim, and the heart of the rash shall understand knowledge. And they shall no more teach every man his neighbour, and every man his brother, saying, Know the Lord, because they shall all know him from the least to the greatest.* A time of general holiness. *Thy people shall be all righteous.* A time of great prevailing of eminent holiness, when little children should, in spiritual attainments, be as though they were *a hundred years old.* Wherein *he that is feeble among God's people should be as David.* A time wherein holiness should be, as it were, inscribed on evething, on all mens' common business and employments, and the common utensils of life, all shall be dedicated to God, and improved to holy purposes. *Her merchandize and hire shall be holiness to the Lord. In that day shall there be upon the bells of the horses,* HOLINESS UNTO THE LORD; *and the pots in the Lord's house shall be like the bowls before the altar; yea, every pot in Jerusalem and in Judah shall be holiness unto the Lord of Hosts.* A time wherein religion and true Christianity shall, in every respect, be uppermost in the world; wherein God will cause his church to *arise and shake herself from the dust, and put on her beautiful garments, and sit down on a throne;* and *the poor shall be raised from the dust, and the beggar from the dunghill, and shall be set among princes, and made to inherit the throne of God's glory.* A time wherein vital piety shall take possession of thrones and palaces, and those that are in most exalted stations shall be eminent in holiness. *And kings shall be thy nursing fathers, and their queens thy nursing mothers. Thou shalt suck the breasts of kings. The daughter of Tyre shall be there with a gift, the rich among the people shall entreat thy favour.* A time of wonderful union, and the most universal peace, love and sweet harmony, wherein the nations shall beat their swords into plow-shares, &c. and God will *cause wars to cease to the ends of the earth, and break the bow, and cut the spear in sunder, and burn the chariot in the fire; and the mountains shall bring forth peace to God's people, and the little hills by righteousness;* wherein *the wolf should dwell with the lamb,* &c. and wherein *God's people shall dwell in a peaceable habita-*

tion, and insure dwellings, and quiet resting places. A time wherein all heresies, and false doctrines shall be exploded, and the church of God shall not be rent with a variety of jarring opinions. *The Lord shall be king over all the earth; in that day there shall be one Lord and his name one.* And all superstitious ways of worship shall be abolished, and all agree in worshipping God in his own appointed way, and agreeable to the purity of his institutions. *I will give them one heart and one way, that they may fear me for ever, for the good of them and their children after them.* A time wherein the whole earth shall be united as one holy city, one heavenly family, men of all nations shall as it were dwell together, and sweetly correspond one with another as brethren and children of the same father; as the prophecies often speak of all God's people at that time as the children of God, and brethren one to another, all appointing over them one head, gathered to one house of God, to worship the king, the Lord of Hosts.—A time wherein this whole great society shall appear in glorious beauty, in genuine amiable christianity, and excellent order, as a city compact together, the perfection of beauty, and eternal excellency, ſhining with a reflection of the glory of Jehovah riſen upon it, which ſhall be attractive and raviſhing to all kings and nations, and it ſhall appear as a bride adorned for her huſband.—A time of great temporal proſperity; of great health. *The inhabitant ſhall not ſay, I am ſick. As the days of a tree, are the days of my people.* A time wherein the earth ſhall be abundantly fruitful. A time wherein the world ſhall be delivered from that multitude of ſore calamities that before had prevailed, and there ſhall be an univerſal bleſſing of God upon mankind, in ſoul and body, and in all their concerns, and all manner of tokens of God's preſence and favour, and *God ſhall rejoice over them, as the bridegroom rejoiceth over his bride, and the mountains ſhall as it were drop down new wine, and the hills ſhall flow with milk.* A time of great and univerſal joy throughout the earth, when *from the utmoſt ends of the earth shall be heard ſongs, even glory to the righteous, and God's people shall with joy draw water out of the well of ſalvation, and God ſhall prepare in his holy mountain, a feaſt of fat things, a feaſt of wines on the lees, of fat things full of marrow, of wines on the lees well refined,* which feaſt is reprefented, as *the marriage fupper of the Lamb.* Yea, the fcriptures reprefent it not only as a time of univerfal joy on earth, but extraordinary joy in heaven, among the angels and faints; the holy apoftles and prophets there. Yea, the fcriptures reprefent it as a time of extraordinary rejoicing with Chrift himfelf, the glorious head, in whom all things in heaven and earth fhall then be gathered together in one. *The Lord thy God in the midft of thee is mighty; he will fave; he will rejoice over thee with joy; he will reft in his love; he will joy over thee with finging.* And the very fields, trees and mountains fhall then, as it were, rejoice, and break forth into finging. *Ye fhall go out with joy, and be led forth with peace; the mountains and the hills fhall break forth before you into finging, and all the trees of the field fhall clap their hands.*— *Sing, O heavens, for the Lord hath done it; fhout, ye lower parts of the earth; break forth into finging, ye mountains; O foreft, and every tree therein; for the Lord hath redeemed Jacob, and glorified himfelf in Ifrael.*

Such being the ftate of things in this future promifed glorious day of the church's profperity, furely it is worth praying for,

Nor is there any one thing whatfoever, if we viewed things aright, which a regard to the glory of God, a concern for the kingdom and honour of our Redeemer, a love to his people, pity to perifhing finners, love to our fellow-creatures in general, compaffion to mankind under its various and fore calamities and miferies, a defire of their temporal and fpritual profperity, love to our country, our neighbours and friends, yea, and to our own fouls, would difpofe us to be fo much in prayer for, as for the dawning of this happy day, and the accomplifhment of that glorious event.'

It may be worthy to be confidered,

3. How much Chrift prayed and laboured and fuffered, in order to the glory and happinefs of that day.

The fum of the bleffings Chrift fought, by what he did and fuffered in the work of redemption, was the Holy Spirit. So is the affair of our redemption conftituted; the Father provides and gives the Redeemer, and the price of redemption is offered to him, and he grants the benefit purchafed; the Son is the redeemer who gives the price, and alfo is the price offered; and the Holy Spirit is the grand bleffing obtained by the price offered, and beftowed on the redeemed. The Holy Spirit, in his in-dwelling, his influences and fruits, is the fum of all grace, holinefs, comfort and joy; or in one word, of all the fpiritual good Chrift pnrchafed for men in this world; and is alfo the fum of all perfection, glory and eternal joy, that he purchafed for them in another world. The Holy Spirit is that great benefit, which is the fubject-matter of the promifes, both of the eternal covenant of redemption, and alfo of the covenant of grace; the grand fubject of the promifes of the Old Teftament, in the prophecies of the bleffings of the Meffiah's kingdom; and the chief fubject of the promifes of the New Teftament; and particularly of the covenant of grace delivered by Jefus Chrift to his difciples, as his laft will and teftament, in the xiv. xv. and xvi. chapters of John; the grand legacy that he bequeathed to them, in that his laft and dying difcourfe with them. Therefore the Holy Spirit is fo often called the fpirit of promife, and emphatically, the promife, the promife of the Father, &c. This being the great bleffing Chrift purchafed by his labours and fufferings on earth, it was the bleffing he received of the Father, when he afcended into heaven, and entered into the holy of holies with his own blood, to communicate to those that he had redeemed. *It is expedient for you, that I go away; for if I go not away, the comforter will not come; but if I depart, I will send him unto you. Being by the right hand of God exalted, and having received of the Father the promise of the Holy Ghost, he hath shed forth this which ye now see and hear.* This is the sum of those gifts, which Christ received for men, even for the rebellious, at his ascension. This is the sum of the benefits Christ obtains for men by his intercession. *I will pray the Father, and he shall give you another comforter, that he may abide with you for ever—even the spirit of truth.* Herein consists Christ's communicative fulness, even in his being full of the Spirit, and so full of grace and truth, that we might of this fulness receive, and grace for grace. He is anointed with the Holy Ghost; and this is the ointment that goes down from the head to the members. God gives the Spirit not by measure unto him, that every one that is his might receive according to the measure of the gift of Christ. This, therefore, was the great blessing he prayed for in that wonderful prayer, that he uttered for his disciples, and all his future church, the evening before he died. The blessing he prayed for to the Father, in behalf of his disciples, was the same he had insisted on in his preceding discourse with them; and this, doubtless, was the blessing he prayed for when, as our High Priest, he offered up strong crying and tears with his blood. The same that he shed his blood for, he also shed tears for, and poured out prayers for.

But the time that we have been speaking of, is the chief time of the bestowment of this blessing—the main season of the success of all that Christ did and suffered in the work of our redemption. Before this the Spirit of God is given but very sparingly, and but few are saved; but then it will be far otherwise; wickedness shall be rare then, as virtue and piety had been before; and, undoubtedly, by far the greatest number of them that ever receive the benefits of Christ's redemption, from the beginning of the world to the end of it, will receive it in that time. The number of the inhabitants of the earth will, doubtless, then be vastly multiplied, and the number of redeemed ones much more. If we should suppose that glorious day to last no more than (literally) a thousand years, and that at the beginning of that thousand years the world of mankind should be but just as numerous as it is now, and that the number should be doubled, during that time of great health and peace, and the universal blessing of heaven, once only in an hundred years, the number at the end of the thousand years would be more than a thousand times greater than it is now; and if it should be doubled once in fifty years, (which probably the number of inhabitants of New-England has ordinarily been, in about half that time) then at the end of the thousand years, there would be more than a million inhabitants on the face of the earth, where there is one now. And there is reason to think, that through the greater part of this period, at least, the number of saints will, in their increase, bear a proportion to the increase of the number of inhabitants. And it must be considered, that if the number of mankind at the beginning of this period be no more than equal to the present number, yet we may doubtless conclude, that the number of true saints will be immensely greater, when instead of the few true and thorough Christians now in some few countries, every nation on the face of the whole earth shall be converted to Christianity, and every country shall be full of true Christians, so that the succeffive multiplication of true faints through the thousand years, will begin with that vast advantage, beyond the multiplication of mankind; where the latter is begun from units, the other, doubtless, will begin with hundreds, if not thousands. How much greater then will be the number of true converts, that will be brought to a participation of the benefits of Christ's redemption, during that period, than in all other times put together? I think, the foregoing things confidered, we shall be very moderate in our conjectures, if we fay, it is probable that there will be an hundred thousand times more, that will actually be redeemed to God by Christ's blood, during that period of the church's prosperity that we have been fpeaking of, than ever had been before, from the beginning of the world to that time.

That time is reprefented in scripture, as the proper appointed feafon of Christ's falvation; eminently the elect feafon, the accepted time and day of falvation, the year of Christ's redeemed. This period is fpoken of as the proper time of the dominion of the

Redeemer, and reign of his redeeming love, in the second and seventh chapters of Daniel, and many other places; the proper time of his harvest, or in-gathering of his fruits from this fallen world; the appointed day of his triumph over Satan, the great destroyer, and the appointed day of his marriage with his elect spouse. The time given to the Sun of Righteousness to rule, as the day is the time God has appointed for the natural sun to bear rule; therefore the bringing on of this time is called *Christ's coming in his kingdom*, wherein *he will rent the heavens and come down,* and *the Sun of Righteousness shall arise.*

The comparatively little saving good there is in the world, as the fruit of Christ's redemption, before that time, is, as it were, granted by way of anticipation; as we anticipate something of the sun's light by reflection before the day-time, the proper time of the sun's rule; and as the first-fruits are gathered before the harvest: Then more especially will be the fulfilment of those great promises, made by God the Father to the Son, for his pouring out his soul unto death; then *shall he see his seed, and the pleasure of the Lord shall prosper in his hand;* then *shall he see of the travail of his soul, and be satisfied, and shall justify many by his knowledge;* then *will God divide him a portion with the great, and he shall divide the spoil with the strong;* then shall Christ, in an eminent manner, obtain his chosen spouse, that *he loved and died for, that he might sanctify and cleanse her, with the washing of water, by the word, and present her to himself, a glorious church.* He will obtain *the joy that was set before him, for which he endured the cross, and despised the shame,* chiefly in the events and consequences of that day: That day, as was observed before, is often represented as eminently the time of the rejoicing of the bridegroom. The fore-knowledge and consideration of it was what supported him, and that which his soul exulted in, at a time when his soul had been troubled at the view of his approaching sufferings; as may be seen in John xii. 23, 24, 27, 31, 32.

Now, therefore, if it be so, that this is what Jesus Christ, our great Redeemer and the Head of the Church, did so much desire, and set his heart upon, from all eternity, and which he did and suffered so much for, offering up strong crying and tears, and his precious blood, to obtain it; surely his disciples and members should also earnestly seek it, and be much and earnest in prayer for it.

Let it be considered,

4. The whole creation is, as it were, earnestly waiting for that day, and constantly groaning and travailing in pain to bring forth the felicity and glory of it. For that day is above all other times, excepting the day of judgment, the day of the manifestation of the sons of God, and of their glorious liberty; and, therefore, that elegant representation the apostle makes of the earnest expectation and travail of the creation, in Rom. viii. 19—22 is applicable to the glorious event of this day. *The earnest expectation of the creature waiteth for the manifestation of the sons of God. For the creature was made subject to vanity, not willingly, but by reason of him who hath subjected the same in hope. Because the creature itself also shall be delivered from the bondage of corruption into the glorious liberty of the children of God. For we know that the whole creation groaneth and travaileth in pain together until now.—* The visible world has now, for many ages,

been subjected to sin, and made, as it were, a servant to it, through the abusive improvement that man, who has the dominion over the creatures, puts the creatures to. Thus the sun is a sort of servant to all manner of wickedness, as its light, and other beneficial influences are abused by men, and made subservient to their lusts and sinful purposes. So of the rain, and fruits of the earth, and the brute animals, and all other parts of the visible creation; they all serve mens' corruption, and obey their sinful will; and God doth, in a sort, subject them to it, for he continues his influence and power to make them to be obedient, according to the same law of nature, whereby they yield to mens' command when used to good purposes. It is by the immediate influence of God upon things, acting upon them, according to those constant methods which we call the laws of nature, that they are ever obedient to mens' will, or that we can use them at all. This influence God continues to make them obedient to mens' will though wicked; which is a sure sign that the present state of things is not lasting, it is confusion, and God would not suffer it to be, but that he designs, in a little time, to put an end to it, when it shall no more be so. Seeing it is to be but a little while, God chuses rather to subject the creature to man's wickedness, than to disturb and interrupt the course of nature according to its stated laws; but it is, as it were, a force upon the creature; for the creature is abused in it, perverted to far meaner purposes than those for which the author of its nature made it, and to which he adapted it. The creature, therefore, is, as it were, unwillingly subject, and would not be subject, but that it is but for a short time, and it, as it were, hopes for an alteration. It is a bondage the creature is subject to, from which it was partly delivered when Christ came, and the gospel was promulgated in the world, and will be more fully delivered at the commencement of the glorious day we are speaking of, and perfectly at the day of judgment. This agrees with the context, for the apostle was speaking of the present suffering state of the church. The reason why the church in this world is in a suffering state, is, that the world is subjected to the sin and corruption of mankind. By vanity, in scripture, is very commonly meant sin and wickedness, and also by corruption, as might be shewn in many places would my intended brevity allow.

Though the creature is thus subject to vanity, yet it does not rest in this subjection, but is constantly acting and exerting itself, in order to that glorious liberty that God has appointed at the time we are speaking of, and, as it were, reaching forth towards it. All the changes that are brought to pass in the world, from age to age, are ordered by infinite wisdom, in one respect or other, to prepare the way for that glorious issue of things, that shall be when truth and righteousness shall finally prevail, and he, whose right it is, shall take the kingdom. All the creatures, in all their operations and motions, continually tend to this; as in a clock, all the motions of the whole system of wheels and movements, tend to the striking of the hammer at the appointed time. All the revolutions and restless motions of the sun and and other heavenly bodies, from day to day, from year to year, and from age to age, are continually tending thither; as all the many turnings of the wheels of a chariot, in a journey, tend to the appointed journey's end.— The mighty struggles and conflicts of nations, and shakings of kingdoms, and those vast successive changes that are brought to pass, in the kingdoms and empires of the world, from one age to another, are, as it were, travail-pangs of the creation, in order to bring forth this glorious event. And the fcriptures reprefent the laſt ſtruggles and changes that ſhall immediately precede this event, as being the greateſt of all—as the laſt pangs of a woman in travail are the moſt violent.

The creature thus earneſtly expecting this glorious manifeſtation and liberty of the children of God, and travailing in pain in order to it, therefore the fcriptures, by a like figure, do very often reprefent, that when this ſhall be accompliſhed, the whole inanimate creation ſhall greatly rejoice: That *the heavens ſhall ſing, the earth be glad, the mountains break forth into ſinging, the hills be joyful together, the trees clap their hands, the lower parts of the earth ſhout, the ſea roar and the fulneſs thereof, and the floods clap their hands.*

All the intelligent elect creation, all God's holy creatures in heaven and earth, are truly and properly waiting for, and earneſtly expecting that event. It is abundantly reprefented in fcripture as the ſpirit and character of all true ſaints, that they ſet their hearts upon, love, long, wait and pray for the promised glory of that day; they are spoken of as those that *prefer Jerusalem to their chief joy; that take pleasure in the stones of Zion, and favour the dust thereof; that wait for the consolation of Israel.* It is the language of the church of God, and the breathing of the soul of every true saint, that we have in Psal. xiv. 7. *O that the salvation of Israel were come out of Zion! when the Lord bringeth back the captivity of his people, Jacob shall rejoice, and Israel shall be glad.* Agreeably to this was the spirit of old Jacob, which he expressed when he was dying, in faith in the great promise made to him and Isaac and Abraham, that *in their seed all the families of the earth should be blessed. I have waited for thy salvation, O Lord.* The same is represented as the spirit of his true children, or the family of Jacob. *I will wait upon the Lord, that hideth himself from the house of Jacob, and I will look for him.*—*They that love Christ's appearing,* is a name that the apostle gives to true christians.

The glorious inhabitants of the heavenly world, the saints and angels there, that rejoice when one sinner repents, are earnestly waiting, in an assured and joyful dependance on God's promifes of that converfion of the world, and marriage of the Lamb, which fhall be when that glorious day comes; and therefore they are reprefented as all with one accord rejoicing and praifing God with fuch mighty exultation and triumph, when it is accomlifhed, in Rom. xix.

5. The word of God is full of precepts, encouragements and examples, tending to excite and induce the people of God to be much in prayer for this mercy.

The fpirit of God is the chief of the bleffings that are the fubject-matter of chriftian prayer; for it is the fum of all fpiritual bleffings; which are thofe that we need infinitely more than others; and are thofe wherein our true and eternal happinefs confifts.— That which is the fum of the bleffings that Chrift purchafed, is the fum of the bleffings that Chriftians have to pray for; but that, as was obferved before, is the Holy Spirit; and therefore when the difciples came to Chrift, and defired him to teach them to pray, Luke xi. he accordingly gave them particular directions for the performance of this duty;—the conclufion of his whole difcourfe, in the 13th verfe, plainly fhews that the Holy Spirit is the fum of the bleffings that are the subject-matter of that prayer about which he had instructed them. *If ye then, being evil, know how to give good gifts unto your children, how much more shall your heavenly Father give the Holy Spirit to them that ask him?* From which words of Christ we may also observe, that there is no blessing that we have so great encouragement to pray for, as the Spirit of God; the words imply, that our heavenly Father is especially ready to bestow his Holy Spirit on them that ask him. Of the more excellent nature any benefit is, which we stand in need of, the more ready God is to bestow it in answer to prayer. The infinite goodness of God's nature is the more gratified, and the grand design and aim of the contrivance and work of our redemption, is the more answered, and Jesus Christ the Redeemer has the greater success in his undertaking and labours; and those desires that are expressed in prayer for the most excellent blessings are the most excellent desires, and consequently such as God most approves of, and is most ready to gratify.

The scriptures do not only direct and encourage us in general to pray for the Holy Spirit above all things else, but it is the expressly revealed will of God, that his church should be very much in prayer for that glorious out-pouring of the Spirit that is to be in the latter days, and the things that shall be accomplished by it. God speaking of that blessed event, Ezek. xxxvi. under the figure of *cleansing the house of Israel from all their iniquities, planting and building their waste and ruined places, and making them to become like the garden of Eden, and filling them with men like a flock, like the holy flock, the flock of Jerusalem in her solemn feasts*; wherein he, doubtless, has respect to the same glorious restoration and advancement of his church that is spoken of in the next chapter, and in all the following chapters to the end of the book, he says, ver. 37. *Thus saith the Lord, I will yet for this be enquired of by the house of Israel, to do it for them.* Which, doubtless, implies, that it is the will of God that extraordinary prayerfulness in his people for this mercy should precede the bestowment of it.

I know of no place in the Bible, where so strong an expression is made use of to signify importunity in prayer, as is used in Isai. lxii. 6, 7. where the people of God are called upon to be importunate for this mercy:

Ye that make mention of the Lord, keep not silence, and give him no rest, till he establish, and till he make Jerusalem a praise in the earth. How strong is the phrase? And how loud is this call to the church of God, to be fervent and incessant in their cries to him for this great mercy? How wonderful are the words to be used, concerning the manner in which such worms of the dust should address the high and lofty One that inhabits eternity? And what encouragement is here, to approach the mercy-seat with the greatest freedom, boldness, earnestness, constancy, and full assurance of faith, to seek of God this greatest thing that can be sought in christian prayer?

It is a just observation of a certain eminent minister of the church of Scotland, in a discourse of his, on social prayer, in which, speaking of pleading for the success of the gospel, as required by the Lord's prayer, he says, " That notwithstanding of its being so
" compendious, yet the one half of it, that
" is, three petitions in six, and these the first
" prescribed, do all relate to this great case;
" so that to put up any one of these petiti-
" ons apart, or all of them together, is upon
" the matter, to pray that the dispensation

"of the gospel may be blessed with divine "power." That glorious day we are speaking of is the proper and appointed time, above all others, for the bringing to pass the things requested in each of these petitions; as the prophecies every where represent that as the time, which God has especially appointed for the hallowing or glorifying his own great name in this world, causing *his glory to be revealed, that all flesh may see it together,* causing it *openly to be manifested in the sight of the heathen,* filling the whole world with the light of his glory to such a degree, that *the moon shall be confounded and the sun ashamed* before that brighter glory; the appointed time for the glorifying and magnifying the name of Jesus Christ, causing *every knee to bow, and every tongue to confess to him.* This is the proper time *of God's kingdom's coming,* or of *Christ's coming in his kingdom:* that is the very time foretold in the iid of Daniel, when the *Lord God of heaven shall set up a kingdom,* in the latter times of the last monarchy, when it is divided into ten kingdoms; and that is the very time foretold in the viith of Daniel, when there should be *given to One like to the Son of Man, dominion, glory, and a kingdom, that all peo-*

ple, nations, and languages, should serve him; and the kingdom and dominion, and the greatness of the kingdom under the whole heaven shall be given to the people of the saints of the most high God, after the destruction of the *little horn,* that should continue *for a time, times, and the dividing of time.* And that is the time wherein *God's will shall be done on earth, as it is done in heaven;* when heaven shall, as it were, be bowed, and come down to the earth, as *God's people shall be all righteous, and holiness to the Lord shall be written on the bells of the horses,* &c. So that the three first petitions of the Lord's prayer are, in effect, no other than requests for the bringing on this glorious day.—And as the Lord's prayer begins with asking for this, in the three first petitions, so it concludes with it, in these words, *For thine is the kingdom, and the power, and the glory for ever. Amen.* Which words imply a request, that God would take to himself his great power, and reign, and manifest his power and glory in the world. Thus Christ teaches us, that it becomes his disciples to seek this above all other things, and make it the first and the last in their prayers, and that every petition should be put up in a subordination to the advancement of God's kingdom and glory in the world.

Befides what has been obferved of the Lord's prayer, if we look through the whole Bible, and obferve all the examples of prayer that we find there recorded, we fhall not find fo many prayers for any other mercy, as for the deliverance, reftoration, and profperity of the church, and the advancement of God's glory and kingdom of grace in the world. If we well confider the prayers that we find recorded in the book of Pfalms, I believe we fhall fee reafon to think, that a very great, if not the greater part of them, are prayers uttered, either in the name of Chrift, or in the name of the church, for fuch a mercy; and undoubtedly, the greateft part of that book of Pfalms, is made up of prayers for this mercy, prophecies of it, and prophetical praifes for it.

The prophets, in their prophecies of the reftoration and advancement of the church, very often fpeak of it as what fhall be done in anfwer to the prayers of God's people. Ifai. xxv. 9.—xxvi. 9, 12, 13, 16, 17. to the end. Chap. xxxiii. 2. Pfal. cii. 13—22. Jer. iii. 21. Ifai. lxv. 24.—xli. 17. Hof. v. 15. with vi. 1, 2, 3. and xiv. 2. to the end.—Zech. x. 6.—xii. x. and xiii. 9. Ifai. lv. 6. with ver. 12, 13. Jer. xxxiii. 3. The prophecies of future glorious times of the church, are often introduced with a prayer of the church for her deliverance and advancement, prophetically uttered, as in Ifai. li. 9, &c. Chap. lxiii. 11. to the end, and lxiv. throughout.

In order to Chrift's being myftically born into the world, in the advancement and flourifhing of true religion, and great increafe of the number of true converts who are fpoken of as having Chrift formed in them, the fcriptures reprefent it as requifite, that the church fhould firft be in travail, crying, and pained to be delivered. And one thing that we have good reafon to underftand by it, is her exercifing ftrong defires, and wreftling and agonizing with God in prayer for this event; becaufe we find fuch figures of fpeech ufed in this fenfe elfewhere. *My little children, of whom I travail in birth again, until Chrift be formed in you. Lord, in trouble have they vifited thee; they poured out a prayer when thy chaftening was upon them. Like as a woman with child, that draweth near the time of her delivery, is in pain, and cryeth out in her pangs, fo have we been in thy fight, O*

Lord. And certainly it is fit, that the church of God fhould be in travail for that, which (as I before obferved) the whole creation travails in pain for.

The fcriptures do not only abundantly manifeft it to be the duty of God's people to be much in prayer for this great mercy, but they alfo abound with manifold confiderations to encourage them in it, and animate them with hopes of fuccefs. There is, perhaps, no one thing that fo much of the Bible is taken up in the promifes of, in order to encourage the faith, hope, and prayers of the faints as this, which at once affords to God's people the cleareft evidences that it is their duty to be much in prayer for this mercy, (for, undoubtedly, that which God does abundantly make the fubject of his promifes, God's people fhould abundantly make the fubject of their prayers) and alfo affords them the ftrongeft affurances that their prayers fhall be fuccefsful. With what confidence may we go before God, and pray for that, of which we have fo many exceeding precious and glorious promifes to plead? The very firft promife of God to fallen man, even that *it fhall bruife thy head,* is a promife which is to have its chief fulfilment at that day; and the whole Bible concludes with a promise of the glory of that day, and a prayer for its fulfilment. *He that testifieth these things, saith—Surely, I come quickly—Amen. Even so, come, Lord Jesus.*

The scripture gives us great reason to think, that when once there comes to appear much of a spirit of prayer in the church of God for this mercy, then it will soon be accomplished. It is evidently with reference to this mercy, that God makes that promise, *When the poor and needy seek water, and there is none, and their tongue faileth for thirst, I, the Lord, will hear them; I, the God of Israel, will not forsake them; I will open rivers in high places, and fountains in the midst of the vallies; I will make the wilderness a pool of water, and the dry land springs of water; I will plant in the wilderness the cedar, the shittah-tree, and the myrtle, and the oil-tree; I will set in the desart the fir-tree, the pine, and the box-tree together.* Spiritual waters and rivers are explained by the apostle John, to be the Holy Spirit. It is now a time of scarcity of these spiritual waters; there are, as it were, none: If God's people, in this time of great drought, were but made duly sensible of this calamity, and their own emptiness and necessity, and brought earnestly to thirst and cry for needed supplies, God would, doubtless, soon fulfil this blessed promise.—We have another promise much like this, in Psal. cii. 16, 17. *When the Lord shall build up Zion, he shall appear in his glory; he will regard the prayer of the destitute, and not despise their prayer.* And remarkable are the words that follow in the next verse: *This shall be written for the generation to come; and the people which shall be created shall praise the Lord.* Which seems to signify, that this promise shall be left on record to encourage some future generation of God's people to pray and cry earnestly for this mercy, to whom he would fulfil the promise, and thereby give them, and great multitudes of others, that should be converted through their prayers, occasion to praise his name. Who knows but that the generation here spoken of, may be this present generation? One thing mentioned in the character of that future generation, is certainly true concerning the present, viz. That it is destitute; the church of God is in very low, sorrowful and needy circumstances; and if the next thing, there supposed, were also verified in us, viz.

That we were made fenfible of our great calamity, and brought to cry earneftly to God for help, I am perfuaded that the third would be alfo verified, viz. That our prayers would be turned into joyful praifes, for God's gracious anfwers of our prayers. It is fpoken of as a fign and evidence, that the time to favour Zion is come, when God's fervants are brought, by their prayerfulnefs for her reftoration, in an eminent manner, to fhew that *they favour her ftones and duft. Thou fhalt arife, and have mercy upon Zion; for the time to favour her, yea, the fet time is come; for thy fervants take pleafure in her ftones, and favour the duft thereof.*

God has refpect to the prayers of his faints in all his government of the world, as we may obferve by the reprefentation made, Revelations viii. at the beginning. There we read of feven angels ftanding before the throne of God, and receiving of him feven trumpets, at the founding of which great and mighty changes were to be brought to pafs in the world, through many fucceffive ages. But when thefe angels had received their trumpets, they muft ftand ftill, and all muft be in filence, not one of them muft be allowed to found, until the prayers of the faints are attended to. The angel of the covenant, as a glorious High Prieſt, comes and ſtands at the altar, with much incenſe, to offer with the prayers of all ſaints upon the golden altar, before the throne; and the ſmoke of the incenſe, with the prayers of the ſaints, aſcends up with acceptance before God, out of the angel's hand; and then the angels prepare themſelves to ſound.—And God, in the events of every trumpet, remembers thoſe prayers, as appears at laſt, by the great and glorious things he accompliſhes for his church, in the iſſue of all, in anſwer to theſe prayers, in the event of the laſt trumpet, which brings the glory of the latter days, when theſe prayers ſhall be turned into joyful praiſes. Rev. xi. 15, 16, 17. *And the ſeventh angel ſounded, and there were great voices in heaven, ſaying—The kingdoms of this world are become the kingdoms of our Lord and of his Chriſt; and he ſhall reign for ever and ever. And the four-and-twenty elders, which ſat before God on their ſeats, fell upon their faces, and worſhipped God, ſaying, We give thee thanks, O Lord God Almighty, which art, and waſt, and art to come, becauſe thou haſt taken to thee thy great power, and haſt reigned.* Since it is thus, that it is the pleaſure of God ſo to honor his people, as to carry on all the deſigns of his kingdom in this way, viz. by the prayers of his ſaints; this gives us great reaſon to think, that whenever the time comes that God gives an extraordinary ſpirit of prayer for the promiſed advancement of his kingdom on earth, (which is God's great aim in all preceding providences, and which is the main thing that the ſpirit of prayer in the ſaints aims at) then the fulfilling this event is nigh.

God, in wonderful grace, is pleaſed to repreſent himſelf, as it were, at the command of his people, with regard to mercies of this nature, ſo as to be ready to beſtow them whenever they ſhall earneſtly pray for them. *Thus ſaith the Lord, the holy One of Iſrael, and his maker, Aſk of me of things to come, concerning my ſons, and concerning the work of my hands, command ye me.* What God is ſpeaking of in this context, is the reſtoration of his church; not only a reſtoration from temporal calamity, and an outward captivity by Cyrus; but alſo a ſpiritual reſtoration and advancement, by God's commanding the heavens to *drop down from above, and the ſkies to pour down righteouſneſs, and cau-*

sing the earth to open and bring forth salvation, and righteousness to spring up together. God would have his people ask of him, or enquire of him by earnest prayer, to do this for them; and manifests himself as being at the command of earnest prayers for such a mercy: and a reason why God is so ready to hear such prayers, is couched in the words, viz. Because it is prayer for his own church, his chosen and beloved people, *his sons and daughters, and the work of his hands;* and he cannot deny any thing that is asked for their comfort and prosperity.

God speaks of himself as standing ready to be gracious to his church, and to appear for its restoration, and only waiting for such an opportunity to bestow this mercy, when he shall hear the cries of his people for it, that he may bestow it in answer to their prayers. *Therefore will the Lord wait, that he may be gracious to thee; and therefore will he be exalted, that he may have mercy upon you: For the Lord is a God of judgment; blessed are all they that wait for him. For the people shall dwell in Zion at Jerusalem.— Thou shalt weep no more; he will be very gracious unto thee, at the voice of thy cry:— when he shall hear it, he shall answer thee.—*

The words imply as much as that when God once sees his people much engaged in praying for this mercy, it shall be no longer delayed. Christ desires to hear the voice of his spouse, *that is in the clefts of the rock, in the secret places of the stairs;* in a low and obscure state, driven into secret corners: he only waits for this, in order to put an end to her state of affliction, and cause *the day to break, and the shadows to flee away.* If he once heard her voice in earnest prayer, he would come swiftly over *the mountains of separation* between him and her, *as a roe, or young hart.* When his church is in a low state, and oppressed by her enemies, and cries to him, he will swiftly fly to her relief, as birds fly at the cry of their young. Yea, when that glorious day comes, that I am speaking of, *before they call, he will answer them, and while they are yet speaking, he will hear;* and, in answer to their prayers, he will make *the wolf and the lamb feed together,* &c. When the spouse prays for the effusion of the Holy Spirit, and the coming of Christ, by granting the tokens of his spiritual presence in the church, saying, *Awake, O north wind, and come, thou south, blow upon my garden, that the spices thereof may flow out:*

let my beloved come into his garden, and eat his pleasant fruits; there seems to be an immediate answer to her prayer, in the next words, in abundant communications of the Spirit, and bestowment of spiritual blessings; *I am come into my garden, my sister, my spouse; I have gathered my myrrh with my spice; I have eaten my honey-comb with my honey; I have drunk my wine with my milk. Eat, O friends; drink, yea, drink abundantly, O beloved.*

Scripture instances and examples of success in prayer, give great encouragement to pray for this mercy. Most of the remarkable deliverances and restorations of the church of God, that we have account of in the scriptures, were in answer to prayer. So was the redemption of the church of God from the Egyptian bondage. The great restoration of the church in the latter day, is spoken of as resembled by this; as in Isai. lxiv. 1—4. xi. 11, 15, 16. xliii. 2, 3, 16 —19. li. 10, 11, 15. lxiii. 11, 12, 13. Zech. x. 10, 11. Hos. ii. 14, 15. It was in answer to prayer, that the sun stood still over Gibeon, and the moon in the valley of Ajalon, and God's people obtained that great victory over their enemies: in which wonderful miracle, God feemed to have fome refpect to a future more glorious event to be accomplifhed for the chriftian church, in the day of her victory over her enemies, in the latter days; even that event foretold, Ifai. xl. 20. *Thy fun fhall no more go down, neither fhall thy moon withdraw itfelf.* It was in anfwer to prayer, that God delivered his church from the mighty hoft of the Affyrians, in Hezekiah's time; which difpenfation is abundantly made ufe of, as a type of the great things God will do for the chriftian church in the latter days, in the prophecies of Ifaiah. The reftoration of the church of God from the Babylonifh captivity, as abundantly appears both by fcripture-prophecies and hiftories, was in anfwer to extraordinary prayer; fee Jer. xxix. 10—14. and l. 4, 5. Dan. ix. throughout. Ezra viii. 21, &c. Neh. i. 4. to the end.—iv. 4, 5. and chap. ix. throughout. This reftoration of the Jewifh church, after the deftruction of Babylon, is evidently a type of the glorious reftoration of the chriftian church, after the deftruction of the kingdom of Antichrift; which, as all know, is abundantly fpoken of in the revelation of St. John, as the anti-type of Babylon. Sampfon, out of

T

weaknefs, received ftrength to pull down Dagon's temple, through prayer. So the people of God, in the latter days, will, out of weaknefs, be made ftrong, and will become the inftruments of pulling down the kingdom of Satan, by prayer.

The Spirit of God was poured out upon Chrift himfelf, in anfwer to prayer. *Now when all the people were baptized, it came to pafs, that Jefus alfo being baptized, and praying, the heaven was opened, and the Holy Ghoft defcended in a bodily fhape like a dove, upon him; and a voice came from heaven, which faid, Thou art my beloved Son, in Thee I am well pleafed.* The Spirit defcends on the church of Chrift, the fame way, in this refpect, that it defcended on the head of the church. The greateft effufion of the Spirit that ever yet has been, even that which was in the primitive times of the chriftian church, which began in Jerufalem on the day of Pentecoft, was in anfwer to extraordinary prayer. When the difciples were gathered together to their Lord, a little before his afcenfion, *he commanded them that they fhould not depart from Jerufalem, but wait for the promife of the Father, which,* faith he, *ye have heard of me,* i. e. the promife of the Holy Ghoft; Acts i. 4. What they had their hearts upon was the reftoration of the kingdom of Ifrael: *Lord,* fay they, *wilt thou, at this time, reftore again the kingdom to Ifrael,* ver. 6. And according to Chrift's direction, after his afcenfion, they returned to Jerufalem, and continued in united fervent prayer and fupplication. It feems they fpent their time in it from day to day, without ceafing; until the fpirit came down in a wonderful manner upon them, and that work was begun which never ceafed, until the world was turned upfide down, and all the chief nations of it were converted to chriftianity; and that glorious deliverance and advancement of the chriftian church, that was in the days of Conftantine the Great, followed the extraordinary cries of the church to God, as the matter is reprefented, Rev. vi. at the opening of the fifth feal. The church, in her fuffering ftate, is reprefented crying with a loud voice, *How long, Lord, holy and true, doft thou not judge, and avenge our blood on them that dwell on the earth?* And the opening of the next feal brings on that mighty revolution, in the days of Conftantine, compared to thofe great changes that fhall be at the end of the world.

As there is so great and manifold reason from the word of God, to think that if a spirit of earnest prayer for that great effusion of the Spirit of God which I am speaking of, prevailed in the christian church, the mercy would be soon granted: so those that are engaged in such prayer might well expect the first benefit. God will come to those that are seeking him and waiting for him; Isai. xxv. 9. and xxxvi. 8. When Christ came in the flesh, he was first revealed to them who were *waiting for the consolation of Israel, and looking for redemption in Jerusalem.* And in that great out-pouring of the Spirit that was in the days of the apostles, which was attended with such glorious effects among the Jews and Gentiles, the Spirit came down first on those that were engaged in united earnest prayer for it.—A special blessing is promised to them that love and pray for the prosperity of the church of God. *Pray for the peace of Jerusalem. They shall prosper, that love thee.*

7. We are presented with many motives in the dispensations of Divine Providence, at this day, to excite us to be much in prayer for this mercy.

There is much in Providence to shew us

our need of it, and put us on defiring it.—
The great outward calamities, in which the
world is involved, and particularly the bloody war that embroils and waftes the nations
of Chriftendom, and in which our nation
has fo great a fhare, may well make all that
believe God's word, and love mankind, earneftly long and pray for that day, when the
wolf fhall dwell with the lamb, and the nations fhall beat their fwords into plow-fhares,
&c. But efpecially do the fpiritual calamities, and miferies of the prefent time, fhew
our great need of that bleffed effufion of
God's Spirit; there having been, for fo long
a time, fo great a with-holding of the Spirit,
from the greater part of the Chriftian world,
and fuch difmal confequences of it, in the
great decay of vital piety, and the exceeding prevalence of infidelity, herefy, and all
manner of vice and wickednefs; and efpecially in our land and nation; of which a
moft affecting account has lately been publifhed in a pamphlet, printed in London,
and re-printed in Scotland, entitled, Britain's
Remembrancer; by which it feems that luxury, and wickednefs of almoft every kind, is
well nigh come to the utmoft extremity in
the nation; and if vice fhould continue to

prevail and increase for one generation more, as it has the generation past, it looks as tho' the nation could hardly continue in being, but must sink under the weight of its own corruption and wickedness. And the state of things in the other parts of the British dominions, besides England, is very deplorable. The church of Scotland has very much lost her glory, greatly departing from her ancient purity, and excellent order; and has of late been bleeding with great and manifold wounds, occasioned by their divisions and hot contentions. And there are frequent complaints from thence, by those that lament the corruptions of that land, of sin and wickedness, of innumerable kinds, abounding and prevailing of late, among all ranks and sorts of men there. And how lamentable is the moral and religious state of these American colonies? Of New-England in particular! How much is that kind of religion, that was professed and much experienced and practised, in the first, and apparently the best times in New-England, grown and growing out of credit? What fierce and violent contentions have been of late among ministers and people, about things of a religious nature? How much is the gospel-ministry grown into contempt? and the work of the ministry, in many respects, laid under uncommon difficulties, and even in danger of sinking amongst us? How many of our congregations and churches rending in pieces? Church-discipline weakened, and ordinances less and less regarded. What wild and extravagant notions, gross delusions of the devil, and strange practices have prevailed, and do still prevail, in many places, under a pretext of extraordinary purity, spirituality, liberty, and zeal against formality, usurpation, and conformity to the world? How strong and deeply rooted and general are the prejudices that prevail against vital religion, and the power of godliness, and almost every thing that appertains to it, or tends to it? How apparently are the hearts of people, every where, uncommonly shut up against all means and endeavours to awaken sinners and revive religion? Vice and immorality, of all kinds, withal increasing and unusually prevailing?—May not an attentive view and consideration of such a state of things well influence the people that favour the dust of Zion, to earnestness in their cries to God for a general out-pouring of his Spirit, which only can be an effectual remedy for these evils?

Besides the things that have been mentioned, the fresh attempts made by the Antichristian powers against the Protestant interest, in their late endeavours to restore a Popish government in Great Britain, the chief bulwark of the Protestant cause; as also the persecution lately revived against the Protestants in France, may well give occasion to the people of God, to renewed and extraordinary earnestness in their prayers to him, for the fulfilment of the promised downfall of Antichrist, and that liberty and glory of his church that shall follow.

As there is much in the present state of things to shew us our great need of this mercy, and to cause us to desire it; so there is very much to convince us, that *God alone can bestow it,* and shew us our entire and absolute dependence on him for it. The insufficiency of human abilities to bring to pass any such happy change in the world as is foretold, or to afford any remedy to mankind, from such miseries as have been mentioned, does now remarkably appear. Those observations of the apostle, 1 Cor. i. *The world by wisdom knows not God, and God makes foolish the wisdom of this world,* never were verified to such a degree as they are now. Great difcoveries have been made in the arts and fciences, and never was human learning carried to fuch a height, as in the prefent age; and yet never did the caufe of religion and virtue run fo low, in nations profeffing the true religion. Never was an age wherein fo many learned and elaborate treatifes have been written, in proof of the truth and divinity of the Chriftian religion; yet never were there fo many infidels among thofe that were brought up under the light of the gofpel. It is an age, as is fuppofed, of great light, freedom of thought, and difcovery of truth in matters of religion, and detection of the weaknefs and bigotry of our anceftors, and of the folly and abfurdity of the notions of thofe that were accounted eminent divines in former generations; which notions, it is imagined, did deftroy the very foundations of virtue and religion, and enervate all precepts of morality, and, in effect, annul all difference between virtue and vice; and yet vice and wickednefs did never fo prevail, like an overflowing deluge. It is an age wherein thofe mean and ftingy principles as they are called, of our forefathers, which, as is fuppofed, deformed religion, and led

U

to unworthy thoughts of God, are very much difcarded, and grown out of credit, and fuppofed more free, noble and generous tho'ts of the nature of religion, and of the Chriftian fcheme are entertained; but yet never was an age, wherein religion in general was fo much defpifed and trampled on, and Jefus Chrift and God Almighty fo blafphemed and treated with open daring contempt.

The exceeding weaknefs of mankind, and their infufficiency in themfelves for the bringing to pafs any thing great and good in the world, with regard to its moral and fpiritual ftate, remarkably appears in many things that have attended and followed the extraordinary religious commotion, that has lately been in many parts of Great Britain and America. The infirmity of the human nature has been manifefted, in a very affecting manner, in the various paffions that men have been the fubjects of, and innumerable ways that they have been moved, as a reed fhaken with the wind, on occafion of the changes and incidents, both public and private, of fuch a ftate of things. How many errors and extremes are we liable to? How quickly over-topped, blinded, mifled, and confounded? And how eafily does Satan make fools of men, if confident in their own wifdom and ftrength, and left to themfelves? Many, in the late wonderful feafon, were ready to admire and truft in men, as if all depended on fuch and fuch inftruments, at leaft did afcribe too much to their fkill and zeal, becaufe God was pleafed to improve them a little while to do extraordinary things; but what great things does the fkill and zeal of inftruments do now, when the Spirit of God is withdrawn?

As the prefent ftate of things may well excite earneft defires, after the promifed general revival and advancement of true religion, and ferve to fhew our dependence on God for it, fo there are many things in Providence, of late, that tend to encourage us in prayer for fuch a mercy. That infidelity, herefy and vice do fo prevail, and that corruption and wickednefs are rifen to fuch an extreme height, is that which is exceeding deplorable; but yet, I think, confidering God's promifes to his church, and the ordinary method of his difpenfations, hope may juftly be gathered from it, that the prefent ftate of things will not laft long, but that a happy change is nigh. We know, that God never will defert the caufe of truth and holiness, nor suffer the gates of hell to prevail against the church; and that it has usually been so from the beginning of the world, that the state of the church has appeared most dark, just before some remarkable deliverance and advancement. *Many a time may Israel say—Had not the Lord been on our side, then our enemies would have swallowed us up quick—The waters had overwhelmed us.* The church's extremity has often been God's opportunity for the magnifying his power, mercy and faithfulness towards her. The interest of vital piety has long been in general decaying, and error and wickedness prevailing; it looks as though the disease were now come to a crisis, and that things cannot long remain in such a state, but that a change may be expected in one respect or other. And not only God's manner of dealing with his church in former ages, and many things in the promises and prophecies of his word, but also several things appertaining to present and late aspects of Divine Providence, seem to give reason to hope that the change will be such, as to magnify God's free grace and sovereign mercy, and not his revenging justice and wrath. There are certain times, that are days of vengeance, appointed for the more special displays of God's justice and indignation; and God has also his days of mercy, accepted times, chosen seasons, wherein it is his pleasure to shew mercy, and nothing shall hinder it; they are times appointed for the magnifying of the Redeemer and his merits, and the triumphs of his grace, wherein his grace shall triumph over mens' unworthiness in its greatest height. And if we consider God's late dealings with our nation and this land, it appears to me that there is much to make us think that this day is such a day; particularly God's preserving and delivering the nation, when in so great danger of ruin by the late rebellion, and his preserving New-England, and the other British colonies in America, in so remarkable a manner, from the great armament from France, prepared and sent against us the last year; and the almost miraculous success given to us against our enemies at Cape-Breton the year before, disappointing their renewed preparations and fresh attempt against these colonies, this present year 1747, by delivering up the strength of their fleet into the hands of the English, as they were in their way hither. And also in protecting us, from time to time, from armies by land, that have come againſt us from Canada ſince the beginning of the preſent war with France. Beſides many ſtrange inſtances of protection of particular forts and ſettlements, ſhewing a manifeſt interpoſition of the hand of heaven, to the obſervation of ſome of our enemies, and even of the ſavages. And added to theſe, the late unexpected reſtoring of the greater part of our many captives in Canada, by thoſe that held them priſoners there. It appears to me, that God has gone much out of his uſual way, in his exerciſes of mercy, patience and long-ſuffering in theſe inſtances. God's patience was very wonderful of old, towards the ten tribes, and the people of Judah and Jeruſalem, and afterwards to the Jews in Chriſt's and the apoſtles times; but it ſeems to me, all things conſidered, not equal to his patience and mercy to us. God does not only forbear to deſtroy us, notwithſtanding all our provocations and their aggravations, which it would be endleſs to recount; but he has, in the fore-mentioned inſtances, wrought great things for us, wherein his hand has been moſt viſible, and his arm made bare; eſpecially thoſe two inſtances in America, God's ſucceeding us againſt Cape-Breton, and confounding the armada from France the laſt year; diſpenſations of Providence which, if conſidered in all their circumſtances, were ſo wonderful, and apparently manifeſting an extraordinary divine interpoſition, that they come, perhaps, the neareſt to a parallel with God's wonderful works of old, in Moſes's, Joſhua's, and Hezekiah's time, of any that have been in theſe latter ages of the world. And it is to my preſent purpoſe to obſerve, that God was pleaſed to do great things for us in both theſe inſtances, in anſwer to extraordinary prayer. Such remarkable appearances of a ſpirit of prayer, on any particular public occaſion, have not been in the land, at any time within my obſervation and memory, as an occaſion of the affair of Cape-Breton.— And it is worthy to be noted and remembered, that God ſent that great ſtorm on the fleet of our enemies the laſt year, that finally diſperſed, and utterly confounded them, and cauſed them wholly to give over their deſigns againſt us, the very night after our day of public faſting and prayer, for our protection and their confuſion.

Thus, although it be a day of great apoſtacy and provocation, yet it is apparently a day of the wonderful works of God; wonders of power and mercy, which may well lead us to think on thofe two places of fcripture, Pfal. cxix. 126. *It is time for thee, Lord, to work, for they have made void thy law.*—And Pfal. lxxv. 1. *That thy name is near, thy wonderous works declare.*—God appears, as it were, loth to deftroy us, or deal with us according to our iniquities, as great and aggravated as they are, and fhews that mercy pleafes him. As corrupt a time as it is, it is plain, by experience, that it is a time wherein God may be found, and ftands ready to fhew mercy in anfwer to prayer. He that has done fuch great things, and has fo wonderfully and fpeedily anfwered prayer for temporal mercies, will much more give the Holy Spirit if we afk him. He marvelloufly preferves us, and waits to be gracious to us, as though he chofe to make us monuments of his grace, and not his vengeance, and waits only to have us open our mouths wide, that he may fill them.

The late remarkable religious awakenings, that have been in many parts of the Chriftian world, are another thing that may juftly encourage us in prayer for the promifed glorious and univerfal out-pouring of

the Spirit of God. " In or about the year
" 1732 or 1733, God was pleafed to pour
" out his Spirit on the people of Saltzburg,
" in Germany, who were living under Pop-
" ifh darknefs, in a moſt uncommon man-
" ner; fo that above twenty thoufand of
" them, merely by reading the Bible, which
" they made a fhift to get in their own lan-
" guage, were determined to throw off Pop-
" ery, and embrace the reformed Religion;
" yea, and to become fo very 'zealous for
" the truth and gofpel of Jefus Chriſt, as to
" be willing to fuffer the lofs of all things in
" the world, and actually to forfake their
" houfes, lands, goods and relations, that
" they might enjoy the pure preaching of
" the gofpel;—with great earneſtnefs, and
" tears in their eyes, befeeching Proteſtant
" miniſters to preach to them, in different
" places where they came, when banifhed
" from their own country."—In the year
1734 and 1735, there appeared a very great
and general awakening in the county of
Hampfhire, in the province of the Maſſa-
chufetts-Bay, in New-England, and alfo in
many parts of Connecticut. Since this, there

has been a far more extenſive awakening of many thouſands in England, Wales, and Scotland, and almoſt all the Britiſh provinces in North America. There has alſo been ſomething remarkable of the ſame kind in ſome places of the United Netherlands; and about two years ago, a very great awakening and reformation of many of the Indians in the Jerſeys and Pennſylvania, even among ſuch as never embraced Chriſtianity before; and within theſe two years, a great awakening in Virginia and Maryland. Notwithſtanding the great diverſity of opinions about the iſſue of ſome of theſe awakenings, yet I know of none that have denied that there have been great awakenings of late, in theſe times and places, and that multitudes have been brought to more than common concern for their ſalvation, and for a time were made more than ordinarily afraid of ſin, and bro't to reform their former vicious courſes, and take much pains for their ſalvation. If I ſhould be of the opinion of thoſe that think theſe awakenings and ſtrivings of God's Spirit have been generally not well improved, and ſo, as to moſt, have not iſſued well, but have ended in enthuſiaſm and deluſion, yet, that the Spirit of God has been of late so wonderfully awakening and striving with such multitudes, in so many different parts of the world, and even to this day, in one place or other, continues to awaken men, is what I should take great encouragement from, that God was about to do something more glorious, and would, before he finishes, bring things to a greater ripeness, and not finally suffer this work of his to be frustrated and rendered abortive by Satan's crafty management; and that these unusual commotions are the forerunners of something exceeding glorious approaching; as the wind, earthquake and fire, at Mount Sinai, were forerunners of that voice, wherein God was, in a more eminent manner; although they also were caused by a divine power, as it is represented, that these things were caused by the *Lord passing by.* 1 Kings xix. 11, 12.

8. How condecent, how beautiful, and of good tendency would it be, for multitudes of Christians, in various parts of the world, by explicit agreement, to unite in such prayer as is proposed to us.

Union is one of the most amiable things that pertains to human society; yea, it is one of the most beautiful and happy things on earth, which indeed makes earth most like heaven. God has made of one blood all nations of men, to dwell on all the face of the earth; hereby teaching us this moral lesson, that it becomes mankind all to be united as one family. And this is agreeable to the nature that God has given men, disposing them to society; and the circumstances God has placed them in, so many ways obliging and necessitating them to it. A civil union, or an harmonious agreement among men, in the management of their secular concerns, is amiable; but much more a pious union, and sweet agreement in the great business for which man was created, and had powers given him beyond the brutes; even the business of religion, the life and soul of which is love. Union is spoken of in scripture as the peculiar beauty of the church of Christ, Cant. vi. 9. *My dove, my undefiled is but one, she is the only one of her mother, she is the choice one of her that bare her; the daughters saw her and blessed her, yea, the queens and the concubines, and they praised her.* Psal. cxxii. 5. *Jerusalem is builded as a city that is compact together.* Eph. iv.

3—6. *Endeavouring to keep the unity of the Spirit in the bond of peace. There is one body and one spirit; even as ye are called in one hope of your calling; one Lord, one faith, one baptism, one God, and Father of all, who is above all, and through all, and in you all.* Ver. 16. *The whole body fitly framed together and compacted, by that which every joint supplieth, according to the effectual working in the measure of every part, maketh increase of the body, unto the edifying itself in love.*

As it is the glory of the church of Christ, that she, in all her members, however dispersed, is thus one, one holy society, one city, one family, one body; so it is very desirable, that this union should be manifested, and become visible; and so, that her distant members should act as one, in those things that concern the common interest of the whole body, and in those duties and exercises wherein they have to do with their common lord and head, as seeking of him the common prosperity. It becomes all the members of a particular family, who are strictly united, and have in so many respects one common interest, to unite in prayer to God for the things they need; it becomes a nation, in days of prayer, appointed by national authority, at certain seasons, visibly to unite in prayer for those public mercies that concern the interest of the whole nation; so it becomes the church of Christ, which is one holy nation, a peculiar people, one heavenly family, more strictly united, in many respects, and having infinitely greater interests that are common to the whole, than any other society; I say, it especially becomes this society, visibly to unite, and expressly to agree together in prayer to God for the common prosperity; and above all, that common prosperity and advancement that is so unspeakably great and glorious, which God has so abundantly promised to fulfil in the latter days.

It is becoming of Christians, with whose character a narrow selfish spirit, above all others, disagrees, to be much in prayer for that public mercy, wherein consists the welfare and happiness of the whole body of Christ, of which they are members, and the greatest good of mankind. And union or agreement in prayer is especially becoming, when Christians pray for that mercy, which above all other things concerns them unitedly, and tends to the relief, profperity and glory of the whole body, as well as of each individual member.

Such an union in prayer for the general out-pouring of the Spirit of God, would not only be beautiful, but profitable too. It would tend very much to promote union and charity between diftant members of the church of Chrift, to promote public fpirit, love to the church of God, and concern for the intereft of Zion, as well as be an amiable exercife and manifeftation of fuch a fpirit.—Union in religious duties, efpecially in the duty of prayer, in praying one with and for another, and jointly for their common welfare, above almoft all other things, tends to promote mutual affection and endearment. And if minifters and people fhould, by particular agreement and joint refolution, fet themfelves, in a folemn and extraordinary manner, from time to time, to pray for the revival of religion in the world, it would naturally tend more to awaken in them a concern about things of this nature, and more of a defire after fuch a mercy; it would engage them to more attention to fuch an affair, make them more inquifitive about it, more ready to ufe endeavours to promote that which they, with so many others, spend so much time in praying for, and more ready to rejoice and praise God when they see or hear of any thing of that nature or tendency; and in a particular manner, would it naturally tend to engage ministers (the business of whose life it is, to seek the welfare of the church of Christ, and the advancement of his kingdom) to greater diligence and earnestness in their work; and it would have a tendency to the spiritual profit and advantage of each particular person. For persons to be thus engaged in extraordinary praying for the revival and flourishing of religion in the world, will naturally lead each one to reflect on himself, and consider how religion flourishes in his own heart, and how far his example contributes to the thing that he is praying for.

9. There is great and particular encouragement given in the word of God, to express union and agreement in prayer. Daniel, when he had a great thing to request of God, viz. That God, by his Holy Spirit, would miraculously reveal to him a great secret, which none of the wise men, astrologers, magicians, or sooth-sayers of Babylon could find out, he goes to Hananiah, Mi-

shael and Azariah, his companions, and they agree together, that they will unitedly defire mercies of the God of heaven, concerning this fecret; and their joint requeft was foon granted; and God put great honor upon them, above all the wife men of Babylon, to the filling their mouths with praife, and to the admiration and aftonifhment of Nebuchadnezzar; infomuch, that that great and haughty monarch, as we are told, fell upon his face and worfhipped Daniel, and owned that *his God was of a truth a God of gods,* and greatly promoted Daniel and his praying companions in the province of Babylon. Efther, when fhe had a yet more important requeft to make, for the faving of the church of God, and whole nation of the Jews, difperfed through the empire of Perfia, when on the brink of ruin, fends to all the Jews in the city Shufhan, to pray and faft with her and her maidens; and their united prayers prevail, fo that the event was wonderful; inftead of the intended deftruction of the Jews, the Jews enemies are deftroyed every where, and they are defended, honored and promoted, and their forrow and diftrefs is turned into great gladnefs, feafting, triumph, and mutual joyful congratulations.

Y

The encouragement to explicit agreement in prayer is great from such instances as these; but it is yet greater from those wonderful words of our blessed Redeemer. Mat. xviii. 19. *I say unto you, that if any two of you shall agree on earth touching any thing that they shall ask, it shall be done for them of my Father which is in heaven.* Christ is pleased to give this great encouragement to the union of his followers in this excellent and holy exercise of seeking and serving God; an holy union and communion of his people being that which he greatly desires and delights in, that which he came into the world to bring to pass, that which he especially prayed for with his dying breath, John xvii. that which he died for, and which was one chief end of the whole affair of our redemption by him. Eph. i. *In whom we have redemption through his blood, the forgiveness of sins, according to the riches of his grace, wherein he hath abounded towards us in all wisdom and prudence; having made known to us the mystery of his will, according to his good pleasure, which he hath proposed in himself; that in the dispensation of the fulness of times, he might gather together in one all things in Christ, both which are in heaven, and which are on earth, even in him.*

OBJECTIONS ANSWERED.

I COME now, as was proposed, in the *third* place, to answer and obviate some objections, which some may be ready to make against the thing that has been proposed to us.

Object. 1. Some may be ready to say, That for Christians, in such a manner to set apart certain seasons, every week, and every quarter, to be religiously observed and kept for the purposes proposed, from year to year, would be, in effect, to establish certain periodical times of human invention and appointment, to be kept holy to God, and so to do the very thing, that has ever been objected against, by a very great part of the most eminent Christians and Divines among Protestants, as what men have no right to do, it being for them to add to God's institutions, and introduce their own inventions and establishments into the stated worship of God, and lay unwarrantable bonds on mens' consciences, and do what naturally tends to superstition.

Ans. To this I would say, There can be no justice in such an objection against this proposal, as made to us in the forementioned memorial. Indeed, that caution and prudence appears in the projection itself, and in the manner in which it is proposed to us, that there is not so much as any colour for the objection. The proposal is such, and so well guarded, that there seems to be no room for the weakest Christian that well observes it, so to mistake it, as to understand those things to be implied in it, that have, indeed, been objected against, by many eminent Christians and Divines among Protestants, as entangling mens' consciences, and adding to divine institutions, &c.—Here is no pretence of establishing any thing by authority; no appearance of any claim of power in the proposers, or right to have any regard paid to their determinations or proposals, by virtue of any deference due to them, in any respect, any more than to every individual person of those that they apply themselves to. So far from that, that they expressly mention that which they have thought of, as what they would propose to the thoughts of others, for their amendments and improvements, declaring that they chuse rather to receive and spread the directions and proposals of others, than to be the first authors of any.—No times, not sanctified by God's own institution, are proposed to be observed more than others, under any notion of such times being, in any respect, more holy, or more honorable, or worthy of any preference, or distinguishing regard; either as being sanctified, or made honorable, by authority, or by any great events of Divine Providence, or any relation to any holy persons or things; but only as circumstantially convenient, helpful to memory, especially free from worldly business, near to the times of the administration of public ordinances, &c. None attempts to lay any bonds on others, with respect to this matter, or to desire that they should lay any bonds on themselves, or look on themselves as under any obligations, either by power or promise; or so much as come into any absolute determination in their own minds, to set apart any stated days from secular affairs, or even to fix on any part of such days, without liberty to alter circumstances, as shall be found expedient, and also liberty left to a future alteration of judgment, as to expediency, on further trial and consideration. All that is proposed is, that such as fall in with what is proposed in their judgments and inclinations, while they do so, shall strengthen, assist and encourage their brethren that are of the same mind, by visibly consenting and joining with them in the affair. Is here any thing like making laws in matters of conscience and religion, or adding mens' institutions to God's, or any shew of imposition, or superstitious esteeming and preferring one day above another, or any possible ground of entanglement of any one's conscience?

For men to go about by law to establish and limit circumstances of worship, not established or limited by any law of God, such as precise time, place, and order, may be in many respects of dangerous tendency. But surely it cannot be unlawful or improper for Christians to come into some agreement with regard to these circumstances, for it is impossible to carry on any social worship without it. There is no institution of scripture requiring any people to meet together to worship God in such a spot of ground, or at such an hour of the day; but yet these must be determined by agreement, or else there will be no social worship, in any place, or any hour. So we are not determined by institution, what the precise order of the different parts of worship shall be, what shall precede, and what shall follow; whether praying or singing shall be first, and what shall be next, and what shall conclude; but yet some order must be agreed on by the congregation that unite in worship, otherwise they cannot jointly carry on divine worship, in any way or method at all. If a congregation of Christians do agree to begin their public worship with prayer, and next to sing, and then to attend on the preaching of the word, and to conclude with prayer; and do by consent carry on their worship in this order from year to year, though this order is not appointed in scripture, none will call this superstition. And if a great number of congregations, through a whole land, or more lands than one do, by common consent, keep the same method of public worship, none will pretend to find fault with it. But yet for any to go about to bind all to such a method, would be usurpation and imposition. And if such a precise order should be regarded as sacred, as though no other could be acceptable to God, this would be superstition. —If a particular number of Christians shall agree, that besides the stated public worship of the sabbath, they will, when their circumstances allow, meet together to carry on some religious exercises on a sabbath-day night, for their mutual edification; or if several societies agree to meet together in different places at that time, this is no superstition, though there be no institution for it. If people in different congregations voluntarily agree to take turns to meet together in the house of God, to worship him and hear a public lecture, once a month, or once in six weeks; it is not unlawful, though there be no institution for it; but yet to do this as a thing sacred, indispensible, and binding on mens' consciences, would be superstition. If Christians of several neighbouring congregations, instead of a lecture, agree on some special occasion to keep a circular fast, each congregation taking its turn in a certain time and order, fixed on by consent; or instead of keeping fast by turns, on different days, one on one week, and one on another, they should all agree to keep a fast on the same day, and to do this either once or frequently, according as they shall judge their own circumstances, or the dispensations of the Divine Providence, or the importance of the mercy they seek, do require; neither is there any more superstition in this than the other.

Object. 2. Some may be ready to say, there seems to be something whimsical in its being insisted on that God's people, in different places, should put up their prayers for this mercy at the same time, as though their prayers would be more forcible on that account, and as if God would not be so likely to hear prayers offered up by many, tho' they happened not to pray at the same time, as he would if he heard them all at the same moment.

Ans. To this I would say, If such an objection be made, it must be through misunderstanding. It is not signified or implied in any thing said in the proposal, or in any arguments made use of to enforce it that I have seen, that the prayers of a great number, in different places, will be more forcible, merely because of that circumstance, of their being put up at the same time. It is, indeed, supposed, that it will be very expedient, that certain times for united prayer should be agreed on; which it may be without implying the thing supposed in the objection, on the following accounts.

1. This seems to be a proper expedient for the promoting and maintaining an uni-

on among Christians of distant places, in extraordinary prayer for such a mercy. It appears, from what was before observed, that there ought to be extraordinary prayers among Christians for this mercy; and that it is fit, that God's people should agree and unite in it. Though there be no reason to suppose that prayers will be more prevalent, merely from that circumstance, that different persons pray exactly at the same time; yet there will be more reason to hope, that prayers for such mercy will be prevalent, when God's people are very much in prayer for it, and when many of them are united in it. If therefore agreeing on certain times for united and extraordinary prayer, be a likely means to promote an union of many in extraordinary prayer, then there is more reason to hope that there will be prevalent prayer for such a mercy, for certain times for extraordinary prayer being agreed on. But, that agreement on certain times for united extraordinary prayer, is a likely and proper means to promote and maintain such prayer, I think will be easily evident to any one that considers the matter. If there should be only a loose agreement or consent to it as a duty, or a thing fit and proper, that Christians fhould be much in prayer for the revival of religion, and much more in it than they ufed to be, without agreeing on particular times, how liable would fuch a lax agreement be to be foon forgotten, and that extraordinary prayerfulnefs, which is fixed to no certain times, to be totally neglected? To be fure, diftant parts of the church of Chrift could have no confidence in one another, that this would not be the cafe. If thefe minifters in Scotland, inftead of the propofal they have made, or any other minifters or Chriftians in any part of the Chriftian world, had fent abroad only a general propofal, that God's people fhould, for the time to come, be much more in prayer for the advancement of Chrift's kingdom, than had been common among Chriftians heretofore; and they fhould hear their propofal was generally allowed to be good, and that minifters and people, in one place and another, that had occafion to fpeak their minds upon it, owned that it was a very proper thing, that Chriftians fhould pray more for this mercy than they generally ufed to do; could they, from this only, have, in any meafure, the like grounds of dependence, that God's people, in various parts of the

Christian world, would, indeed, henceforward act unitedly, in maintaining extraordinary prayer for this mercy, as if they should not only hear that the duty in general was approved of, but also that particular times were actually fixed on for the purpose, and an agreement and joint resolution was come into, that they would, unless extraordinarily hindered, set apart such particular seasons to be spent in this duty, from time to time, maintaining this practice for a certain number of years?

2. For God's people, in distant places, to agree on certain times for extraordinary prayer, wherein they will unitedly put up their requests to God, is a means fit and proper to be used, in order to the visibility of their union in such prayer. Union among God's people in prayer is truly beautiful, as has been before observed and shewn; it is beautiful in the eyes of Christ, and it is justly beautiful and amiable in the eyes of Christians. And if so, then it must needs be desirable to Christians that such union should be visible. If it would be a lovely sight in the eyes of the church of Christ, and much to their comfort, to behold various and dif-

ferent parts of the church united in extraordinary prayer for the general out-pouring of the Spirit, then it muſt be defirable to them that ſuch an union ſhould be viſible, that they may behold it; for if it be not viſible, it cannot be beheld. But agreement and union in a multitude in their worſhip becomes viſible, by an agreement in ſome external viſible circumſtances. Worſhip itſelf becomes viſible worſhip, by ſomething external and viſible belonging to the worſhip, and no other way; therefore union and agreement of many in worſhip becomes viſible no other way, but by union and agreement in the external and viſible acts and circumſtances of the worſhip. Such union and agreement becomes viſible, particularly by an agreement in thoſe two viſible circumſtances, time and place. When a number of Chriſtians live near together, and their number and ſituation is convenient, and they have a deſire viſibly to unite in any acts of worſhip, they are wont to make their union and agreement viſible by an union in both theſe circumſtances. But when a much greater number of Chriſtians, dwelling in diſtant places, ſo that they cannot unite by worſhipping in the ſame place, yet deſire a viſible union in some extraordinary worship, they are wont to make their union and agreement visible, by agreeing only in the former of those circumstances, viz. that of time; as is common in the appointment of public fasts and thankfgivings; the same day is appointed, for the performance of that extraordinary worship, by all those Christians, in different places, that it is intended should be united therein, as a visible note of their union. This the common light and sense of God's people leads Christians to in all countries. And the wisdom of God seems to dictate the same thing, in appointing that his people, through the world, in all ages, in their stated and ordinary public worship, every week, should manifest this union and communion one with another, in their worship, as one holy society, and great congregation of worshippers, and servants of God, by offering up their worship on the same day, for the greater glory of their common Lord, and the greater edification and comfort of the whole body.

If any yet find fault with the proposal of certain times to be agreed on by God's people in different places, in the manner set forth in the memorial, I would ask whether they object againſt any ſuch thing, as a viſible agreement of God's people, in different parts of the world, in extraordinary prayer, for the coming of Chriſt's kingdom? Whether ſuch a thing, being viſible, would not be much for the public honor of God's name? And whether it would not tend to Chriſtians aſſiſtance, quickening and encouragement in the duty united in, by mutual example, and alſo to their mutual comfort, by a manifeſtation of that union which is amiable to Chriſt and Chriſtians, and to promote a Chriſtian union among profeſſing Chriſtians in general? And whether we have not reaſon to think, from the word of God, that before that great revival of religion foretold is accompliſhed, there will be a viſible union of the people of God, in various parts of the world, in extraordinary prayer, for this mercy? If theſe things are allowed, I would then aſk further, whether any method can be thought of or deviſed, whereby an expreſs agreement, and viſible union of God's people, in different parts of the world, can be come into, and maintained, but this, or ſome other equivalent to it? If there be any expreſs agreement about any extraordinary prayer at all, it muſt firſt be propoſed by ſome, and others muſt fall in, in the manner as is repreſented in my text. And if extraordinary prayer be agreed on and maintained by many in different places, viſibly one to another, then it muſt be agreed in ſome reſpect, and with regard to ſome circumſtances, what extraordinary prayer ſhall be kept up; and it muſt be ſeen and heard of, from one to another, what extraordinary prayer is kept up. But how ſhall this be, when no times are agreed upon, and it is never known nor heard, by thoſe in different parts, nor is in any reſpect viſible to them, when, or how often, thoſe in one town or country, and another do attend this extraordinary prayer? The conſequence muſt neceſſarily be, that it can never be known how far, or in what reſpect others join with them in extraordinary prayer, or whether they do it at all; and not ſo much as one circumſtance of extraordinary prayer will be viſible; and indeed nothing will be viſible about it. So that I think any body that well conſiders the matter, will ſee, that he who determines to oppoſe ſuch a method as is propoſed to us in the memorial, and all others equivalent to it is, in effect, determined to oppose there ever being any such thing at all, as an agreed and visibly united extraordinary prayer, in the church of God, for a general out-pouring of the Spirit.

3. Though it would not be reasonable to suppose, that merely such a circumstance of prayer, as many people's praying at the same time will directly have any influence or prevalence with God, to cause him to be the more ready to hear prayer; yet such a circumstance may reasonably be supposed to have influence on the minds of men; as the consideration of it may tend to encourage and assist those in praying, that are united in prayer. Will any deny, that it has any reasonable tendency to encourage, animate, or in any respect to help the mind of a Christian in serving God in any duty of religion, to join with a Christian congregation, and to see an assembly of his dear brethren around him, at the same time engaged with him in the same duty? And supposing one in this assembly of saints is blind, and sees no one there, but has by other means ground of satisfaction that there is present at that

time a multitude of God's people, that are united with him in the same service, will any deny, that his suppofing this, and being fatisfied of it, can have any reafonable influence upon his mind, to excite and encourage him, or in any refpect to affift him in his worfhip? The encouragement or help that one that joins with an affembly in worfhipping God, has in his worfhip, by others being united with him, is not merely by any thing that he immediately perceives by fight, or any other of the external fenfes (for union in worfhip is not a thing objected to the external fenfes;) but by the notice or knowledge the mind has of that union, or the fatisfaction the underftanding has that others, at that time, have their minds engaged with him in the fame fervice; which may be when thofe unitedly engaged are at a diftance one from another, as well as when they are prefent. If one be prefent in a worfhipping affembly, and is not blind, and fees others prefent, and fees their external behaviour, their union and engagednefs with him in worfhip is what he does not fee, and what he fees encourages and affifts him in his worfhip, only as he takes it as an evidence of that union and concurrence in his worfhip, that is out of his fight. And perfons may have evidence of this concerning perfons that are abfent, that may give him as much fatisfaction of their union with him, as if they were prefent. And therefore the confideration of others being at the fame time engaged with him in worfhip, that are abfent, may as reafonably animate and encourage him in his worfhip as if they were prefent.

There is no wifdom in finding fault with human nature, as God has made it. Things that exift now, at this prefent time, are, in themfelves, no more weighty or important, than like things, and of equal reality, that exifted in time paft, or are to exift in time to come; yet it is evident, that the confideration of things being prefent (at leaft in moft cafes) does efpecially affect human nature. As for inftance, if a man fhould be certainly informed, that his dear child, at a diftance, was now under fome extreme fuffering, or that an abfent moft dear friend was at this time thinking of him, and in the exercife of great affection towards him, or in the performance of fome great deed of friendfhip; or if a pious parent fhould know that now his child was in the act of fome enormous wickednefs; or that, on the contrary, he was now in some eminent exercise of grace, and in the performance of an extraordinary deed of virtue and piety; would not those things, be more affecting to the human nature, for being considered as things that are in existence at the present time, than if considered as at some distance of time, either past or future? Hundreds of other instances might be mentioned wherein it is no less plain, that the consideration of the present existence of things gives them advantage to affect the minds of men. Yea, it is undoubtedly so with things in general, that take any hold at all of our affections, and towards which we are not indifferent. And if the mind of a particular child of God is disposed to be affected by the consideration of the religion of other saints, and with their union and concurrence with him in any particular duty or act of religion, I can see no reason why the human mind should not be more moved by the object of its affection, when considered as present, as well in this case, as in any other case; yea, I think, we may on good grounds determine there is none.

Nor may we look upon it as an instance of the peculiar weakness of the human nature, that men are more affected with things that are confidered as prefent, than thofe that are diftant; but it feems to be a thing common to finite minds, and fo to all created intelligent beings. Thus, the angels in heaven have peculiar joy, on occafion of the converfion of a finner, when recent, beyond what they have in that which has been long paft. If any therefore shall call it filly and whimfical in any, to value and regard fuch a circumftance, in things of religion, as their exifting at the prefent time, fo as to be the more affected with them for that, they muft call the hoft of angels in heaven a parcel of filly and whimfical beings.

I remember, the Spectator (whom none will call a whimfical author) fomewhere fpeaking of different ways of dear friends mutually expreffing their affection, and maintaining a kind of intercourfe, in abfence one from another, mentions fuch an inftance as this, with much approbation, viz. That two friends, that were greatly endeared one to another, when about to part, and to be for a confiderable time neceffarily abfent, that they might have the comfort of the enjoyment of daily mutual expreffions of friendfhip, in their abfence, agreed that they would, every day, precisely at such an hour, retire from all company and business, to pray for one another. Which agreement they so valued, and so strictly observed, that when the hour came, scarce any thing would hinder them. And rather than miss this opportunity, they would suddenly break off conversation, and abruptly leave the company they were engaged with.—If this be a desirable way of intercourse of particular friends, is it not a desirable and amiable way of maintaining intercourse and fellowship between brethren in Christ Jesus, and the various members of the holy family of God, in different parts of the world, to come into an agreement, that they will set apart certain times, which they will spend with one accord, in extraordinary prayer to their heavenly Father, for the advancement of the kingdom, and the glory of their common dear Lord and Saviour, and for each other's prosperity and happiness, and the greatest good of all their fellow-creatures through the world?

Object. 3. Some perhaps may object, That it looks too much like Pharisaism, when persons engage in any such extraordinary religious exercises, beyond what is appointed by express institution, for them thus design-edly to make it manifest abroad in the world, and so openly to distinguish themselves from others.

Ans. 1. All openly engaging in extraordinary exercises of religion, not expressly enjoined by institution, is not Pharisaism, nor has ever been so reputed in the Christian church. As when a particular church or congregation of Christians agree together to keep a day of fasting and prayer, on some special occasion; or when public days of fasting and thanksgiving are kept, throughout a Christian province or country; and though it be ordinarily the manner for the civil magistrate to lead, in the setting apart such days, yet that alters not the case; if it be Pharisaism in the society openly to agree in such extraordinary exercises of religion, it is not less Pharisaism for the heads of the society leading in the affair. And if that were now the case with the Christian church, that once was, for about three hundred years together, that the civil magistrate was not of the society of Christians, nor concerned himself in their affairs; yet this would not render it the less suitable for Christians, on proper occasions, jointly, and visibly one to another, to engage in such extraordinary exercises of religion, and to keep days of fasting and thanksgiving by agreement.

Ans. 2. As to the latter part of the objection, there can be no room for it in this case. It cannot be objected against what is proposed in the memorial, that if persons should comply with it, it would look like affecting singularity, and open distinction from others of God's professing people, in extraordinary religion, such as was in the Pharisees of old; because it is evident, the very design of the memorial, is not to promote singularity and distinction, but as much as possible to avoid and prevent it. The end of the memorial is not to confine and limit the thing proposed, that it may be practised only by a few, in distinction from the generality; but on the contrary to extend it, and make it as general among professing Christians as possible. Some had complied with the extraordinary duty proposed, and therein had been distinguished from others, for two years, before the memorial was published; and they were more distinguished than they desired, and therefore send abroad this memorial, that the practice might be more spread, and become more general, that they might be less distinguished. What they evidently seek, is to bring to pass as general a compliance as possible of Christians of all denominations, "intreating, that the desire of concurrence "and assistance, contained in the memorial, "may by no means be understood, as restric- "ting to any particular denomination or "party, or those who are of such or such "opinions about any former instances of re- "markable religious concern; but to be ex- "tended to all, who shall vouchsafe any at- "tention to the proposal, and have at heart "the interest of vital Christianity, and the "power of godliness; and who, however dif- "fering about other things, are convinced "of the importance of fervent prayer, to "promote that common interest, and of "scripture persuasives, to promote such "prayer.

Object. 4. Another objection, that is very likely to arise in the minds of many against such extraordinary prayer as is proposed for the speedy coming of Christ's kingdom, is that we have no reason to expect it, until there first come a time of most extreme calamity to the church of God, and prevalence of her anti-christian enemies against her; even that which is represented, Rev. xi. by the slaying of the witnesses; but have reason to determine the contrary.

Ans. It is an opinion that seems pretty much to have obtained, that before the fulfilment of the promises relating to the church's latter-day glory, there must come a most terrible time, a time of extreme suffering, and dreadful persecution of the church of Christ, wherein Satan and Antichrist are to obtain their greatest victory over her, and she is to be bro't lower than ever by her enemies. Which opinion has chiefly risen from the manner of interpreting and applying the fore-mentioned prophecy of the slaying of the witnesses. This opinion, with such persons as retain it, must needs be a great restraint and hindrance, with regard to such an affair as is proposed to us in the memorial. If persons expect no other, than that the more the glorious times of Christ's kingdom are hastened, the sooner will come this dreadful time, wherein the generality of God's people must suffer so extremely, and the church of Christ be almost extinguished, and blotted out from under heaven; how can it be otherwise, than a great damp to their hope, courage and activity, in praying for and reaching after the speedy introduction of those glorious promised times? As long as this opinion is retained, it will undoubtedly ever have this unhappy influence on the minds of those that wish well to Zion, and favor her stones and dust. It will tend to damp, deaden, and keep down life, hope, and joyful expectation in prayer; and even in great measure, to prevent all earnest, animated and encouraged prayer, in God's people, for this mercy, at any time before it is actually fulfilled. For they that proceed on this hypothesis in their prayers, must, at the same time that they pray for this glorious day, naturally conclude within themselves, that they shall never live to see on the earth any dawning of it, but only to see the dismal time that shall precede it, in which the far greater part of God's people, that shall live until then, shall die under the extreme cruelties of their persecutors. And the more they expect that God will answer their prayers, by speedy bringing on the promised glorious day, the more must they withal expect themselves to have a share in those dreadful things, that nature shrinks at the thoughts of, and also expect to see things that a renewed nature shrinks at and dreads; even the prevailing of God's enemies, and the almost total extinguishing the true religion in the world. And on this hypothesis, these discouragements are like to attend the prayers of God's people, until that dismal time be actually come; and when that is come, those that had been prophesying and praying in sackcloth, shall generally be slain; and after that time is over, then the glorious day shall immediately commence. So that this notion tends to discourage and hinder all earnest prayer in the church of God for that glorious coming of Christ's kingdom, until it be actually come; and that is to hinder its ever being at all.

It being so, this opinion being of such hurtful tendency, certainly it is a thousand pities it should prevail and be retained, if truly there be no good ground for it.

Therefore in answer to this objection, I would, with all humility and modesty, examine the foundation of that opinion, of such a dreadful time of victory of Antichrist over the church, yet to be expected: and particularly shall endeavour to shew that the *slaying of the witnesses*, foretold, Rev. xi. 7—10. is not an event that remains yet to be fulfilled.—To this end, I would propose the following things to consideration.

1. The time wherein the *witnesses lie dead in the streets of the great city*, doubtless, signifies the time wherein the true church of Christ is lowest of all, most of all prevailed against by Antichrist, and nearest to an utter extinction; the time wherein there is left the least visibility of the church of Christ yet subsisting in the world, least remains of any thing appertaining to true religion, whence a revival of it can be expected, and wherein all means of it are most abolished, and the state of the church is, in all respects, furthest from any thing whence any hopes of its ever flourishing again might arise. For before this the witnesses *prophesy in sackcloth*, but now they are *dead;* before this they were kept low indeed, yet there was life, and power to bring plagues on their enemies, and so much of true religion left, as to be a continual eye-sore and torment to them; but now their enemies rejoice and feast, and have a general public triumph, as having obtained a full victory over them, and having entirely extirpated them, and being completely delivered from them, and all that might give them any fear of being troubled with them any more. This time, wherever it be fixed, doubtless, is the time, not only wherein fewest

professors of the true religion are left in the world, but a time wherein the truth shall be farthest out of sight, and out of reach, and most forgotten; wherein there are left fewest beams of light, or traces of truth, fewest means of information, and opportunities of coming to the knowledge of the truth; and so a time of the most barbarous ignorance, most destitute of all history, reliques, monuments and memory of things appertaining to true religion, or things, the knowledge of which hath any tendency to bring truth again to light, and most destitute of learning, study and enquiry.

Now, if we confider the prefent ftate of mankind, it is credible that a time will yet come in the world, that in thefe refpects exceeds all times that were before the Reformation? And that fuch a time will come before the fall of Antichrift, unlefs we fet that at a much greater diftance, than the fartheft that any yet have fuppofed? It is next to impoffible, that fuch a change fhould be brought about in fo fhort a time—it cannot be without a miracle. In order to it, not only muft the Popifh nations fo prevail, as utterly to extirpate the Proteftant religion through the earth, but muft do many other things, far more impoffible for them to effect, in order to cover the world with fo grofs and confirmed a darknefs, and to bury all light and truth in fo deep an oblivion, and fo far out of all means and hopes of a revival. And not only muft a vaft change be made in the Proteftant world, but the Popifh nations muft be ftrangely metamorphofed, and they themfelves muft be terribly perfecuted by fome other power, in order to bring them to fuch a change; nor would perfecution without extirpation be fufficient for it. If there fhould be another univerfal deluge, it might be fufficient to bring things in the world to fuch a pafs, provided a few ignorant barbarous perfons only were preferved in an ark; and it would require fome cataftrophe, not much fhort of this, to effect it.

2. In the Reformation, that was in the days of Luther, Calvin, and others their contemporaries, the threatened deftruction of Antichrift, that dreadful enemy that had long oppreffed and worn out the faints, was begun; nor was it a fmall beginning, but Antichrift hath fallen, at leaft, halfway to the ground, from that height of power and

grandeur, that he was in before. Then began the vials of God's wrath to be *poured out on the throne of the beast,* to the great shaking of its foundations, and diminution of its extent; so that the Pope lost near half of his former dominions, and as to degree of authority and influence over what is left, he is not possessed of what he had before. God now at length, in answer to the long continued cries of his people, awaked as one out of sleep, and began to deliver his church from her exceeding low state, that she had continued in for many ages, under the great oppression of this grand enemy, and to restore her from her exile and bondage in the spiritual Babylon and Egypt. And it is not agreeable to the analogy of God's dispensations, that after this, God should desert his people, and hide himself from them, even more than before, and leave them more than ever in the hands of their enemy, and all this advantage of the church against Antichrist should be entirely given up and lost, and the power and tyranny of Antichrist be more confirmed, and the church brought more under, and more entirely subdued than ever before, and further from all help and means to recover. This is not God's way

of dealing with his people, or with their e-
nemies; his work of salvation is perfect—
when he has begun such a work he will carry it on—when he once causes the day of
deliverance to dawn to his people, after such
a long night of dismal darkness, he will not
extinguish the light, and cause them to return again to midnight darkness—when he
has begun to enkindle the blessed fire, he
will not quench the smoaking flax, until he
hath brought forth judgment unto victory.
When once the church, after her long labour and sore travail, has brought forth her
man-child, and wrought some deliverance,
her enemies shall never be able to destroy
this child, though an infant, but it shall ascend up to heaven, and be set on high out
of their reach.

The destruction that God often foretold
and threatened to ancient Babylon (which
is often referred to in the Revelation, as a
great type of the anti-christian church) was
gradually accomplished, and fulfilled by various steps, at a great distance of time one
from another; it was begun in the conquest
of Cyrus, and was further accomplished by
Darius, about eighteen years after, by a yet

greater deſtruction, wherein it was brought much nearer to utter deſolation; but it was about two hundred and twenty-three years after this, before the ruin of it was perfected, and the prophecies againſt it fully accompliſhed, in its being made an utter and perpetual deſolation, without any human inhabitant, becoming the dwelling-place for owls, dragons, and other doleful creatures. But yet when God had once begun to deſtroy her, he went on until he finiſhed, and never ſuffered her any more to recover and eſtabliſh her former empire. So the reſtitution of the Jewiſh church, after the Babyloniſh captivity, was gradual, by various ſteps; there were ſeveral times of return of the Jews from captivity, and ſeveral diſtinct decrees of the Perſian emperors, for the reſtoring and rebuilding Jeruſalem, and re-eſtabliſhing the Jewiſh church and ſtate; and it was done in turbulent times, there were great interruptions and checks, and violent oppoſitions, and times wherein the enemy did much prevail: But yet, when God had once begun the work he alſo made an end; he never ſuffered the enemies of the Jews to bring Jeruſalem to ſuch a ſtate of deſolation as it had been in before, until the promised restoration was complete. Again, the deliverance of God's church from the oppression of Antiochus Epiphanes, (another known type of Antichrist) was gradual; they were first assisted in a small degree, by the Maccabees, and afterwards the promised deliverance was completed, in the recovery of Jerusalem, the restoration of the temple, the miserable end of Antiochus, and the consequent more full deliverance of the whole land. But after God once began to appear for the help of his church in that instance, after it seemed dead and past all hope, he never suffered Antiochus to prevail against his people, to that degree, again; though the utmost strength of this great monarch was used, from time to time, in order to it, and his vast empire was engaged against an handful that opposed them: God never forsook the work of his own hands; when he had begun to deliver his people, he also made an end. And so Haman, that proud and inveterate enemy of the Jews, that tho't to extirpate the whole nation, who also was probab'y another type of Antichrist, when he began to fall before Esther and Mordecai, never stayed, until his ruin, and the church's deliverance was complete. Haman's wife speaks of it, as an argument of his approaching inevitable full destruction, that he *had begun to fall*, Esth. vi. 15.

3. If it should be so, that anti-christian tyranny and darkness should hereafter so prevail against the Protestant church, and the true religion, and every thing appertaining to it, as to bring things to the pass forementioned, this would hardly so properly answer the prophecy of slaying the two witnesses; for, doubtless, one reason why they are called two witnesses is, that the number of the remaining witnesses for the truth was, though sufficient, yet very small. Which was remarkably the case, in the dark times of Popery; but since the Reformation the number of those appearing on the side of true religion, has been far from being so small. —The visible church of Christ has been vastly large, in comparison of what it was before; the number of Protestants has sometimes been thought nearly equal to that of the Papists; and, doubtless, the number of true saints has been far greater than before.

4. It seems to be signified in prophecy, that after the Reformation, Antichrist should never prevail against the church of Christ any more, as he had done before. I cannot

but think, that whoever reads and well considers what the learned Mr. Lowman has written on the five first vials, Rev. xvi. in his late Exposition on the Revelation, must think it to be very manifest, that what is said, verse 10, of the pouring out of the fifth vial *on the throne of the beast,* (for so it is in the original) is a prophecy of the Reformation. Then the vial of God's wrath was poured out on the throne of the beast, *i. e.* according to the language of scripture, on his authority and dominion, greatly to weaken and diminish it, both in extent and degree. But when this is represented in the prophecy, then it is added, *and his kingdom was full of darkness, and they gnawed their tongues for pain.* If we consider what is commonly intended by such like phrases in the scripture, I think we shall be naturally, and, as it were, necessarily led to understand those words thus: Their policy, by which heretofore they have prevailed, shall now fail them; their authority shall be weakened, and their dominion greatly diminished, and all their craft and subtilty shall not avail them to maintain and support the throne of the beast, or even again to extend his authority so far as it had been before extended, and to recover what it loft; but all their crafty devices to this end fhall be attended with vexatious tormenting difappointment; they that have the management of the affairs of the beaft's kingdom, fhall henceforward grope as in the dark, and ftumble, and be confounded in their purpofes, plots and enterprizes; formerly their policy was greatly fuccefsful, was as a light to guide them to their ends, but now their kingdom fhall be full of darknefs, and their wifdom fhall fail them in all their devices to fubdue, and again to bring under the church of God.—The fcripture takes notice of the great policy and fubtilty of the powers that fupport this kingdom, Dan. vii. 8. *And, behold, in this horn were eyes like the eyes of a man.* So it is faid of Antiochus Epiphanes, that great type of Antichrift, Dan. viii. 23. *A king of fierce countenance, and underftanding dark fentences, fhall ftand up.* Ver. 25. *And thro' his policy alfo, fhall he caufe craft to profper in his hand.* This underftanding and policy is the light of this kingdom, as true wifdom is the light of the fpiritual Jerufalem. And, therefore, when the light fails, then may the kingdom of this fpiritual Egypt be faid to be full of darknefs. God henceforward will defend his people from thefe myftical Egyptians, as he defended Ifrael of old from Pharaoh and his hoft, when purfuing after them, by placing a cloud and darknefs in their way, and fo not fuffering them to come nigh. So he will protect his church from the men of that city that is fpiritually called Sodom, as Lot's houfe, wherein were the angels, was defended from the men of Sodom, by their being fmitten with darknefs or blindnefs, fo that they wearied themfelves to find the door; and as God defended the city in which was Elifha the prophet, and witnefs of the Lord, from the Syrians, when they compaffed it about with horfes and chariots, and a great hoft to apprehend him, by fmiting them with blindnefs. The fcripture teaches us, that God is wont in this way to defend his church and people from their crafty and powerful enemies, Job v. 11, &c. *To fet up on high thofe that be low, that thofe which mourn may be exalted to fafety: He difappointeth the devices of the crafty, fo that their hands cannot perform their enterprize: He taketh the wife in their own craftinefs, and the counfel of the forward is carried headlong: They meet with darknefs in the day-time, and grope in the* noon-day as in the night; but he saveth the poor from the sword, from their mouth, and from the hand of the mighty. Psal. xxxv. 4. 6. *Let them be confounded and put to shame, that seek after my soul; let them be turned back, and brought to confusion, that devise my hurt —Let their way be dark and slippery.*

Upon the account of such defence of God's Protestant church, and disappointment and confusion of all the subtle devices, deep-laid schemes, and furious attempts of their anti-christian enemies, to bring them under, and root them out, and their seeing them still maintaining their ground, and subsisting in an independency on them, in spite of all that they do, it makes them as it were gnash their teeth, and bite their tongues for mere rage and vexation; agreeable to Psal. cxii. 9, 10. *His righteousness endureth for ever, his horn shall be exalted with honour: The wicked shall see it and be grieved, and gnash with his teeth and melt away: The desire of the wicked shall perish.*

Hitherto this prophecy has been very signally fulfilled; since the Reformation, the kingdom of Antichrist has been remarkably filled with darkness in this respect. Innumerable have been the crafty devices, and great attempts of the church of Rome, wherein they have exerted their utmost policy and power, to recover their lost dominions, and again to subjugate the Protestant nations, and subdue the northern heresy, as they call it. They have wearied themselves in these endeavours for more than two hundred years past; but have hitherto been disappointed, and have often been strangely confounded. When their matters seemed to be brought to a ripeness, and they triumphed as though their point was gained, their joy and triumph has suddenly turned into vexation and torment. How many have been their politic and powerful attempts against the Protestant interest in our nation in particular? And how wonderfully has God disappointed them from time to time! And as God has hitherto so remarkably fulfilled his word in defending his Protestant church from Antichrist, so I think we have ground to trust in him, that he will defend it to the end.

5. The hypothesis of those who suppose the slaying of the witnesses is a thing that yet remains to be fulfilled, makes the prophecies of the Revelation to be inconsistent

one with another. According to their hypothesis, that battle, Rev. xi. 7. wherein the beast makes war with the witnesses, and overcomes them, and kills them, is the last and greatest conflict between Antichrist and the church of Christ, which is to precede the utter overthrow of the anti-christian kingdom. And they must suppose so, for they suppose, that immediately after the sufferings the church shall endure in that war, she shall arise, and, as it were, ascend into heaven; *i. e.* as they interpret it, the church shall be directly advanced to her latter-day rest, prosperity and glory. And consequently, this conflict must be the same with that great battle between Antichrist and the Church, that is described, chap. xvi. 13. to the end, and more largely, chap. xix. 11. to the end. For that which is described in these places, is most evidently and indisputably the greatest and last battle or conflict that shall be between the church and her anti-christian enemies, on which the utter downfall of Antichrist, and the church's advancement to her latter-day glory, shall be immediately consequent. And so the earthquake that attends the resurrection of the witnesses, chap. xi. 13. must be the same with that great earthquake that is defcribed, chap. xvi. 18. And the falling of the tenth part of the city muft be the fame with that terrible and utter deftruction of Antichrift's kingdom, chap. xvi. 17. to the end.

But thefe things cannot be. The battle. chap. xi. 7. cannot be the fame with that laft and great battle between the Church and Antichrift, defcribed, chap xvi. and xix.—For the things that are faid of one and the other, and their iffue, are in no wife confiftent. In that battle, chap. xi. the church of God conflicts with her enemies in forrow, fackcloth, and blood; but in the other the matter is reprefented exceedingly otherwife—the church goes forth to fight with Antichrift, not in fackcloth and blood, but cloathed in white raiment, Chrift himfelf before them, as their captain, going forth in great pomp and magnificence, upon a *white horfe*, and *on his head many crowns*, and *on his vefture, and on his thigh, a name written*, KING OF KINGS AND LORD OF LORDS; and the faints who follow fo glorious a leader to this great battle, follow him on *white horfes, cloathed in fine linen, white and clean*, in garments of ftrength, joy, glory and triumph; in the fame kind of raiment, that the saints appear in, when they are reprefented as triumphing with Chrift, with palms in their hands, chap. vii. 9. And the iffue of the latter of thefe conflicts, is quite the reverfe of the former. In the battle, chap. xi. 7. *The beaft makes war with the witneffes, and* OVERCOMES THEM, AND KILLS THEM; the fame is foretold, Dan. vii. 21. *I beheld, and the fame horn made war with the faints, and prevailed againft them.*—And Rev. xii. 7. *And it was given unto him to make war with the faints, and to overcome them.* But in the iffue of that laft and great battle, which the church fhall have with her anti-chriftian enemies, the church fhall OVERCOME THEM, AND KILL THEM, Rev. xvii. 14. *Thefe fhall make war with the Lamb, and the Lamb fhall overcome them; for he is Lord of Lords, and King of Kings; and they that are with him, are called, and chofen, and faithful,* compared with chapter xix. 16, and following verfes, and chapter xvi. 16, 17. In the conflict that the beaft fhall have with the witneffes, the *beaft kills them, and their dead bodies lie unburied;* as though they were to be meat for the beafts of the earth, and fowls of heaven; but in that laft battle, it is reprefented that Chrift and his church *fhall flay their e-*

nemies, and give their dead bodies to be meat for the fowls of heaven, chap. xix. 17. to the end. There is no manner of appearance, in the defcriptions which are given of that laft great battle, of any advantages gained in it, by the enemies of the church, before they themfelves are overcome, but all appearance of the contrary. Be fure the defcriptions in the xvi. and xix. chapters of the Revelation will, by no means, allow of fuch an advantage, as the overcoming God's people, and flaying them, and their lying dead for fome time, and unburied, that their dead bodies may be for their enemies to abufe, and trample on, and make fport with. In chap. xvi. we read of their being gathered together againft the church, a mighty hoft, into the place called Armageddon, and then the firft thing we hear of, is the pouring out the feventh vial of God's wrath, and a voice faying—*It is done.* And fo in the xix. chap. we have an account of the *beaft, and the kings of the earth, and their armies, being gathered together to make war againft him that fat on the horfe, and againft his army.* And then the next thing we hear of is, that *the beaft is taken, and with him the falfe prophet;* and that *thefe are both caft alive into the lake of fire;* and that *the remnant of their vaſt army are ſlain, and all the fowls filled with their fleſh.* The iſſue of the conflict of the beaſt with the witneſſes, is the triumph of the church's enemies over God's people, looking on them as entirely vanquiſhed, and their intereſt utterly ruined, paſt all poſſibility of recovery: *They that dwell on the earth ſhall ſee the dead bodies of the ſaints lying in the ſtreets of the great city, and ſhall rejoice over them, and make merry, and ſend gifts one to another.*— But the iſſue of that great and laſt battle is quite the reverſe; it is the church's triumph over her enemies, as being utterly and for ever deſtroyed.

Here, if any one ſhall ſay, that the aſcenſion of the witneſſes into heaven in the ſight of their enemies, may, as has more generally been ſuppoſed, ſignify the church's laſt victory and triumph over her anti-chriſtian enemies, and final deliverance from them, and yet the battle between Antichriſt and the witneſſes, ſpoken of, Rev. xi. 7. wherein the witneſſes are ſlain, may not be the ſame with that laſt and greateſt battle between Antichriſt and the church, chap. xvi. and xix. which immediately precedes and iſſues in the church's final victory and deliverance; there may be two great battles, soon following one another, though both are not mentioned in the same place; one a conflict, wherein Antichrist prevails against the witnesses, and overcomes them, and kills them, and another that great battle described, chap. xvi. and xix. after the witnesses resurrection, before their ascension into heaven, wherein they shall prevail and overcome their enemies, and kill them: I say, if any one shall say thus, they will say that which the prophecies give no reason, nor allow any room to suppose. That last battle between the Church and Antichrist, wherein Christ and his people obtain a complete victory, is evidently one of the greatest and remarkable events foretold in all the Apocalypse; and there is no one thing, unless it be the consummation of all things, in the two last chapters, that is described in so solemn and august a manner. And the description shews that it is an event which, with its circumstances, must take up much time. There is vast preparation made for it by the church's enemies; the devils, in order to stir men up, and gather them together, to this *battle of that great day of God Almighty, go forth unto the kings of the earth, and of the whole world,* to propagate various kinds of delusions, far and wide, all over the world; which, undoubtedly, must take up many years time, chap xvi. 13, 14. And then great preparation is made in the church of God, to make opposition, chap. xix. 11—17. Now can any reasonably suppose, that in what is represented, chap. xi. of a great conflict between Antichrist and God's people, wherein the latter are overcome and slain, and lie dead three days (or three years) and a half, and their enemies triumphing over them, but God's people rising again from the dead in the midst of this triumph of their enemies, and ascending into heaven, while the enemies stand astonished and amazed spectators—that the manner of the description leaves fair room for us to suppose, that after this resurrection of God's people, they continue long before they ascend, to encounter with Antichrist in a new conflict, wherein their enemies, after long time to prepare, should engage with them with vastly greater preparations, strength and violence than before, and should wage war with the mightiest army that ever was gathered against the church, and in the greatest battle that ever was fought!

And besides, the witnesses ascending into heaven in the sight of their enemies, spoken of chap. xi. cannot be the same with the church's gaining a glorious ascendant over her enemies, in her final victory over Antichrist, spoken of chap. xvi. and xix. because the descriptions of the events that attend the one and the other do by no means answer each other. For, observe, it is said, that when the witnesses *arose, and stood on their feet, and ascended into heaven, the same hour there was a great earthquake;* but this does not seem to answer to what is described, chap. xvi. 18. *And there were voices, and thunders, and lightnings, and there was a great earthquake, such as was not since men were upon the earth, so mighty an earthquake, and so great.* —It is said, that at the same time of the first earthquake, chap. xi. 13. *The tenth part of the city fell;* but how far does this fall short of what is described, as attending the great earthquake? chap. xv. 19, 20. *And the great city was divided into three parts, and the cities of the nations fell; and great Babylon came into remembrance before God, to give unto her the cup of the wine of the fierceness of his wrath; and every island fled away, and the mountains were not found.* It is said of the earthquake, chap. xi. *And in the earthquake were slain of men seven thousand;* but how far is this from answering the slaughter described, chap. xix. 17, &c. Which is represented as a general slaughter of the kings, captains, mighty men, horses, and armies of the earth, and of the whole world; so that all the fowls that fly in the midst of heaven, as far as the sun shines, are filled with the flesh of the dead carcases, it being the *flesh of all men, both free and bond, both small and great;* (compare chap. xvi. 14.) who can think, that this great slaughter, that is thus represented, should, in chap. xi. be only called a *slaying of seven thousand men?*

If we read this very eleventh chapter thro', we shall see that the falling of the tenth part of the city, and the witnesses rising and ascending into heaven, are entirely distinct from the final destruction of Antichrist, and that advancement of the church to her latter-day glory, that is consequent upon it.— The judgments here spoken of, as executed on God's enemies, are under another woe; and the benefits bestowed on the church, are under another trumpet. For immediately after the account of the rising and ascending of the witnesses, and the tenth part of the city's falling, and the slaying of the seven thousand men, and the affrighting of the rest, and their giving glory to the God of heaven, follow these words in the 14th and 15th verses, *The second woe is past, and behold the third woe cometh quickly. And the seventh angel sounded, and there were great voices in heaven, saying—The kingdoms of this world are become the kingdoms of our Lord, and of his Christ, and he shall reign for ever and ever.* And in the following verses, we have an account of the praises sung to God on this occasion. And then in that last verse, we have a brief hint of that same earthquake, and the great hail, and those thunders, and lightnings, and voices, that we have an account of in the latter part of chap. xvi. So that the earthquake mentioned in the last verse of chap. xi. is that great earthquake that attends the last great conflict of the church and her enemies, and not that mentioned ver. 13.

The three woes are the woes of God on Antichrist and his subjects; and the third and last of them evidently signifies the terrible judgments of God on Antichrist, by which God's wrath upon him shall be fulfilled in his utter deſtruction; but the calamities on Antichriſt, ſpoken of as attending the riſing and aſcending of the witneſſes, ſuch as the falling of the tenth part of the city, and ſlaying ſeven thouſand men, do not belong to this laſt woe, and therefore do not ſignify the final deſtruction of Antichriſt; for the words of verſe 14. will by no means allow of ſuch a ſuppoſition; for there, immediately after giving an account of theſe calamities, it is added—*The ſecond woe is paſt; and, behold, the third woe cometh quickly;* making a moſt plain and expreſs diſtinction between theſe calamities that had already been mentioned, and eſpecially theſe that were juſt then mentioned in the very laſt words, and the calamities that belong to the third woe, that yet remain to be mentioned; for by being paſſed, the prophet is to be underſtood no otherwiſe than paſſed in the declaration and repreſentation—it was not paſt in any other reſpect; it is as much as to ſay, Thus an account has been given of the calamities upon Antichriſt that belong to the ſecond woe; now I proceed to give an account of thoſe diſpenſations of Providence that belong to the third and laſt woe, which ſhall prove Antichriſt's final deſtruction, and

in the kingdoms of this world becoming the kingdoms of our Lord, and of his Christ.

What was fulfilled in the Reformation, well answers the representation made concerning the witnesses, Rev. xi. 11. 12. *Of the spirit of life from God entering into them, and their standing on their feet, and ascending up to heaven, in the sight of their enemies.* A little before the Reformation, the state of the church of God, and of true religion was lowest of all, and nearest to utter extinction.— Antichrist had, after great and long struggles, prevailed against the Waldenses, Albigenses, and Bohemians. The war with the Albigenses seems especially to be intended by the war of the beast with the witnesses, spoken of verse 7. These were witnesses to the truth that were the most numerous and considerable, and those that most tormented the church of Rome. And the war that was maintained against them, was, by far, the greatest that ever Antichrist had against any of the professors of the truth, before the Reformation, and was properly the war of the beast; it was the Pope that proclaimed the war, and that raised the soldiers by his emissaries and priests, preaching the cross, gathering innumerable multitudes of pilgrims from all parts of Christendom, and raising one croisade after another, which were conducted and managed by the Pope's legates; and it was the Pope that paid the soldiers with pardons, indulgences, promises of Paradise, and such like trumpery. When Antichrist had gradually prevailed against these witnesses, with much difficulty, and long continued violent struggling, and after innumerable vexatious disasters and disappointments, the church of God, in the time of Luther, and other reformers, on a sudden, in a wonderful manner, revives, when such an event was least expected, (to the surprize and amazement of their anti-christian enemies) and appears in such strength, that the reformed are able to stand on their own legs, and to withstand all the power and rage of the church of Rome. Presently after this revival, the people of God are set on high, having the civil magistrate in many countries on their side, and henceforward have the power of many potent princes engaged for their protection. And this, in sight of their enemies, and greatly to their grief and vexation; who, though they, from time to time, exert their utmost, never are able to prevail against them, to bring them under any more, as they had done in former wars. Oftentimes, in fcripture, God's church's dwelling in fafety, out of the reach of their enemies, is reprefented by their dwelling on high, or being fet on high; as Pfal. lix. 1. lxix. 29. xci. 14. cvii. 41. Prov. xxix. 25. Ifai. xxxiii. 16. The children of Ifrael, in their deliverance out of Egypt, from their cruel tafk-mafters, who would fain have brought them into bondage again, were faid *to be carried on eagle's wings,* which is lofty in its flight, flies away towards heaven, fo that the Egyptians could not come at them; and they were protected by the cloud that went with them, as the witneffes are faid to be caught up to heaven in a cloud. Compare this with Ifai. iv. 5. *And the Lord will create upon every dwelling-place of Mount Zion, and upon her affemblies, a cloud and fmoke by day, and the fhining of a flaming fire by night; for upon all the glory fhall be a defence.*

I fhall not pretend to explain the myftery of the three days and a half of the witneffes lying dead, or to determine the precife duration fignified by that myftical reprefentation. Poffibly no particular meafure of time may be intended by it, and yet it may not be without significancy.* As no particular number of persons is intended by the two witnesses, but, in general, it intends a small number, and yet a sufficient number; and as small as might be, and yet be sufficient; as less than two witnesses was not sufficient, so, perhaps, no particular duration of that low state that the church was in before the Reformation, may be intended by three days and an half, but, in general, it may be hereby signified, that this time of the triumphing of the wicked, and extremity of God's church, should be but short. Possibly three days and an half may be mentioned, because that is the utmost space of time that a dead body can be ordinarily supposed to lie without putrefaction, signifying that at this time the church should be brought to the very brink of utter ruin, and yet should be preserved, and revive again. And half a day may be mentioned to

NOTE.

* Mr. Lowman, in the preface to his Paraphrase on the Revelation, page 8, observes as follows: *Prophetic numbers do not always express a determinate duration, or space of time, any more than they always express a certain number. Prophecy, I acknowledge, uses numbers sometimes as other expressions, in a figurate meaning, as symbols and hieroglyphics. Thus the number* SEVEN *sometimes does not denote the precise number seven; but figuratively denotes perfection, or a full and complete number; and the number ten sometimes does not mean precisely ten in number, but many in general, or a considerable number.*

signify the particular care of Providence in exactly determining this time of his church's extremity. And probably there may be some reference to the three times (or three years) and an half of the witnesses prophesying in sackcloth: the more apparently to shew the disproportion between the time of the church's welfare, and the time of her enemies victory and triumph; the time of the church's affliction and conflict may be long, and in the issue she may be overcome; but the time of this victory shall be but short, in comparison with the other, but as a day to a year; she may, as it were, be killed, and lie dead, until she comes to the very brink of utter and hopeless ruin, but yet God will not suffer her to see corruption; but at that very time, when her enemies expected that she should putrify, she shall rise, and be set on high, out of their reach, greatly to their astonishment.

The grand objection against all this is, that it is said, that *the witnesses should prophesy twelve hundred and sixty days cloathed in sackcloth; and when they have finished their testimony, the beast should make war against them, and kill them,* &c. and that it seems manifest, that after this, they are no longer in fackcloth, for henceforward they are in an exalted ftate in heaven; and that, therefore, feeing the time of their wearing fackcloth is twelve hundred and fifty days, which is the time of the continuance of Antichrift; hence their being flain and rifing again, muft be at the conclufion of this period, and fo at the end of Antichrift's reign.

In anfwer to which I would fay, that we can juftly infer no more from this prophecy than this, viz. That the twelve hundred and fixty days is the proper time of the church's trouble and bondage, or being cloathed in fackcloth, becaufe it is the appointed time of the reign of Antichrift. But this does not hinder but that God, out of his great compaffion to his church, fhould, in fome refpect, fhorten the days, and grant that fhe fhould, in fome meafure, anticipate the appointed great deliverance that fhould be at the end of thofe days; as he has, in fact, done in the Reformation, whereby the church has had a great degree of reftoration granted, from the darknefs and power of Antichrift, before her proper time of reftoration, which is at the end of the twelve hundred and fixty days. Thus the church of Chrift, through the tender mercies of her Father and Redeemer, in some respects, anticipates her deliverance from her sorrows and sackcloth; as many parts of the church are hereby brought from under the dominion of the anti-christian powers, into a state of power and liberty, though, in other respects, the church may be said to continue in sackcloth, and in the wilderness, until the end of the days; many parts of it still remaining under grievous persecution.

What we render, *When they shall have finished their testimony*, Mr. Lowman, from Mr. Daubuz, renders, *While they shall perform their testimony;* and observes, that the original may mean the time of their testimony, as well as the end of it.

I might here observe, that we have other instances of God's shortening the days of his church's captivity and bondage, either at the beginning or end, very parallel with what has been now supposed in the case of the witnesses. Thus the proper time of the bondage of the posterity of Abraham in Egypt, was four hundred years, Gen. xv. 13. But yet God in mercy deferred the beginning of their bondage, whereby the time was much shortened at the beginning. So the time wherein it was foretold, that the *whole land of Is-*

rael should be a desolation and an astonishment, and the land should enjoy her sabbaths, by the Babylonish captivity, was seventy years, Jer. xxv. 11, 12. and these seventy years are dated in 2d Chro. xxxvi. 20, 21. from Zedekiah's captivity; and yet, from that captivity to Cyrus's decree, was but fifty-two years; though it was indeed seventy years before the more full restoration of the Jewish church and state by Darius's decree, Ezra vi. So the proper time of the oppression and bondage of the Jewish church under Antiochus Epiphanes, wherein *both the sanctuary and host should be trodden under foot by him, was two thousand three hundred days,* Dan. viii. 13, 14. The time from Antiochus's taking Jerusalem, and polluting the sanctuary, to Antiochus's death, seems to have been about so long; but God shortened the days, by granting remarkable help to his people by means of the Maccabees, before that time; yea, the temple and sanctuary were restored, and the altar rebuilt and dedicated before that time.

Upon the whole, I think there appears to be no reason from the prophecy concerning the two witnesses, Rev. xi. to expect any such general and terrible destruction of the church of Christ, before the utter downfal of

Antichrift, as fome have fuppofed, but good reafon to determine the contrary. It is true, there is abundant evidence in fcripture, that there is yet remaining a mighty conflict between the church and her enemies, the moft violent ftruggle of Satan and his adherents, in oppofition to true religion, and the moft general commotion that ever was in the world, fince the foundation of it to that time; and many particular Chriftians, and fome parts of the church of Chrift, may fuffer hard things in this conflict; but, in the general, Satan and Antichrift fhall not get the victory, nor greatly prevail, but, on the contrary, be entirely conquered, and utterly overthrown, in this great battle. So that I hope this prophecy of the flaying of the witneffes will not ftand in the way of a compliance with the propofal made to us in the memorial, as a prevalent objection and difcouragement.

Object. 5. A late very learned and ingenious Expofitor of the Revelation, viz. Mr. Lowman, fets the fall of Antichrift, and confequently the coming of Chrift's kingdom, at a great diftance, fuppofing that the twelve hundred and fixty years of Antichrift's reign did not begin till the year feven hundred and fifty-six; and confequently, that it will not end until after the year two thoufand, more than two hundred and fifty years hence, and this opinion he confirms by a great variety of arguments.

Anf. 1. If this objection be allowed to be valid, and that which ought to determine perfons in an affair of this nature, and thofe things concerning God's people praying for this glorious event, be alfo allowed to be true, which before were fhewn to be the will of God abundantly revealed in his word, then the following things muft be fuppofed, viz. That it is the will of God that his people be much in prayer for this event, and particularly that it is God's revealed will and purpofe, that, a little before the accomplifhment of it, his people be earneftly feeking and waiting, and importunately and inceffantly crying to God for it; but yet that it was God's defign, that before this time comes of extraordinary prayer and importunity of his church, for the bringing on this glorious event, his church fhould have it given them to underftand precifely when the appointed time fhould be, and that accordingly he has now actually brought the fixed time to light by means of Mr. Lowman.—

But is it reasonable to suppose, that this should be God's manner of dealing with his church, first to make known to them the precise time which he has unalterably fixed for the shewing this mercy to Zion, and then make it the duty of his church, in an extraordinary manner, to be, by prayer, enquiring of him concerning it, and saying—*How long, Lord!* and waiting for it, day and night, crying to him, with exceeding importunity, that he would bring it on, that he would come quickly, that he would hide himself no longer, but would arise and have mercy upon Zion, and awake as one out of sleep, openly manifest himself, and make bare his holy arm for the salvation of his people? That *they that make mention of the Lord should not keep silence, nor give him any rest, until he establish and make Jerusalem a praise on the earth?* And that the church should then say to Christ, *Make haste, my beloved, and be thou like a roe or a young hart on the mountain of spices?*

It may be many ways for the comfort and benefit of God's church in her afflicted state, to know that the reign of Antichrist is to be no more than one thousand two hundred and sixty years; and some things in general may be argued concerning the approach of it, when it is near: as the Jews could argue the approach of Chrift's firft coming, from Daniel's prophecy of the feventy weeks, though they knew not precifely when that feventy weeks would end. But it is not reafonable to expect that God fhould make known to us beforehand, the precife time of Chrift's coming in his kingdom. The difciples defired to know this, and manifefted their defire to their Lord, but he told them plainly, that *it was not for them to know the times and feafons, which the Father hath put in his own power*, Acts i. 6, 7. and there is no reafon to think that it is any more for us than for them, or for Chrift's difciples in thefe days, any more than for his apoftles in thofe days. God makes it the duty of his church to be importunately praying for it, and praying that it may come fpeedily; and not only to be praying for it, but to be feeking for it, in the ufe of proper means, endeavouring that religion may now revive every where, and Satan's kingdom be overthrown; and always to be waiting for it, being in a conftant preparation for it, as fervants that wait for the coming of their lord, or virgins for the coming of the bridegroom, not knowing at what hour he will come.—But God's making known beforehand the precife time of his coming, does not well confift with thefe things.

It is the revealed will of God, that he fhould be enquired of by his people, by extraordinary prayer, concerning this great mercy, to do it for them, before it be fulfilled. And if any fuppofe, that it is now found out precifely when the time is to be, and (the time being at a confiderable diftance) that now is not a proper feafon to begin this extraordinary prayer, I would, on this fuppofition, afk—When we fhall begin? How long before the fixed and known time of the beftowment of this mercy comes, fhall we begin to cry earneftly to God that this mercy may come, and that Chrift would make hafte and be like a roe, &c. For us to delay, fuppofing that we know the time to be far off, is not agreeable to the language of God's people in my text—*Come, let us go* SPEEDILY, *and pray before the Lord, and feek the Lord of Hofts.*

Anf. 2. I acknowledge that Mr. Lowman's Expofition of the Revelation is, on many accounts, excellently written, giving great light into some parts of that prophecy, and an instance of the fulfillment of that prediction, Dan. xii. 4. *Many shall run to and fro, and knowledge shall be increased;* and especially in his Interpretation of the Five First Vials, (which he supposeth already poured out) exceedingly satisfying. But yet the opinion of Mr. Lowman, with regard to the particular time of the beginning and end of the time, times, and an half of Antichrist's reign, and of all others that pretend to fix the time, is the least to be regarded, because it is clearly revealed, and expressly declared by God, that that matter shall be sealed up and hid, and not known until the time of the end of this time, times, and an half. Daniel, in the last chapter of his prophecy, gives us an account, how the angel told him of a future time of great trouble and affliction to the church of God, and then said to him, ver. 4. *But thou, O Daniel,* SHUT UP THE WORDS, AND SEAL THE BOOK, EVEN TO THE TIME OF THE END. And then the prophet proceeds to give an account of a vision that he had of one earnestly enquiring of the angel of the Lord *how long it would be to the end of this remarkable and wonderful time of the church's trouble,* saying, *How long shall it be to the end of these wonders?* ver. 5, 6. The answer was, that *it should be for a time, times, and an half,* and that when so long a time was past, then this wonderful affliction and scattering of the holy people should be finished, ver. 7. But then Daniel tells us, in the next verse, that *he heard, but he understood not,* and said, *O, my Lord, what shall be the end of these things?* He did not understand that general and mystical answer, that those things should have an end at the end of a time, times, and an half; he did not know by it, when this period would have an end; and therefore he enquires more particularly what the time of the end was. But the angel replies, ver. 9. *Go thy way, Daniel, the words are closed and sealed up, until the time of the end.* I do not know what could have been more express. The angel gently rebukes this over inquisitiveness of Daniel, very much as Christ did a like inquisitiveness of the disciples concerning the same matter, when he said to them—*It is not for you to know the times and seasons, that the Father hath put in his own power.*—I think there can be no doubt but that this space, of a time, times, and an half of the church's great trouble, about the end of which Daniel enquires, is the same with that time, times, and half, that is spoken of, chap. vii. 25. and Rev. xii. 14. as the time of Antichrist's reign, and the church's being in the wilderness, and not merely the time of the church's troubles by Antiochus Epiphanes. But we see, when Daniel has a mind to know particularly when this time would come to an end, he is bid to go away, and rest contented in ignorance of this matter; for, says the man cloathed in linen, THE WORDS ARE CLOSED UP, AND SEALED, UNTIL THE TIME OF THE END. That is, very plainly, the matter that you enquire about, when the end of this time, and times, and half shall come, shall not be known, but be kept a great secret, until the time of the end actually comes, and all attempts to find it out before that shall be in vain. And therefore when a particular divine appears, that thinks he has found it out, and has unsealed this matter, and made it manifest with very manifold and abundant evidence, we may well think he is mistaken, and doubt whether those supposed evidences are truly solid ones, and such as are indeed sufficient to make that matter manifest, which God has declared should be kept hid, and not made manifest before it is accom-

plished. Mr. Lowman's own words in his preface, p. 24, 25. are here worthy to be repeated: " It will (says he) ever be a point
" of wisdom, not to be over busy, or over
" confident in any thing, especially in fix-
" ing periods of time, or determining sea-
" sons, which it may be are not to be deter-
" mined, it may be are not fit to be known.
" It is a maxim, of greater wisdom than is
" usually thought, *Seek not to know what*
" *should not be revealed.* Such are many
" future events. The precise time of our Sa-
" viour's coming to judgment, was not re-
" vealed, because not fit to be revealed.—
" The uncertainty of his appearance was of
" greater service to preserve a care of reli-
" gion, than the revelation of it would have
" been; for the uncertainty itself gives many
" useful exhortations—*Watch, for ye know not*
" *what hour the Son of Man cometh.* Sup-
" pose then some of the events described in
" this prophecy should be of doubtful ap-
" plication; suppose the precise time of the
" downfall of the beast, the slaying and re-
" surrection of the witnesses, and the begin-
" ning of the thousand years happy state of
" the church, should not be so determined,
" but it would admit of different calcula-

"tions; may it not be wise, and therefore fit, it should be so? The certainty of those events in a proper time, though that time should not be precisely determined, will answer the greater ends of useful instruction. And if the revelation should go no farther than this, it would yet be a revelation, of great benefit and advantage, as the certainty of the day of judgment in its proper time surely is, though of that day and hour knoweth no man."

Ans. 3. Though it is not for us to know the precise time of the fall of Antichrist, yet I humbly conceive that we have no reason to suppose the event principally intended, in the prophecies, of Antichrist's destruction, to be at so great a distance, as Mr. Lowman places it, but have reason to think it to be much nearer. Not that I would set up myself as a person of equal judgment with Mr. Lowman in matters of this nature. As he differs from most others of the most approved expositors of the Apocalypse, in this matter, so I hope it will not appear vanity and presumption in me, to differ from this particular expositor, and to agree with the greater number. And since his opinion stands so much in the way of that great and important affair, to promote which is the very end of this whole difcourfe, I hope it will not look as though I affected to appear confiderably among the interpreters of prophecy, and as a perfon of fkill in thefe myfterious matters, that I offer fome reafons againft Mr. Lowman's opinions. It is furely a great pity, that it fhould be received as a thing clear and abundantly confirmed, that the glorious day of Antichrift's fall is at fo great a diftance, (fo directly tending to damp and difcourage all earneft prayers for, or endeavours after its fpeedy accomplifhment) unlefs there be good and plain ground for it. I would therefore offer fome things to confideration, which, I think, may juftly make us look upon the opinion of this learned interpreter, of this happy event's being at fo great a diftance, not fo certain and indubitable, as to hinder our praying and hoping for its being fulfilled much fooner.

The period of Antichrift's reign, as this author has fixed it, feems to be the main point infifted on in his Expofition of the Revelation, which he fuppofes a great many things in the fcheme of prophecies delivered in that book do concur to eftablifh. And, indeed, it is fo, with refpect to the fcheme of interpretation of these prophecies, which he goes into, and finds it requisite to maintain, in order to confirm this point. But there are several things in that scheme, that appear to me justly liable to exception.

Whereas it is represented, Rev. xvii. 10, 11. that there are seven different successive heads of the beast; that five were past, and another was to come, and to continue a short space, that might, on some accounts, be reckoned a seventh; and that Antichrist was to follow next after this, as the eighth; but yet the foregoing not being properly one of the heads of the beast, he was properly the seventh. Mr. Lowman does not think with others, that by the seventh that was to continue a short space, which would not be properly one of the heads of the beast, is meant Constantine, and the other Christian emperors; (for he thinks they are reckoned as properly belonging to the sixth head of the beast) but that hereby is intended the government that Rome was subject to under the Gothic princes, and the exarchate of Ravenna, after the imperial form of government in Rome ceased in Augustulus, until the Pope was invested with his temporal dominion, called St. Peter's Patrimony, by Pipin, king of France, in the year seven hundred and fifty-six. And he supposes, that that wounding of one of the heads of the beast with a sword of death, that we read of, chap. xiii. 3 and 14. was not fulfilled in the destruction of the heathen empire, and the giving the imperial power unto Christians, but in the destruction of the imperial form of government, by the sword of the Goths, in the time of Augustulus. But it seems to me to be very unlikely, that the Spirit of God should reckon Constantine and the Christian emperors as proper members, and belonging to one of the heads, of that monstrous wild and cruel beast, that is compared to a leopard and a bear, and a devouring lion, and that had a mouth speaking great things and blasphemies, and that rules by the power and authority of the dragon, or the devil;* which beast is represented in this 17th chapter, as full of names of blasphemy, and of a bloody colour, denoting his exceeding cruelty in persecuting the Christian church. For Constantine, instead of

NOTE.

* The word *Therion* signifies a wild savage beast, as Mr. Lowman himself observes, page 127.

this was a member of the Christian church, and set by God in the most eminent station in his church, and was honoured above all other princes that ever had been in the world, as the great protector of his church, and her deliverer from the persecuting power of that cruel scarlet-coloured beast. Mr. Lowman himself styles him *a Christian Prince, and Protector of the Christian Religion.* God is very careful not to reckon his own people among the Gentiles, the visible subjects of Satan, Num. xxiii. 9. *The people shall not be reckoned among the nations.* God will not enroll them with them; if they happen to be among them, he will be careful to set a mark upon them, as a note of distinction, Rev. vii. 3, &c. when God is reckoning up his own people, he leaves out those that have been noted for idolatry. As among the tribes that were sealed, Rev. viii. those idolatrous tribes of Ephraim and Dan are left out, and in the genealogy of Christ, Matth. i. those princes that were chiefly noted for idolatry, are left out. Much more would God be careful not to reckon his own people, especially such Christian princes as have been the most eminent instruments of overthrowing idolatry, amongst idolaters, and as members and heads of that kingdom that is noted in scripture as the most notorious and infamous of all, for abominable idolatry, and opposition and cruelty to the true worshippers of God. And especially not to reckon them as properly belonging to one of those seven heads of this monarchy, of which very heads it is particularly noted that they had on them the names of BLASPHEMY, which Mr. Lowman himself supposes to signify idolatry. It was therefore worthy of God, agreeable to his manner, and what might well be expected, that when he was reckoning up the several successive heads of this beast, and Constantine and his successors came in the way, and there was occasion to mention them, to set a mark, or note of distinction on them, signifying that they did not properly belong to the beast, nor were to be reckoned as belonging to the heads, and therefore are to be skipped over in the reckoning, and Antichrist, though the eighth head of the Roman empire, is to be reckoned the seventh head of the beast. This appears to me abundantly the most just and natural interpretation of Rev. xvii. 10, 11. It is reasonable to suppose, that God would take care to make such a note in this prophetical description of this dreadful beast, and not, by any means to reckon Constantine as belonging properly to him.—If we reckon Constantine as a member of this beast having seven heads and ten horns, described chap. xvii. and as properly one of his heads, then he was also properly a member of the great red dragon with seven heads and ten horns that warred with the woman, chap. xii. For the seven heads and ten horns of that dragon, are plainly the same with the seven heads and ten horns of the beast. So that this makes Constantine a visible member of the devil; for we are told expressly of that dragon, ver 9. that he was *that old serpent, called the Devil and Satan.* And to suppose that Constantine is reckoned as belonging to one of the heads of that dragon, is to make these prophecies inconsistent with themselves. For here in this 12th chapter, we have represented a war between the dragon and the woman cloathed with the sun; which woman, as all agree, is the church; but Constantine, as all do also agree, belonged to the woman, was a member of the Christian church, and was on that side in the war against the dragon; yea, was the main instrument of that great victory that was obtained over the dragon there spoken of, ver. 9—12. What an inconsistency therefore is it, to suppose that he was at the same time a member and head of that very dragon, which fought with the woman, and yet which Constantine himself fought with, overcame, and gloriously triumphed over! It is not therefore to be wondered at, that God was careful to distinguish Constantine from the proper heads of the beast; it would have been a wonder if he had not. God seems to have been careful to distinguish him, not only in his word, but in his providence, by so ordering it that this Christian emperor should be removed from Rome, the city that God had given up to be the seat of the power of the beast, and of its heads, and that he should have the seat of his empire elsewhere.

Constantine was made the instrument of giving a mortal wound to the heathen Roman empire, and giving it a mortal wound in its head, viz. the heathen emperors that were then reigning, Maxentius and Licinius.— But more eminently was this glorious change in the empire owing to the power of God's word, the prevalence of the glorious gospel, by which Constantine himself was converted, and so became the instrument of the overthrow of the heathen empire in the east and west. The change that was then bro't to pass, is represented as the destruction of the heathen empire, or the old heathen world, and therefore seems to be compared to that dissolution of heaven and earth that shall be at the day of judgment, Rev. vi. 12. to the end. And therefore well might the heathen empire, under the head which was then reigning, be represented as wounded to death, chap. xiii. 3. It is much more likely, that the wound the beast had by a sword, in his head, spoken of ver. 14. was the wound that the heathen empire had in its head, by that sword which we read of, chap. i. 16. and xix. 15. that proceeds out of the mouth of Christ, than the wound that was given to the Christian empire and emperor by the sword of the heathen Goths. It is most likely that this deadly wound was by that sword with which Michael made war with him, and overcame him, and cast him to the earth, chap. xii. 9. and that the deadly wound which was given him, was given him at that very time. It is most likely, that the sword that gave him this deadly wound, after which he strangely revived, as though he rose from the dead, was the same sword with that which is spoken of, as what shall at last utterly destroy him, so that he shall never rise more, chap. xix. 15, 19, 20, 21. This wounding of the head of the beast by the destruction of the heathen empire, and conversion of the emperor to the Christian truth, was a glorious event indeed of Divine Providence, worthy to be so much spoken of in prophecy. It is natural to suppose, that the mortal wounding of the head of that savage cruel beast, that is represented as constantly at war with the woman, and persecuting the church of Christ, should be some relief to the Christian church; but, on the contrary, that wounding to death, that Mr. Lowman speaks of, was the victory of the enemies of the Christian church over her, and the wound received from them.

It is said of that head of the empire that shall be next after the sixth head, and next before Antichrist, and that is not reckoned as properly one of the number of the heads of the beast, that *when it comes, it shall continue a short space,* chap. xvii. 10. By which we may understand, at least, that it shall be one of the shortest, in its continuance, of the successive heads. But the government seated at Ravenna, in the hands of the Goths, or of the deputies of the Greek emperors, (which Mr. Lowman ſuppoſes to be meant by the head) continued, as Mr. Lowman himſelf takes notice, very near three hundred years. And if ſo, its continuance was one of the longeſt of the heads mentioned.

And beſides, if the government that Rome was under, from the time that Auguſtulus abdicated, to the time when the Pope was confirmed in his temporal dominion, was meant by the ſeventh head that was to be between the imperial head and the papal, there would doubtleſs have been two different heads mentioned, inſtead of one, between the Emperor and the Pope, viz. Firſt, the Gothic princes, which reigned near an hundred years. Secondly, the Exarchs of Ravenna, which governed for about one hundred and eighty-five years. The Gothic kingdom was much more properly a diſtinct government from the Imperial, than the Exarchate of Ravenna; for during the Exarchate, Rome was under the government of the emperor, as much as it was in Conſtantine's time.

In Rev. xvii. 12. it is ſaid, the *ten horns are ten kings, which are to receive power as kings one hour with the beaſt*, or (as Mr. Lowman ſays, it ought to have been tranſlated) *the same hour*, or *point of time with the beast*. This will not allow the time when Antichrist first receives power as king, to be so late as Mr. Lowman supposes. This division of the empire into many kingdoms, denoted by the number ten, was about the year four hundred and fifty-six, after Gensericus had taken the city of Rome; but Mr. Lowman places the beginning of the reign of Antichrist in the year seven hundred and fifty-six, which is three hundred years later. I know, such an expression as *in one hour*, or *the same hour*, may allow some latitude, but surely not such a latitude as this. This is a much longer time, than it was from the time of the vision to Constantine: much longer than the space of all the first six seals, longer than it was from Christ's ascension to Constantine, and near as long as the time of all the reigns of the heathen emperors put together, from Augustus Cæsar to Constantine. An hour is every where, in the other places in this book of Revelation, used to signify a very short time, as may be seen in places cited in the margin.* And the expression, *the same*

NOTE.
* Rev. xviii. 10, 17, 19. Chap. iii. 3, 10.—viii. 1.—ix. 15.—xiv. 7.

hour, every where elfe in the Bible, intends near the fame point of time.† The phrafe *one hour* is ufed feveral times in the next chapter, fpeaking of the downfall of Antichrift;‡ and each time, evidently fignifies a very fhort fpace of time. And there is no reafon why we fhould not underftand the fame phrafe in the fame fenfe, when it is ufed here concerning the rife of Antichrift.

Mr. Lowman greatly infifts upon it, that what is fpoken as continuing one thoufand two hundred and fixty days, is not fo much any fpiritual authority or ecclefiaftical power of the Pope, over the nations of Chriftendom, as his temporal government and dominion in that individual city of Rome, and therefore to determine when thefe one thoufand two hundred and fixty days or years began, and when they will end, we muft confider when the Pope firft received this his temporal power over the city of Rome, and the neighbouring regions, called St. Peter's Patrimony. But I can fee no good reafon for this. Indeed it is ftrange, if it be fo.— God has been pleafed in thefe revelations

---

NOTES.

† Dan. iii. 6.—iv. 33.—v. 5. Matth. viii. 13.—x. 19.—Luke vii. 21.—xii. 12.—xx. 19.—xxiv. 33. John iv. 53. Acts xvi. 18, 33.—xxii. 13. Rev. xi. 13. ‡ Ver. 10, 17, 19.

and prophecies, which he has given for the benefit of his church in general, to speak much concerning an anti-christian power that should arise, that should *persecute the saints, and scatter the power of the holy people*, and be an occasion of great affliction to the church of Christ; and in these revelations, in both Old Testament and New, has declared, and often repeated it, that his dominion shall continue so long, and no longer; and for the comfort of his church in general, Christ hath sworn with great solemnity, that the continuance of this persecuting power shall be limited, Dan. xii. 7. Now it would be strange if, in all this, the thing principally intended is not that dominion of this anti-christian power which chiefly concerns the church of Christ in general, but merely his temporal dominion over one province in Italy, called St. Peter's Patrimony. Doubtless, that dominion of Antichrist, which the prophecies insist upon and describe, is the dominion whose duration and limits those prophecies declare. But the dominion of Antichrist which the prophecies insist upon and describe, is not any dominion over a particular province in Italy, but the dominion by which he succeeds the four great *monarchies of the world,* Dan. vii. The dominion by which he *succeeds the dragon in his power, throne and great authority,* Rev. xiii. 2. The dominion in which he has *power given him over all kindreds, tongues and nations,* ver. 7. The dominion by which *the great whore sits on many waters,* chap. xvii. 1. which the angel explains to be *peoples, and multitudes, and nations, and tongues,* ver. 15. and the dominion in which he *reigns over the ten kings,* into which the Roman empire is divided, Rev. xiii. 1. and xvii. 3. 12, 13. The beast that had ten horns, is not the city of Rome, and the neighbouring region, but the Roman empire; they are the horns or the kings, not of the city, but of the empire. If we consider what is expressed in the passages themselves, which speak of the three years and an half of Antichrist, they will lead us to understand something very diverse from the duration of his temporal dominion over St. Peter's Patrimony. In Dan. vii. 25. the time, times, and half of the little horn, is expresly the continuance of time, wherein *it shall be given to him to change times and laws, and wear out the saints of the Most High;* and in chap. xii. 7. it is spoken of as *the time of his scattering the power of the holy people;* in Rev. xi. 2. the forty and two months is spoken of as the time of Antichrist's *treading under foot the court of the temple and the holy city;* i. e. the external and visible Christian church abroad in the world, or the nations of Christendom. In ver. 3. the one thousand two hundred and sixty days of Antichrist are spoken of as the time of the *witnesses prophesying in sackcloth;* and in chap. xii. 6. and 14. the time of the *woman's being in the wilderness,* which was through the great power that Antichrist had over the Christian world, and not his small temporal dominion in Italy.

It is true, some regard is had in the prophecies to the city of Rome, the city built on seven hills; which being the fountain of all rule and authority in the Roman monarchy, and the capital city in the empire, from whence the whole empire was denominated, and the place where the head of the empire usually resided, was properly made use of by the angel, Rev. xvii. 9, 18. to shew what empire Antichrist should rule over, and what city he should usually reside in. And this is all that can be meant by the words of the angel; and not that those streets and walls, and the very ground, were such main and essential things in what the prophecy intended by the beast; that when Antichrist's dominion ceases in that place, then the beast ceases. For, if so, then it will follow, that the beast had his head wounded to death a second time, and ceased to be, when the Popes resided at Avignon in France, for the best part of a century; when not only the Popes did not reside in Rome, nor in any part of St. Peter's Patrimony, nor any part of Italy, but some of them were neither Romans nor Italians. Though the angel says of the great whore, Rev. xvii. 18. *The woman which thou sawest, is the great city which reigns over the kings of the earth;* yet by the city, in this case, is not meant so much what was contained within those Roman walls, as the Roman empire, as is evident by chap. xi. 8. *And their dead bodies shall lie in the street of the great city, which is spiritually called Sodom and Egypt.* Here, by that great city, neither Mr. Lowman himself, nor, I suppose, any other Protestant interpreter, understands the city of Rome, strictly speaking, but the Roman monarchy.

And though it be true, as Mr. Lowman observes, the Pope's ecclesiastical monarchy, and power and influence through Christendom, was greatly eſtabliſhed and advanced by Pepin's making him a temporal prince over the Exarchate of Ravenna; yet, I would aſk, whether the Pope's power and influence in the world, and his ability to diſturb the quiet of the nations of Chriſtendom, and (as it is expreſſed in Daniel) *to change times and laws,* and to carry his own deſigns, in the various countries and kingdoms of Europe, was not greater before Pepin, than it is now, and has been for a long time? And yet Mr. Lowman ſuppoſes that now is properly the time of Antichriſt's reign, that the one thouſand two hundred and ſixty years of his reign continues, and will continue for about two hundred and ſeventy years longer; tho' his power be now ſo ſmall, and has been declining ever ſince the reformation, and ſtill declines continually.

One thing that Mr. Lowman ſuppoſes confirms his opinion of ſo late a beginning of the one thouſand two hundred and ſixty years of the reign of the beaſt, is the order of the ſeveral periods of this prophecy, and the manner of their ſucceeding one another.

As to his particular ſcheme of the ſeven periods, ſo divided and limited, and ſo obviouſly ranked in ſuch order, and following one another in such direct and continual succession, and each ending in a state of peace, safety and happiness to the church of God, it seems to me to be more ingenious than solid, and that many things might be said to demonstrate it not to be founded in the truth of things, and the real design of the divine author of this prophecy. But now to enter into a particular and full examination of it, would be to lengthen out this discourse far beyond its proper limits. I would only observe, (which directly concerns my present purpose) that to make out this scheme, Mr. Lowman supposes that the fifth and sixth trumpets, that bring on the two first woes, and the whole ninth chapter of the Revelation, altogether respects the Saracens. But it appears to me not very credible, that the Saracens should have so much said of them in this prophecy, as to have a whole chapter taken up about them, and not a word in the prophecy be said about the Turks, who immediately succeeded them* in the same

NOTE.

* For though it be true, that the reign of Othman, or Ottoman, who began what they call the Ottoman empire, was a long time after this; yet the Turks themselves, under other princes, in the government they set up in territories that had formerly been possessed by Christians, and in their over-running and ravaging Chris-

religion, and proceeding on the same principles, and were so much more considerable, and brought vastly greater calamities on the Christian world, and have set up and long maintained one of the greatest, strongest and most extraordinary empires that ever the world saw, and have been the most terrible scourge to Christendom, that ever Divine Providence made use of, and one of the greatest of all God's plagues on the world of mankind.

Mr. Lowman, in pursuance of his scheme, also supposes, (which is yet more incredible) this period of the trumpets ends in *a state of safety, peace and happiness to the church of God;* so that, on that occasion, *there are great voices in heaven, saying, The kingdoms of this world are become the kingdoms of our Lord, and of his Christ.* And yet he supposes, that it issues in setting up the kingdom of Antichrist; and that about that very time, when these heavenly voices so joyfully proclaimed this, the beast was enthroned, and the time, times and half, or one thousand two

NOTE.

tian countries, immediately succeeding the Saracens; and from thenceforward have been a terrible, and almost continual scourge to the church.

hundred and sixty days of his reign began, which is spoken of every where, as the time of the church's greatest darkness and trouble, the time wherein *the little horn should wear out the saints of the Most High. The time appointed for his scattering the power of the holy people. The time of the woman's being in the wilderness. The time of treading under foot the court of the temple.* And *the time of the witnesses prophesying in sackcloth.*

However, I do not deny that the time when Mr. Lowman supposes the reign of the beast began, even the time when Pepin confirmed to the Pope his temporal dominions in Italy, was a time of the great increase and advancement of the power of Antichrist in the world, and a notable epoch. And if I may be allowed humbly to offer what appears to me to be the truth with relation to the rise and fall of Antichrist, it is this—As the power of Antichrist, and the corruption of the apostate church, rose not at once, but by several notable steps and degrees, so it will in the like manner fall; and that divers steps and seasons of destruction to the spiritual Babylon, and revival and advancement of the true church, are prophesied of under one. Though it be true, that there is some particular event, that prevails above all others in the intention of the prophecy, some remarkable season of the destruction of the church of Rome, and the papal power and corruption, and advancement of true religion, that the prophecies have a principal respect to.

It was certainly thus with regard to the prophecies of the destruction of old Babylon, and the church's deliverance from captivity and oppression by that city and kingdom, which is abundantly alluded to in these prophecies of the Revelation, as a noted type of the oppression of the church of Christ by the church of Rome, calling the latter so often by the name of Babylon, and the church of Christ Jerusalem. The captivity of the Jews by the Babylonians was not perfected at once, but was brought on by several notable steps. So neither was the restoration of the Jewish church, after the captivity, perfected at once. It was several times foretold, that the duration of the captivity should be seventy years; and also, that after seventy years were accomplished, God would destroy Babylon. But this period had manifestly several different beginnings, and several endings. Thus from Jehoiakim's captivity to Cyrus's decree, for the return of the Jews, and the rebuilding of Jerusalem, was seventy years. And from Zedekiah's captivity to Darius's decree seventy years. And from the last carrying away of all, to the finishing and dedication of the temple, was also seventy years. So also the prophecies of Babylon's destruction were fulfilled by several steps. These prophecies seem to have a principal respect to that destruction that was accomplished by Cyrus, at the end of the first seventy years fore-mentioned; but there were other things in the very same prophecies, that were not fulfilled until the fourth year of Darius, when what remained of Babylon was subjected to another dreadful destruction, which, in a great measure, completed its desolation, which was at the end of the second seventy years, and at the same time that the restoration of the Jews was perfected by the decree of Darius.*— But yet, there were many other things contained in the same prophecies of Babylon's destruction, rendering it thenceforward perfectly and perpetually desolate, and the haunt

NOTE.
* Prideaux's Connection, part I. p. 183, 184, and 267, 268, 269. Edit. 9, and p. 271 and 272.

of serpents and wild beasts, that were not fulfilled until more than two hundred years after, in the time of Seleucus king of Syria.* So also it was with respect to the prophecies of the destruction of Tyre, in the xxvith, xxviith and xxviiith chapters of Ezek. from which many of the expressions used in the Revelation, concerning the destruction of the kingdom of Antichrist, are taken, and which is evidently made use of in scripture as a type of the latter. These prophecies of the destruction of Tyre were fulfilled by various steps. Many things were fulfilled in the destruction of the old city by Nebuchadnezzar,† and yet other parts of the same prophecies were fulfilled by Alexander,‡ which was about two hundred and forty years afterwards. And yet both these desolations are prophesied of under one.

And thus it seems to me very probable, that it will prove, with respect to the prophecies of the destruction of mystical Babylon. It is, I think, pretty manifest by the prophecies, that this anti-christian hierarchy and apostate church will at last be so destroyed, that there shall be no remainders of

NOTES.
* Prid. Connect. Part I. p. 808—812. † Ibid. 128, 129, 130.
‡ Ibid. p. 693.

it left, and shall have as perfect a desolation, before God has done with her, as old Babylon had; there shall be no such thing as Pope or church of Rome in the world.* It seems also pretty manifest, that after that event that is chiefly intended in the prophecies of Antichrist's destruction, there will be some remains of the Romish church. This appears by that most particular and large description of that destruction, Rev. xviii. There it seems to be implied, not only that many shall yet remain of the church of Rome, that shall bewail her overthrow, of her people and clergy, but that there should be some princes among them, *Kings of the earth, that have committed fornication, and lived deliciously with her.* And it is exceeding improbable in itself, that every Papist, in each quarter of the world, should be destroyed, or cease from the world, at one blow. And as long as so considerable a number remains, as may be gathered from the prophecy, they will doubtless have an hierarchy, and there will be one among them that will bear the name of a Pope, although the church of Rome shall be mainly destroyed, and the interest of Popery shall be sunk very low in the world,

NOTE.
* See Rev. xviii. 21—23. and xix. 20, 21. Dan. vii. 26, 27.

so that there will yet remain such a thing as a papal church and hierarchy in the world, to be wholly extirpated at another period,* sometime after that great overthrow principally infisted on in the prophecies. And this second destruction of Antichrist, or rather extirpation of his remains, together with the complete extirpation of all remains of mahometanism, heathenism and herefy thro' the world, and the finishing stroke towards the overthrow of Satan's visible kingdom on earth, and so the beginning of the Millennium, or spiritual rest of the world, may, for ought I know, be about the time Mr. Lowman speaks of; agreeable to the opinion of the ancient Jews, and many Christian divines that have followed them, that the world would stand six thousand years, and then, the seventh thousand years should be the world's rest or sabbath. The ruin of the Popish interest is but a small part of what is requisite, in order to introduce and settle such a state of things, as the world is represented as being in, in that Millennium that is described, Rev. xx. wherein Satan's visible kingdom is every where totally extir-

NOTE.

* At the pouring out of the seventh vial upon the air, the principalities and powers of Satan.

pated, and a perfect end put to all heresies, delusions, and false religions whatsoever, through the whole earth, and Satan henceforward *deceives the nations no more*, and has no place any where but in hell. This is the sabbatism of the world, when all shall be in a holy rest; when the wolf shall dwell with the lamb, and there shall be nothing to hurt or offend, and there shall be abundance of peace, and the earth shall be full of the knowledge of the Lord as the waters cover the seas, and God's people shall dwell in quiet resting-places. There is not the least reason to think, that all this will be brought to pass as it were at one stroke, or that from the present lamentable state of things, there should be brought about and completed the destruction of the church of Rome, the entire extirpation of all infidelity, heresies superstitions and schisms, through all Christendom, and the conversion of all the Jews, and the full enlightening and conversion of all Mahometan and heathen nations, thro' the whole earth, on every side of the globe, and from the north to the south pole, and the full settlement of all in the pure Christian faith and order, all as it were in the issue of one battle, and by means of the victory of the church in one great conflict with her enemies. This would contradict many things in fcripture, which reprefent this great event to be brought to pafs by a gradual progrefs of religion; as leaven that gradually fpreads, until it has diffufed itfelf, through the whole lump, and a plant of muftard, which from a very fmall feed, gradually becomes a great tree. *And like feed which a man cafts upon the ground, that fprings and grows up, night and day; and firft brings forth the blade, then the ear, then the full corn in the ear.* And efpecially would this contradict the prophetical reprefentation in Ezek. xlvii. where the progrefs of religion is reprefented by the gradual increafe of the waters of the fanctuary: being firft a fmall fpring iffuing out from under the threfhold of the temple, and then after they had run a thoufand cubits, being up to the ankles; and at the end of another thoufand cubits, up to the knees; and at the end of another thoufand, up to the loins; and afterwards a great river, that could not be paffed over; and being finally brought into the fea, and healing the waters even of the vaft ocean. If the Spirit of God fhould be immediately poured out, and that work of God's power and grace should now begin, which, in its progress and issue, should complete this glorious effect; there must be an amazing and unparalleled progress of the work and manifestation of divine power to bring so much to pass, by the year two thousand. Would it not be a great thing, to be accomplished in one half century, that religion, in the power and purity of it, should so prevail, as to gain the conquest over all those many things that stand in opposition to it among Protestants, and gain the upper hand through the Protestant world? And if in another, it should go on so to prevail, as to get the victory over all the opposition and strength of the kingdom of Antichrist, so as to gain the ascendancy in that which is now the Popish world? And if in a third half century, it should prevail and subdue the greater part of the Mahometan world, and bring in the Jewish nation, in all their dispersions? And when in the next whole century, the whole heathen world should be enlightened and converted to the Christian faith, throughout all parts of Africa, Asia, America and Terra Australis, and be thoroughly settled in Christian faith and order, without any remainders of their old delufions and fuperftitions, and this attended with an utter extirpation of the remnant of the church of Rome, and all the relicts of mahometanifm, herefy, fchifm and enthufiafm, and a fuppreffion of all remains of open vice and immorality, and every fort of vifible enemy to true religion, through the whole earth, and bring to an end all the unhappy commotions, tumults, and calamities occafioned by fuch great changes, and all things be fo adjufted and fettled through the world, that the world henceforward fhould enjoy an holy reft or fabbatifm.

I have thus diftinguifhed what belongs to a bringing of the world from its prefent ftate, to the happy ftate of the Millennium, the better to give a view of the greatnefs of the work; and not, that I pretend fo much as to conjecture, that things will be accomplifhed juft in this order. The whole work is not the lefs great and wonderful, to be accomplifhed in fuch a fpace of time, in whatever order the different parts of it fucceed each other. They that think that what has been mentioned would not be fwift progrefs, yea, amazingly fwift, do not confider how great the work is, and the vaft and innumerable obftacles that are in the way. It was a wonderful thing, when the Christian religion, after Christ's ascension, so prevailed, as to get the ascendancy in the Roman empire in about three hundred years, but that was nothing to this.

Ansf. 4. There are, as I apprehend, good reasons to hope, that that work of God's Spirit will begin in a little time, which in the progress of it will overthrow the kingdom of Antichrist, and, in its issue, destroy Satan's visible kingdom on earth.

The prophecy of the sixth Vial, Rev. xvi. 12—16. if we take it in its connection with the other Vials, and consider those providential events, by which the preceding Vials have manifestly been fulfilled, I humbly conceive, affords just ground for such a hope.

It is very plain, from this whole chapter, as also the preceding and following, that all these seven Vials are Vials of God's wrath on Antichrist; one is not poured out on the Jews, another on the Turks, another on Pagans, another on the church of Rome; but they all signify God's successive judgments or plagues on the beast and his kingdom, which is in this chapter and almost every where in this book, called GREAT BABYLON. And therefore undoubtedly, when it is said, *The sixth angel poured out his Vial on the river Euphrates, and the water thereof was dried up, that the way of the kings of the east might be prepared.* By the river Euphrates is meant something some way appertaining to this mystical Babylon, as that river that ran thro' Chaldea, called Euphrates, was something appertaining to the literal Babylon. And it is very manifest, that here is in the prophecy of this Vial an allusion to that by which the way was prepared for the destruction of Babylon by Cyrus, which was by turning the channel of the river Euphrates, which ran through the midst of the city, whereby the way of the kings of the east, the princes of Media and Persia, was prepared to come in under the walls of the city, at each end, where the waters used to run, and destroy it; as they did that night wherein Daniel interpreted the hand-writing on the wall, against Belshazzar, Dan. v. 30. The prophecies of Babylon's destruction do, from time to time, take notice of this way of destroying her, by drying up the waters of the river Euphrates, to prepare the way for her enemies, Isai. xliv. 27, 28. *That saith to the deep—Be dry—and I will dry up thy rivers; that saith of Cyrus—He is my servant, and shall perform all my pleasure.* Jer. li. 31, 32. *One post shall run to meet another, to shew the king of Babylon that his city is taken at one end, and that the passages are stopped, and the reeds they have burnt with fire, and the men of war are affrighted.* And ver. 36. *I will dry up her sea, and make her springs dry.*—The Medes and Persians, the people that destroyed Babylon, dwelt to the eastward of Babylon, and are spoken of as coming from the east to her destruction, Isai. xlvi. 11. *Calling a ravenous bird from the* EAST, *the man that executeth my counsel, from a far country.* And the princes that joined with this ravenous bird from the east, in this affair of destroying Babylon, are called kings, Jer. li. 11. *The Lord hath raised up the spirit of the* KINGS *of the Medes; for his device is against Babylon to destroy it.* Ver. 28. *Prepare against her the nations, with the* KINGS *of the Medes, the captains thereof, and the rulers thereof.*—The drying the channel of the river Euphrates, to prepare the way for these kings and captains of the east, to enter into that city, under its high walls, was the last thing done by the besiegers of Babylon, before her actual destruction; as this sixth Vial is the last Vial of God's wrath but one, on the myſtical Babylon, and the effect of it, the drying up the channel of the river Euphrates, is the laſt thing done againſt it, before its actual deſtruction by the ſeventh Vial, and opens the way for thoſe that fight in a ſpiritual war againſt it, ſpeedily to bring on its ruin.

Hence I think it may, without diſpute, be determined, that by the river Euphrates in the prophecy of this Vial, is meant ſomething appertaining or relating to the myſtical Babylon, or the anti-chriſtian church and kingdom, that ſerves that, or is a benefit to it, in a way anſwerable to that in which the river Euphrates ſerved old Babylon, and the removal of which will in like manner prepare the way for her enemies to deſtroy her. And therefore what we have to do in the firſt place, in order to find out what is intended by the river Euphrates, in this prophecy, is to conſider how the literal Euphrates ſerved old Babylon. And it may be noted, that Euphrates was of remarkable benefit to that great city in two reſpects; it ſerved the city as a ſupply—it was let thro' the midſt of the city by an artificial canal, and ran through the midſt of the palace of the king of Babylon; that part of his palace called the Old Palace, standing on one side, and the other part called the New Palace, on the other; with communications from one part to another, above the waters, by a bridge, and under the waters, by a vaulted or arched passage, that the city, and especially the palace, might have the convenience of its waters, and be plentifully supplied with water. And another way that the waters of Euphrates served Babylon, was as an impediment and obstacle in the way of its enemies, to hinder their access to it to destroy it; for there was a vast moat round the city, without the walls, of prodigious width and depth, filled with the water of the river, to hinder the access of her besiegers; and at each end of the city, the river served instead of walls. And therefore when Cyrus had dried up the river, the moat was emptied, and the channel of the river under the walls left dry, and so his way was prepared.

And therefore it is natural to suppose, that by drying up the waters of the river Euphrates, in the prophecy of the destruction of the new Babylon, to prepare the way of her enemies, is meant the drying up her incomes and supplies, and the removal of those things that hitherto have been the chief obstacles in the way of those that, in this book, are represented as at war with her, and seeking her destruction, (spoken of Rev. xix. 11. to the end, and chap. xii. 7.) that have hindered their progress and success, or that have been the chief impediments in the way of the Protestant religion. The first thing is the drying the streams of the wealth of the new Babylon, the temporal supplies, revenues, and vast incomes of the Romish church, and the riches of the Popish dominions. Waters in scripture language very often signify provision and supplies, both temporal and spiritual, as in Prov. ix. 17. Isai. xxxiii. 16.—xliii. 20.—lv. 1. and lviii. 11. Jer. ii. 13 and 18.—xvii. 8 and 13. and in other places innumerable. The temporal supplies of a people are very often in scripture called waters, as Isai. v. 13. *Therefore my people is gone into captivity, and their honourable men are famished, and their multitude dried up with thirst,* i. e. deprived of the supports and supplies of life. And the drying up the waters of a city or kingdom, is often used in scripture prophecy, for the depriving them of their wealth, as the scripture explains itself, Hof. xiii. 15. *His springs shall become dry, and his fountain shall be dried up: He shall spoil the treasure of all pleasant vessels.* Isai. xv. 6, 7. *The waters of Nimrim shall be desolate, for the hay is withered, the grass faileth, there is no green thing.— Therefore the abundance they have gotten, and that which they have laid up, shall they carry away to the brook of the willows.* By the brook of the willows there seems to be a reference to the waters of Assyria or Chaldea, whose streams abounded with willows. So that the carrying away the treasures of Moab, and adding of them to the treasures of Assyria, is here represented by the figure of turning away the waters of Nimrim from the country of Moab, and adding them to the waters of Assyria, as the prophecy explains itself. Yea, even in the prophecies of the destruction of Babylon itself, the depriving her of her treasures, seems to be one thing intended by the drying up of her waters.— This seems manifest by the words of the prophecy in Jer. l. 37, 38. *A sword is upon her treasures, and they shall be robbed; a drought is upon her waters, and they shall be dried up.* Compared with chap. li. 15. *O thou that dwellest upon many waters, abundant in trea-*

sures; with ver. 36. *I will dry up her sea, and make her springs dry.* The wealth, revenues, and vast incomes of the church of Rome, are the waters by which that Babylon has been nourished and supported; these are the waters which the Popish clergy and members of the Romish hierarchy thirst after, and are continually drinking down, with insatiable appetite; and they are waters that have been flowing into that spiritual city like a great river; ecclesiastical persons possessing a very great part of the Popish dominions; as this Babylon is represented as vastly rich, in the prophecy of the Apocalypse, especially in the 17th and 18th chapters. These are especially the waters that supply the palace of the king of this new Babylon, viz. the Pope, as the river Euphrates ran through the midst of the palace of the king of old Babylon. The revenues of the Pope have been like waters of a great river, coming into his palace, from innumerable fountains, and by innumerable branches and lesser streams, coming from many various and distant countries.

This prophecy represents to us two cities very contrary the one to the other—viz. New Babylon and the New Jerusalem, and a river running through the midſt of each.—The New Jeruſalem, which ſignifies the church of Chriſt, eſpecially in her beſt eſtate, is deſcribed as having a river running thro' the midſt of it, Rev. xxii. 1, 2. This river, as might eaſily be made moſt evident, by comparing this with abundance of other ſcriptures, undoubtedly ſignifies the divine ſupplies, and rich and abundant ſpiritual incomes and proviſion of that holy city. Mr. Lowman, in his late Expoſition, ſays, " It " repreſents a conſtant proviſion for the com- " fortable and happy life of all the inhabi- " tants of this city of God." And in his notes on the ſame place, obſerves as follows: " Water, (ſays he), as neceſſary to the ſup- " port of life, and as it contributes in great " cities, eſpecially in hot eaſtern countries, " to the ornament of the place, and delight " of the inhabitants, is a very proper repre- " ſentation of the enjoyment of all things, " both for the ſupport and pleaſure of life." As the river that runs through the new Jeruſalem, the church of Chriſt, that refreſhes that holy ſpiritual ſociety, ſignifies their ſpiritual ſupplies, to ſatisfy their ſpiritual thirſt, ſo the river that runs through the new Babylon, the anti-chriſtian church, that wicked carnal society, signifies, according to the opposite character of the city, her worldly, carnal supplies, to satisfy their carnal desires and thirstings.

This new Jerusalem is called in this book the Paradise of God, and therefore is represented as having the tree of life growing in it. And it being described, as though a river ran through the midst of it, there seems to be some allusion to the ancient paradise in Eden, of which we are told that there ran a river through the midst of it to water it; *i. e.* to supply the plants of it with nourishment. And this river was this very same river Euphrates, that afterwards ran through Babylon. And in one and the other, it represented the divers supplies of two opposite cities; in Eden, it represented the spiritual supplies and wealth of the true Christian church, in her spiritual advancement and glory, and seems to be so made use of, Rev. xxii. 1, 2. In the other it represented the outward carnal supplies of the false antichristian church, in her worldly pomp and vain glory, chap. xvi. 12.

When the waters, that supply this mystical Babylon, come to be dried up in this sense, it will prepare the way for the enemies of anti-chriſtian corruption, that ſeek her overthrow. The wealth of the church of Rome, and of the powers that ſupport it, is very much its defence. After the ſtreams of her revenues and riches are dried up, or very greatly diminiſhed, her walls will be as it were broken down, and ſhe will become weak and defenceleſs, and expoſed to eaſy ruin.

When Joab had taken that part of the city of Rabbah, that was called the City of Waters, whence the city had its ſupply of water, the fountains of the brook Jabbok being probably there, and which was alſo called the royal city, probably becauſe there the king had his palace and gardens, on the account of its peculiar pleaſantneſs; I ſay, when he had taken this, the conqueſt of the reſt of the city was eaſy; his meſſage to David implies, that the city now might be taken at pleaſure, 2 Sam. xii. 27, 28. It is poſſible that by the pouring out of the ſixth Vial to dry up the river of the myſtical Babylon, there might be ſomething like the taking the City of Waters in Rabbah; ſome one of the chief of the Popiſh powers, that has been the main ſtrength and ſupport of the Popiſh cauſe, or from whence that church has its chief supplies, may be destroyed, or converted, or greatly reduced. But this events must determine.

In the prophecies of Egypt's destruction, it is signified, that when their rivers and waters should be dried up, in that sense, that the streams of their temporal supplies should be averted from them, their defence would be gone, Isai. xix. 4, &c. *The Egyptians will I give over into the hand of a cruel lord, and the waters shall fail from the sea, and the river shall be wasted and dried up, and the brooks of* DEFENCE *shall be emptied and dried up, and the reeds and flags shall wither— Every thing sown by the brooks shall wither: The fishers also shall mourn—*

Those whose way was prepared to come in and destroy Babylon, by the drying up the river of Euphrates, were the army that was at war with Babylon, Cyrus the king, and his host, that fought her overthrow; so there seems to be all reason to suppose, that those whose way will be prepared to come in and destroy mystical Babylon, by drying up the mystical Euphrates, are that king and army that are, in this book of Revelation, represented as at war with Antichrist. And what king and army that is, we may see in chap. xii. 7. and xix. 11. to the end—Michael the king of angels, and his angels; he *whose name is called the Word of God, and that has on his vesture, and on his thigh, a name written, King of Kings, and Lord of Lords; and the heavenly armies that follow him, cloathed in fine linen, white and clean.* Cyrus, the chief of the kings of the east, that destroyed Babylon, and redeemed God's church from thence, and restored Jerusalem, seems, in that particular affair, very manifestly to be spoken of as a type of Christ: God calls him *his shepherd, to perform his pleasure, to say to Jerusalem—Thou shalt be built, and to the temple—Thy foundation shall be laid.* God calls him his Messiah. *Thus saith the Lord to his anointed,* (in the original *to his Messiah) to Cyrus.* He is spoken of as one *that God had raised up in righteousness, that he might build his city, and freely redeem his captives, or let them go without price or reward.* He is said to be one whom *God had loved;* in like manner as the Messiah is said to be *God's elect, in whom his soul delighteth.* As by Babylon, in the Revelation, is meant that anti-christian society that is typified by old Babylon; so by the kings of the east, that should destroy this anti-christian church, must be meant those enemies of it that were typified by Cyrus, and other chieftians of the east, that destroyed old Babylon; viz. Christ, who was born, lived, died, and rose in the east, together with those spiritual princes that follow him, the principalities and powers in heavenly places, and those ministers and saints that are kings and priests, and shall reign on earth; especially those leaders and heads of God's people—those Christian ministers and magistrates, that shall be distinguished as public blessings to his church, and chief instruments of the overthrow of Antichrist.

As the river Euphrates served the city of Babylon as a supply, so it also was before observed, it served as an impediment or obstacle to hinder the access of its enemies; as there was a vast moat round the city, filled with the water of the river, which was left empty when Euphrates was dried up. And therefore we may suppose, that another thing meant by the effect of the sixth Vial, is the removal of those things which hitherto have been the chief obstacles in the way of the progress of the true religion, and the victory of the church of Christ over her enemies;

which have been the corrupt doctrines and practices that have prevailed in Protestant countries, and the doubts and difficulties that attend many doctrines of the true religion, and the many divisions and contentions that subsist among Protestants. The removal of those would wonderfully prepare the way for Christ and his armies, to go forward and prevail against their enemies, in a glorious propagation of true religion. So that this Vial, which is to prepare the way for Christ and his people, seems to have respect to that remarkable preparing the way for Christ, by *levelling mountains, exalting valleys, drying up rivers,* and *removing stumbling-blocks,* which is often spoken of in the prophecies, as what shall next precede the church's latter-day glory, as Isai. xlii. 13, &c. *The Lord shall go forth as a mighty man; he shall stir up jealousy as a man of war; he shall prevail against his enemies.—I will make waste mountains and hills, and dry up all their herbs; and I will make the rivers islands, and I will dry up the pools; and I will bring the blind by a way that they know not, and I will lead them in paths that they have not known; I will make darkness light before them, and crooked things straight: these things will I do unto them, and not forsake them.* Chap. xl. 3, 4, 5. *Prepare ye the way of the Lord; make straight in the desart an high-way for our God: every valley shall be exalted, and every mountain and hill shall be made low, and the crooked shall be made straight, and rough places plain; and the glory of the Lord shall be revealed, and all flesh shall see it together.* Chap. xi. 15, 16. *And the Lord shall destroy the tongue of the Egyptian sea, and with his mighty wind shall he shake his hand over the river, and shall smite it in the seven streams thereof, and make men go over dry shod; and there shall be an high-way for the remnant of his people which shall be left, from Assyria, like as it was to Israel, in the day that he came out of the land of Egypt.* Chap. lvii. 14. *Cast ye up, cast ye up, prepare the way, take up the stumbling-block out of the way of my people.* And chap. lxii. 10. *Go through, go through the gates; prepare ye the way of the people; cast up, cast up the high-way; gather out the stones; lift up a standard for the people.* Zech. x. 10, 11, 12. *I will bring them again also out of the land of Egypt, and gather them out of Assyria; and I will bring them into the land of Gilead and Lebanon; and place shall not be found for them. And he shall pass through the sea with affliction, and shall smite the waves of the sea; and all the deeps of the river shall dry up; and the pride of Assyria shall be brought down, and the sceptre of Egypt shall depart away: And I will strengthen them in the Lord, and they shall walk up and down in his name, saith the Lord.* And it is worthy to be remarked, that as Cyrus's destroying Babylon, and letting go God's captives from thence, and restoring Jerusalem, is certainly typical of Christ's destroying mystical Babylon, and delivering his people from her tyranny, and gloriously building up the spiritual Jerusalem in the latter days; so God's preparing Cyrus's way, by drying up the river Euphrates, is spoken of in terms like those that are used in those prophecies that have been mentioned, to signify the preparing Christ's way, when he shall come to accomplish the latter event. Thus God says concerning Cyrus, Isai. xlv. 2. *I will go before thee, and* MAKE CROOKED PLACES STRAIGHT. And ver. 13. *I will direct,* or *make straight* (as it is in the margin) *all his ways.* This is like chap. xl. 2, 4. *Prepare ye the way of the Lord; make straight in the desart an high-way for our God.*—*The crooked things shall be made straight.* Chap.

xlii. 16. *I will make darkness light before them, and crooked things straight.*

If any should object against understanding the river Euphrates, in Rev. xvi. 12. as signifying what has been supposed, that when mention is made of the river Euphrates, in another place in this prophecy, it is manifestly not so to be understood, viz. in chap. ix. 14. *Saying to the sixth angel which had the trumpet—Loose the four angels which are bound in the great river Euphrates;* and that there is no reason to understand the river Euphrates in the vision of the sixth Vial, as signifying something diverse from what is meant by the same river in the vision of the sixth trumpet.

I answer, That there appears to me to be good reason for a diverse understanding of the river Euphrates in these two different places; the diversity of the scene of the vision, and of the kind of representation, in those two divers parts of this prophecy, naturally leads to it, and requires it. It is in this book as in the Old Testament; when the river Euphrates is spoken of in the Old Testament, both in the histories and prophecies, it is mentioned, with respect to the twofold relation of that river, viz. 1st, with regard to its relation to Babylon. And as it was related to that, it was something belonging to that city, as its defence and supply, as has been represented. Thus the river Euphrates is spoken of in many places that have been already observed, and others that might be mentioned. 2dly. This river is spoken of with regard to its relation to the land of Israel, God's visible people; and as it was related to that, it was its eastern boundary. It is so spoken of, Gen. xv. 18. Exod. xxiii. 31. Deut. i. 7. and xi. 24. Josh. i. 4. 2 Sam. viii. 3. 1 Chron. xviii. 3. 1 Kings iv. 21. Ezra iv. 20. Agreeable to this diverse respect or relation of this river, under which it is mentioned in the Old Testament, so must we understand it differently in different parts of the prophecy of this book of Revelation, according as the nature and subject of the vision requires. In the xvth chapter, where the prophecy is about Babylon, and the vision is of God's plagues on Babylon, preparing the way for her destruction, there, when the river Euphrates is mentioned, we are naturally and necessarily led to consider it as something belonging to Babylon, appertaining to the mystical Babylon, as Euphrates did to old Babylon. But we cannot understand it so in the ixth chapter, for there the prophecy is not about Babylon. To mention Euphrates there, as something belonging to Babylon, would have been improper; for the nature of the vision, and prophetical representation, did not lead to it, nor allow it. John had had no vision of Babylon; that kind of representation had not been made to him; there is not a word said about Babylon till we come to the second part of this prophecy, after John had the vision of the second book, and Christ had said to him— *Thou must prophecy again before peoples, and nations, and kings,* chap. xi. The scene of the vision, in the former part of the prophecy, had been more especially the land of Israel, and the vision is concerning two sorts of persons there, viz. those of the tribes of Israel that had the seal of God in their foreheads, and those wicked apostate Israelites that had not this mark. Compare chap. vii. 3—8. and chap. ix. 4. The vision in this ixth chapter, is of God's judgments on those of the tribes of Israel, or in the land of Israel, which had not the seal of God in their foreheads; and therefore when mention is made, ver. 14. of a judgment coming on them from the river Euphrates, this river is here spoken of in the former respect, viz. with regard to its relation to the land of Israel, as its eastern border; and thereby we must understand that God would bring some terrible calamity on Christendom from its eastern border, as he did when the Turks were let loose upon Christendom.

If these things that have been spoken of, are intended in the prophecy of the sixth Vial, it affords, as I conceive, great reason to hope that the beginning of that glorious work of God's Spirit, which, in the progress and issue of it, will overthrow Antichrist, and introduce the glory of the latter days, is not very far off.

Mr. Lowman has, I think, put it beyond all reasonable doubt, that the fifth Vial was poured out in the time of the Reformation. It also appears satisfyingly, by his late Exposition, that take one Vial with another, it has not been two hundred years from the beginning of one Vial to the beginning of another, but about one hundred and eighty years. But it is now two hundred and twenty years since the fifth Vial began to be poured, and it is a long time since the main effects of it have been finished. And therefore if the sixth Vial has not already began to be poured out, it may well be speedily expected.

But with regard to the first thing that I have supposed to be signified by the effect of this Vial, viz. The drying up the fountains and streams of the wealth and temporal incomes and supplies of the antichristian church and territories, I would propose it to consideration, whether or no many things that have come to pass within these twenty years past, may not be looked upon as probable beginnings of a fulfilment of this prophecy; particularly what the kings of Spain and Portugal did some years since, when displeased with the Pope, forbidding any thenceforward going to Rome for investitures, &c. thereby cutting off two great streams of the Pope's wealth, from so great and rich a part of the Popish world; and its becoming so frequent a thing of late for Popish princes, in their wars, to make bold with the treasure of the church, and to tax the clergy within their dominions, as well as laity; or which is equivalent, to oblige them to contribute great sums, under the name of a free gift; and also the late peeling and impoverishing the Pope's temporal dominions in

Italy, by the armies of the Auſtrians, Neapolitans and Spaniards, paſſing and repaſſing through them, and living ſo much at diſcretion in them, of which the Pope has ſo loudly complained, and in vain; receiving nothing but menaces, when he has objected againſt giving liberty for the like paſſage for the future. Theſe things make it hopeful that the time is coming when the princes of Europe, *the ten horns, ſhall hate the whore, and make her deſolate and naked, and eat her fleſh,* as Rev. xvii. 16. which will prepare the way for what next follows, *her being burnt with fire;* even as the ſixth Vial poured out, to conſume the ſupplies of Antichriſt, and ſtrip him naked of his wealth, and, as it were, to pick his fleſh off from his bones, will make way for what next follows, the ſeventh Vial, that will conſume Antichriſt, by the fierceneſs of God's wrath.

Theſe things duly conſidered, I imagine, afford us ground to ſuppoſe, not only that the effect of this ſixth Vial is already begun, but that ſome progreſs is already made in it, and that this Vial is now running apace. And when it ſhall be finiſhed, there is all reaſon to ſuppoſe that the deſtruction of Antichriſt will very ſpeedily follow, and that the two laſt Vials will ſucceed one another more cloſely than the other Vials. When once the river Euphrates was dried up, and Cyrus's way was prepared, he delayed not, but immediately entered into the city to deſtroy it. Nor is it God's manner, when once his way is prepared, to delay to deliver his church, and ſhew mercy to Zion. When once impediments are removed, Chriſt will no longer remain at a diſtance, but will be like a roe or a young hart, coming ſwiftly to the help of his people. When that cry is made, *Caſt ye up, caſt ye up, prepare the way*, &c. *The high and lofty One that inhabits eternity, is repreſented as very near to revive the ſpirit of the contrite, and deliver his people with whom he had been wroth.* When that cry is made, Iſai. xl. *Prepare ye the way of the Lord, make ſtraight in the deſart an high-way for our God; every valley ſhall be exalted,* &c. God tells his church, *that her warfare is accompliſhed, and the time to comfort her is come, and that the glory of the Lord now ſhall be revealed, and all fleſh ſee it together.* And agreeably to theſe things, Chriſt, on the pouring ou tthe ſixth Vial, ſays, *Behold I come.* The ſixth Vial is the forerunner of the ſeventh or laſt, to prepare its way. The angel that pours out this Vial is the harbinger of Chrift, and when the harbinger is come, the king is at hand. John the Baptift, that was Chrift's harbinger, who came to level mountains and fill up vallies, proclaimed, *The kingdom of heaven is at hand;* and when he had prepared Chrift's way, then *the Lord fuddenly came into his temple, even the meffenger of the covenant.* Mal. iii. 1.

It is true, that we do not know how long this Vial may continue running, and fo Chrift's way preparing, before it is fully prepared; but yet if there be reafon to think the effect of this Vial is begun, or is near, then there is reafon alfo to think that the beginning of that great work of God's Spirit, in reviving of religion, which, before it is finifhed, will iffue in Antichrift's ruin, is not far off. For it is pretty manifeft, that the beginning of this work will accompany the fixth Vial; for the gathering together of the armies on both fides, on the fide of Chrift and Antichrift, to that great battle that fhall iffue in the overthrow of the latter, will be under this Vial; (compare Rev. xvi. 12, 13, 14. with chap. xix. 11. to the end.) And it is plain, that Chrift's manifefting himfelf, and wonderfully appearing after long hiding himself, to plead his own and his people's cause, and riding forth against his enemies in a glorious manner, and his people's following him in pure linen, or the practice of righteousness and pure religion, will be the thing that will give the alarm to Antichrist, and cause him to gather that vast host to make the utmost opposition. But this alarm and gathering together is represented as being under the sixth Vial; so that it will be a great revival, and mighty progress of true religion under the sixth Vial, eminently threatening the speedy and utter overthrow of Satan's kingdom on earth, that will so mightily rouse the old serpent, to exert himself with such exceeding violence, in that greatest conflict and struggle that ever he had with Christ and the church, since the world stood.*

All the seven Vials bring terrible judgments upon Antichrist; but there seems to be something distinguishing of the three last, the fifth, sixth and seventh, viz. That they

NOTE.

* If there be any mistake here, it is an anticipation of the destruction of Antichrist, through the prevalence of vital religion, instead of the present rod of the divine indignation; but, it may be, there is a warfare between truth and error yet to come, towards which our author's views might be directed, and for which it becomes us all to be prepared. EDITOR.

more directly tend to the overthrow of his kingdom, and accordingly each of them is attended with a great reviving of religion. The fifth Vial was attended with such a revival and reformation, that greatly weakened and diminished the throne or kingdom of the beast, and went far towards its ruin. It seems as though the sixth Vial should be much more so, for it is the distinguishing note of this Vial, that it is the preparatory Vial, which more than any other Vial prepares the way for Christ's coming to destroy the kingdom of Antichrist, and to set up his own kingdom in the world. A great outpouring of the Spirit accompanied that dispensation which was preparatory to Christ's coming in his public ministry, in the days of his flesh; so, much more, will a great outpouring of the Spirit accompany the dispensation that will be preparatory to Christ's coming in his kingdom.

And besides those things which belong to the preparation of Christ's way, which are so often represented by levelling mountains, drying up rivers, &c. viz. The unravelling intricacies, and removing difficulties attending Christian doctrines, the distinguishing between true religion and its false appearances, the detecting and exploding errors and corrupt principles, and the reforming the wicked lives of profeſſors, which have been the chief ſtumbling-blocks and obſtacles that have hitherto hindered the progreſs of true religion; I ſay, theſe things, which ſeem to belong to this preparatory Vial, are the proper work of the Spirit of God, promoting and advancing divine light and true piety, and can be the effect of nothing elſe.

Agreeably to what has been ſuppoſed, that an extraordinary out-pouring of the Spirit of God is to accompany this ſixth Vial; ſo the beginning of a work of extraordinary awakening has already attended the probable beginning of this Vial; and has been continued in one place or other, for many years paſt; although it has been, in ſome places, mingled with much enthuſiaſm, after the manner of things in their firſt beginnings, unripe, and mixed with much crudity. But it is to be hoped, a far more pure, extenſive and glorious revival of religion is not far off, which will more properly be the beginning of that work, which, in its iſſue, ſhall overthrow the kingdom of Antichriſt, and of Satan through the world. But God *will be enquired of for this, by the houſe of Iſrael to do it for them.*

Anſ. 5. If, notwithſtanding all that I have ſaid, it be ſtill judged that there is ſufficient reaſon to determine that the ruin of Antichriſt is at a very great diſtance, and if all that I have ſaid, as arguing that there is reaſon to hope the beginning of that glorious revival of religion, which, in its continuance and progreſs, will deſtroy the kingdom of Antichriſt, is not very far off, be judged to be of no force; yet it will not follow, that our complying with what is propoſed to us in the late memorial from Scotland, will be in vain, or not followed with ſuch ſpiritual bleſſings, as will richly recompence the pains of ſuch extraordinary prayer for the Holy Spirit, and the revival of religion. If God does not grant that greateſt of all effuſions of his Spirit, ſo ſoon as we deſire, yet we ſhall have the ſatisfaction of a conſciouſneſs of our having employed ourſelves in a manner that is certainly agreeable to Chriſt's will and frequent commands, in being much in prayer for this mercy, and much more in it than has heretofore been common with Chriſtians; and there will be all reaſon to hope, that we ſhall receive ſome bleſſed token of his acceptance. If the fall of myſtical Babylon, and the work of God's Spirit that shall bring it to pass, be at several hundred years distance, yet it follows not that there will be no happy revivals of religion before that time, which shall be richly worth the most diligent, earnest and constant praying for.

I would say something to one objection more, and then hasten to a conclusion of this discourse.

Object. 6. Some may be ready to object, that what is proposed in this memorial is a new thing, such as never was put in practice in the church of God before.

Ans. 1. If there be something circumstantially new in it, this cannot be a sufficient objection. The duty of prayer is no new duty; for many of God's people expressly to agree, as touching something they shall ask in prayer, is no new thing; for God's people to agree on circumstances of time and place for united prayer, according to their own discretion, is no new thing; for many, in different places, to agree to offer up extraordinary prayers to God, at the same time, as a token of their union, is no new thing, but has been commonly practised in the appointment of days of fasting and prayer for special mercies. And if the people of God should engage in the duty of prayer, for the coming of Christ's kingdom, in a new manner, in that respect, that they resolve they will not be so negligent of this duty, as has been common with professors of religion heretofore, but will be more frequent and fervent in it; this would be such a new thing as ought to be, and would be only to reform a former negligence. And for the people of God, in various parts of the world, visibly, and by express agreement, to unite for this extraordinary prayer, is no more than their duty, and no more than what it is foretold the people of God should actually do, before the time comes of the church's promised glory on earth. And if this be a duty, then it is a duty to come into some method to render this practicable; but it is not practicable (as was shewn before) but by this method, or some other equivalent.

Ans. 2. As to this particular method, proposed to promote union in extraordinary prayer, viz. God's people, in various parts, setting apart fixed seasons, to return at certain periods, wherein they agree to offer up their prayers at the same time, it is not so new as some may possibly imagine. This may appear by what follows, which is part of a paper, difperfed abroad in Great Britain and Ireland, from London, in the year 1712, being the latter end of queen Anne's reign, and very extenfively complied with, entitled, " A ferious Call from the City to " the Country, to join with them in fetting " apart fome time, viz. from feven to eight, " every Tuefday morning, for folemn feek- " ing of God, each one in his clofet, now in " this fo critical a junéture."

Jonah i. 6. *Call upon God, if fo be that God will think upon us, that we perifh not.*— What follows is an extract from it.

" You have formerly been called upon to " the like duty, and have complied with it, " and that not without fuccefs. It is now " thought highly feafonable to renew the " call. It is hoped that you will not be more " backward, when it is fo apparent that there " is even greater need. It is fcarce imagin- " able how a profeffing people fhould ftand " in greater need of prayer, than we do at " this day. You were formerly befpoke from " that very pertinent text, Zech. viii. 21. " *The inhabitants of one city fhall go to ano-* " *ther, faying, Let us go fpeedily to pray be-* " *fore the Lord,* or, (as the marginal reading,

" more expreffive of the original reading,
" is,) *continually, from day to day, to entreat*
" *the face of the Lord.* According to this ex-
" cellent pattern, we of this city, the metro-
" polis of our land, think ourfelves obliged
" to call upon our brethren in Great Britain
" and Ireland, at a time when our hearts can-
" not but meditate terror, and our flefh trem-
" ble for fear of God, and are afraid of his
" righteous judgments; thofe paft being for
" the moft part forgotten, and the figns of
" the times foreboding evil to come, being
" by the generality little, if at all, regarded;
" we cannot therefore but renew our earneft
" requeft, that all who make confcience of
" praying for the peace of Jerufalem, who
" wifh well to Zion, who would have us and
" our pofterity a nation of Britifh Protef-
" tants, and not of Popifh bigots and French
" flaves, would give us (as far as real and
" not pretended neceffity will give leave) a
" meeting at the throne of grace, at the hour
" mentioned, there to wreftle with God for
" the turning away his anger from us, for
" our deliverance from the hands of his and
" our enemies, for the turning the councils
" of all Ahitophels, at home and abroad, in-
" to foolifhnefs, for mercy to the queen and

" kingdom, for a happy peace or succefsful
" war, so long as the matter shall continue
" undetermined; for securing the Proteftant
" succeffion in the illustrious house of Ha-
" nover, (by good and evil wishes to which,
" the friends and enemies of our religion and
" civil rights, are so effentially diftinguish-
" ed,) and especially for the influences of di-
" vine grace upon the rising generation, par-
" ticularly the seed of the righteous, that the
" offspring of our Christian heroes may ne-
" ver be the plague of our church and coun-
" try. And we desire that this solemn pray-
" er be begun the first Tuesday after sight,
" and continued at least the summer of this
" present year 1712. And we think, every
" modeft, reasonable and juft requeft, such
" as this, should not on any account be de-
" nied us, since we are not laying a burden
" on others, to which we will not moft wil-
" lingly put our own shoulders; nay, indeed,
" count it much more a blefling than a bur-
" den. We hope this will not be efteemed,
" by serious Proteftants, of any denomina-
" tion, a needless ftep; much less do we fear
" being censured by any such, as fanciful
" and melancholy, on account of such a pro-
" posal. We, with them, believe a provi-

"dence, know and acknowledge that our God is a God hearing prayer. Scripture recordeth, and our age is not barren of inftances of God's working marvellous deliverances for his people in anfwer to humble, believing and importunate prayer, efpecially when prayer and reformation go together, which is what we defire. Let this counfel be acceptable to us, in this day of the church's calamity, and our common fears. Let us feek the Lord while he may be found, and call upon him while he is near. Let us humble ourfelves under the mighty hand of God. Let us go and pray unto our God, and he will hearken unto us. We fhall feek him and find him, when we fearch for him with all our hearts. Pray for the peace of Jerufalem; they fhall profper that love her. And may Zion's friends and enemies both cry out with wonder, when they fee the work of God—Behold they pray!—What hath God wrought! Verily there is a God that judgeth in the earth.

"*Poftfcript.* It is defired and hoped, that if any are hindered from attending this work at the above-mentioned hour, they will neverthelefs fet apart an hour weekly for it."

God speedily and wonderfully heard and answered those who were united in that extraordinary prayer, proposed in the above-mentioned paper, in suddenly scattering those black clouds which threatened the nation and the Protestant interest with ruin, at that time; in bringing about, in so remarkable a manner, that happy change in the state of affairs in the nation, which was after the queen's death, by the bringing in king George the First. just at the time when the enemies of the religion and liberties of the nation had ripened their designs to be put in speedy execution. And we see in the beginning of this extract, this which is proposed, is mentioned as being no new thing, but that God's people in Great Britain had formerly been called upon to the like duty, and had complied, and that not without success. Such like concerts or agreements have several times been proposed in Scotland, before this which is now proposed to us, particularly there was a proposal published for this very practice, in the year 1732, and another in 1735; so that it appears that this objection of novelty is built on a mistake.

THE CONCLUSION.

And now, upon the whole, I desire every

serious Christian, that may read this discourse, calmly and deliberately to consider whether he can excuse himself from complying with what has been proposed to us and requested of us, by those ministers of Christ in Scotland, who are the authors of the late memorial. God has stirred up a part of his church, in a distant part of the world, to be in an extraordinary manner seeking and crying to him, that he would appear to favour Zion, as he has promised. And they are applying themselves to us, to join with them, and make that very proposal to us which is spoken of in my text, and in like manner and circumstances. The members of one church, in one country, are coming to others, in other distant countries, saying, *Let us go speedily and constantly to pray before the Lord, and to seek the Lord of Hosts.* Will it not become us readily to say, *I will go also?* What these servants of Christ ask of us, is not silver or gold, or any of our outward substance, or that we would put ourselves to any cost, or do any thing that will be likely to expose us to any remarkable trouble, difficulty or suffering in our outward interest, but only that we would, help together with them, by our prayers to God, for the greatest mercy in the world, and that a mercy which as much concerns us as them, for the glory of their Lord and ours, for the great advancement of our common interest and happiness, and the happiness of our fellow-creatures through all nations; a mercy, which, at this day especially, there is great need of; a mercy, which we, in this land, do stand in particular need of; a mercy, which the word of God requires us to make the subject-matter of our prayers, above all other mercies, and gives us more encouragement to pray earnestly and unitedly to him for, than any other mercy; and a mercy, which the providence of God towards the world of mankind, at this day, does loudly call the people of God to pray for. I think we cannot reasonably doubt but that these ministers have acted a part becoming disciples of the great Messiah, and ministers of his kingdom, and have done the will of God, and according to his word, in setting forward such an affair at this day, and in proposing it to us; and therefore I desire it may be considered, whether we shall not really sin against God, in refusing to comply with their proposal and request, or in neglecting it, and turning it by, with but little notice and attention, therein difregarding that which is truly a call of God to us.

The minifters that make this propofal to us, are no feparatifts or fcnifmatics, promoters of no public diforders, nor of any wildnefs or extravagance in matters of religion, but are quiet and peaceable members and minifters of the church of Scotland, that have lamented the late divifions and breaches of that church. If any fhall fay, that they are under no advantage to judge of their character, but muft take it on truft from others, becaufe they conceal their names; in anfwer to this, I would fay, That I prefume no fober perfon will fay that he has any reafon to fufpect them, to be any other than gentlemen of honeft intention. Befure there is no appearance of any thing elfe, but an upright defign in their propofal, and that they have not mentioned their names, is an argument of it. It may well be prefumed, from the manner of their expreffing themfelves, in the memorial itfelf, they concealed their names from that, which, perhaps, may be called an excefs of modefty, chufing to be at the greateft diftance from appearing to fet forth themfelves to the view of the world, as the heads of a great affair, and the first projectors and movers of something extraordinary, that they defire should become general, and that God's people, in various diftant parts of the world, should agree in. And therefore, they are moreover careful to tell us, that they do not propofe the affair, as now fetting it on foot, but as a thing already fet on foot, and do not tell us who firft projected and moved it. The propofal is made to us in a very proper and prudent manner, with all appearance of Chriftian modefty and fincerity, and with a very prudent guard againft any thing that looks like fuperftition, or whatfoever might entangle a tender confcience, and far from any appearance of a defign to promote any particular party or denomination of Chriftians, in oppofition to others, but with all appearance to the contrary, in their charitable requeft, that none would, by any means, conceive of any fuch thing to be in their view, and that all, of every denomination and opinion concerning the late religious commotions, would join with them, in feeking the common intereft of the kingdom of Chrift; and, therefore, I think, none can be in the way of their duty, in neglecting a propofal in itfelf excellent, and that which they have reafon to think is made with upright intentions, merely because the propofers modeftly conceal their names. I do not fee how any ferious perfon, that has an ill opinion of late religious ftirs, can have any colour of reafon to refufe a compliance with this propofal, on that account; the more diforders, extravagancies and delufions of the devil have lately prevailed, the more need have we to pray earneftly to God, for his Holy Spirit, to promote true religion, in oppofition to the grand deceiver, and all his works; and the more fuch prayer, as is propofed, is anfwered, the more effectually will all that is contrary to fober and pure religion be extirpated and exploded.

One would think that every one who favours the duft of Zion, when he hears that God is ftirring up a confiderable number of his minifters and people, to unite in extraordinary prayer, for the revival of religion and advancement of his kingdom, fhould greatly rejoice on this occafion. If we lay to heart the prefent calamities of the church of Chrift, and long for that blefled alteration which God has promifed, one would think it fhould be natural to rejoice at the appearance of fomething in fo dark a day, which is so promising a token. Would not our friends that were lately in captivity in Canada, who earnestly longed for deliverance, have rejoiced to have heard of any thing that seemed to forebode the approach of their redemption? And particularly may we not suppose such of them as were religious persons, would greatly have rejoiced to have understood that there was stirred up in God's people an extraordinary spirit of prayer for their redemption? And I do not know why it would not be as natural for us to rejoice at the like hopeful token of the redemption of Zion, if we made her interest our own, and preferred Jerusalem above our chief joy.

If we are indeed called of God to comply with the proposal now made to us, then let me beseech all that do sincerely love the interest of real Christianity, notwithstanding any diversity of opinion, and former disputes, now to unite in this affair, with one heart and voice—and *let us go speedily to pray before the Lord.* There is no need that one should wait for another. If we can get others, that are our neighbours, to join with us, and so can conveniently spend the quarterly seasons with praying societies, this is desirable; but if not, why should we wholly neglect the duty proposed? Why should not we perform it by ourselves, uniting in heart and practice, as far as we are able, with those who, in distant places, are engaged in that duty at that time?

If it be agreeable to the mind and will of God, that we should comply with the memorial, by praying for the coming of Christ's kingdom, in the manner therein proposed, then doubtless it is the duty of all to comply with the memorial, in that respect also, viz. in endeavouring, as far as in us lies, to promote others joining in such prayer, and to render this union and agreement as extensive as may be. Private Christians may have many advantages and opportunities for this; but especially ministers, inasmuch as they not only are by office overseers of whole congregations of God's people, and their guides in matters of religion, but ordinarily have a far more extensive acquaintance and influence abroad, than private Christians in common have.

And I hope that such as are convinced it is their duty to comply with and encourage this design, will remember we ought not only to go speedily to pray before the Lord, and to seek his mercy, but also to go constantly. We should unite in our practice these two things, which our Saviour unites in his precept, praying and not fainting. If we should continue some years, and nothing remarkable in Providence should appear, as though God heard and answered, we should act very unbecoming believers, if we should therefore begin to be disheartened, and grow dull and slack, in our seeking of God so great a mercy. It is very apparent from the word of God, that God is wont often to try the faith and patience of his people, when crying to him for some great and important mercy, by with-holding the mercy sought, for a season, and not only so, but at first to cause an increase of dark appearances, and yet, without fail, at last, to succeed those who continue instant in prayer with all perseverance, and will not let God go except he blesses. It is now proposed that this extraordinary united prayer should continue for seven years, from November, 1746. Perhaps some that appear forward to engage, may begin to think the time long, before the seven years are out, and may account it a dull story, to go on, for so long a time, praying in this extraordinary method, while all yet continues dark and dead, without any dawnings of the wished-for light, or new promising appearance in Providence of the near approach of the desired mercy. But let it be considered, whether it will not be a poor business, if our faith and patience is so short-winded, that we cannot be willing to wait upon God one seven years, in a way of taking this little pains, in seeking a mercy so infinitely vast. For my part, I sincerely wish and hope, that there may not be an end of extraordinary united prayer, among God's people, for the effusions of the blessed Spirit, when the seven years are ended, but that it will be continued, either in this method, or some other, by a new agreement, that will be entered into, with greater engagedness, and more abundant alacrity, than this is; and that extraordinary united prayer for such a mercy will be further propagated and extended, than it can be expected to be in one seven years. But yet, at the same time, I hope, God's people, that unite in this agreement, will see some tokens for good, before these seven years are out, that shall give them to see, that God has not said to the seed of Jacob—Seek ye me in vain; and shall serve greatly to animate and encourage them to go on in united prayers for the advancement of Chrift's kingdom, with en-creafing fervency. But whatever our hopes may be in this refpect, we muft be content to be ignorant of the times and feafons, which the Father hath put in his own power; and muft be willing that God fhould anfwer prayer, and fulfil his own glorious promifes, in his own time; remembering fuch inftructions, counfels and promifes of the word of God as thefe—*Wait on the Lord, be of Good courage, and he fhall ftrengthen thine heart; wait, I fay, on the Lord. For the vifion is yet for an appointed time; but in the end it will fpeak, and not lie: though it tarry, wait for it, becaufe it will furely come, it will not tarry. I will look unto the Lord, I will wait for the God of my falvation; my God will hear me. God will wipe away tears from off all faces, and the rebuke of his people fhall he take away from off all the earth; for the Lord hath fpoken it. And it fhall be faid in that day, Lo, this is our God! we have waited for him, and he will fave us: This is* JEHOVAH! *we have waited for him, we will be glad and rejoice in his falvation.* Amen.

DOWNFALL

OF

MYSTICAL BABYLON;

OR, A

KEY TO THE PROVIDENCE OF GOD,

IN THE

POLITICAL OPERATIONS OF 1793-4.

BEING THE SUBSTANCE OF A DISCOURSE, PREACHED, FIRST, AT ELIZABETH TOWN, AND AFTERWARDS AT NEW-YORK, ON THE EVENING OF THE LORD'S DAY, APRIL 7, 1793, AND NOW OFFERED, WITH NOTES AND ILLUSTRATIONS, IN EVIDENCE OF THE SENTIMENTS THEN DELIVERED.

By *DAVID AUSTIN*, A. M.
Minister of the First Presbyterian Church at Elizabeth Town.

APOLOGY.

AS the following discourse was delivered from short notes, it is hoped that any little difference in arrangement, or any additional proofs or illustrations, now observed, will be readily excused by any who heard the discourse preached; especially, whilst it is remembered, that in a printed discourse much higher authorities are expected, than what is necessary in the common course of parochial preaching.

For any sentiments observed to be omitted, the reader is referred to the tenor of the preceding discourses; and if any should be ready to say, that proofs and illustrations are needlessly multiplied, it may not be improper to answer, that on the subject of prophecy, as well as in respect to every other, the truth gains in proportion to the evidence by which it is attested; and shines much brighter whilst supported by a cloud of approved witnesses, than whilst resting on the opinion of any single interpreter.

THE DOWNFALL OF MYSTICAL BABYLON.

REVELATION xviii. 20.

Rejoice over her thou heaven, and ye holy apostles and prophets, for God hath avenged you on her.

IN all the calamities which it pleases God to bring upon his enemies, or upon the enemies of his church, all holy beings have cause to rejoice. The ground of their joy, in such events, however awful to the sufferers, is founded in the reason and nature of things as well as in the express appointment and call of God.

The cause of God in heaven, and the cause of Christ and of his church on the earth are one and the same; and so far as either the former or the latter, or both unitedly, may be employed, in their usual methods of exertion, in counteracting, and in overturning the purposes of the Grand Adversary or of his instruments; in the same degree may the struggle be stiled a common cause, or a general war. The enemies of God are the enemies of his church, and they who seek the overthrow of the latter, would, if possible, dethrone the former. On this account, therefore, it is, that all holy beings, whether in the heaven of heavens, on high, or whether in the heavens of the Christian church, (for so, in prophetic stile, the word sometimes signifies,) are called upon to rejoice at the calamities which God, in judgment for their sins, brings on his enemies, and on the enemies of his Zion.

All holy beings have cause to rejoice in the downfall of the wicked, as such a disaster, under the management of heaven, may tend to the upbuilding of the kingdom of Christ, and of the truth in the world. By such events victory is, renewedly, ascribed to God. The faith and hope of the pious are revived and confirmed.—That such effects, by such disasters upon the wicked, have been produced, the scriptures plainly teach. The drowning of the old world, and the destruction of Pharaoh and his host are instances in point. In view of the latter, *sang Moses and the children of Israel this song unto the Lord, and spake, saying—I will sing unto the Lord, for he hath triumphed gloriously: the horse and his rider hath he thrown into the sea. The Lord is my strength and song, and he is become my salvation: he is my God, and I will prepare him an habitation; my father's God, and I will exalt him. The Lord is a man of war: the Lord is his name.*

Not only is the confidence of the righteous maintained by such displays of vindictive power, but the same events load, with increasing danger, the interests of Satan and of the wicked in general.

To revive the interests of truth and of grace—to support the cause of God in the bosoms of the righteous, and to accumulate the degrees of danger, apprehension and final destruction, on the part of the wicked, have no doubt been important, if not leading objects to be accomplished, in all the denunciations and executions which, in all ages, have been, in a higher or less degree, emptied forth upon the wicked, from the vials of the divine indignation.

In pursuance of the same important objects, a call is issued, on a mighty and solemn occasion, to all friends to God, and to his government to rejoice. *Rejoice over her thou heaven, and ye holy apostles and prophets, for God hath avenged you on her.*

Unfolding this passage I propose to shew,

I. Who it is over whose destruction holy beings are called upon to rejoice.

II. The cause of this disaster.

III. Notice the means employed to bring this event to pass. And,

IV. Shew the foundation the event lays for universal joy; concluding with some reflections from the whole.

And will a very gracious God so enlighten the mind, both of the speaker and of the hearers, that truths may be opened, impressions made, and effects wrought answerable to the nature and import of so solemn and momentous a subject.—I am,

I. To shew who it is over whose destruction, or downfall, all holy beings are called upon to rejoice.

For this knowledge we must repair to the first and second verses of the context. *And after these things,* saith the inspired apostle, *I saw another angel come down from heaven, having great power, and the earth was lightened with his glory. And he cried mightily with a strong voice, saying,* BABYLON THE GREAT IS FALLEN, IS FALLEN.

It is very generally, if not unanimously, agreed by Protestant writers, that by Babylon, as used in this place, you are to understand the extensive, once triumphant, and persecuting power of anti-christian Papal Rome, stiled BABYLON, because there are so many appendages to this idolatrous power, which so nearly resemble, and so exactly answer the prophetic description of Babylon, of the Chaldees—the inveterate, the powerful, and, for a season, the successful enemy of the people of God, in ancient time.

Figures of speech, especially in the prophetic parts, are very frequent in the scriptures. Indeed, almost the whole of this book of *the Revelation of Jesus Christ which God gave unto him, to shew unto his servants things which must shortly come to pass*, is made up of figures. Sometimes, lest the figure should be unintelligible, the angel sent to communicate the very interesting intelligence of this invaluable book, explains the figure.— And sometimes the prophetic herald gives a different view of the same object in different figures. Of this method we have an example in the subject before us.

Papal Rome, here stiled BABYLON THE GREAT, in the chapter preceding is called, because of her idolatrous practices, and because of her forsaking her original faithful Lord and Husband—the GREAT WHORE: And that it might be known to be the same power, as is here described, the word Babylon is annexed or interwoven with the other characters of this mystical harlot. This fact will be yet more clear if you listen to the testimony itself. *So he carried me away in the spirit into the wilderness: and I saw a woman sit upon a scarlet-coloured beast, full of names of blasphemy, having seven heads and ten horns. And the woman was arrayed in purple and scarlet-colour, and decked with gold, and precious stones, and pearls, having a golden cup in her hand, full of abominations and filthiness of her fornication. And upon her forehead was a name written,* MYSTERY, BABYLON THE GREAT, THE MOTHER OF HARLOTS AND ABOMINATIONS OF THE EARTH.

In supporting the allusion, or in running the parallel between ancient heathenish and modern anti-christian Papal Babylon, you will permit, that I but touch upon the different branches of fimilarity, leaving the more full illuftration to be fupplied by your own recollection and ftudy.

As in the prophetic writings the words Jerufalem, Zion, the Temple of the living God, &c. are ufed to exprefs the ftate of the church under the Jewifh, fo the fame words are fometimes applied to exprefs the ftate and character of the church under the Chriftian difpenfation. On the other hand, as Sodom, Egypt and Babylon were names given to the enemies of God, and of his church, in ancient time, fo, under the fame names, their fucceffors are fet forth and defcribed as to exift in later times.

All thefe dark fhades of national character, and many more, did time allow, might be proved to be, with juftice, applicable to this anti-chriftian power of Papal Rome.— To Sodom this power may be likened for her fin, and to Egypt for her darknefs, idolatry and oppreffion. And, without doubt, by the angel of God, in his addrefs to St. John on the fubject of the flaughter of the witneffes, thefe dark fhades are applied to this tyrannical dominion. *And their dead bodies fhall lie in the ftreet of the great city,* *which spiritually is called Sodom and Egypt, where, also, our Lord was crucified.* On these words, saith an approved commentator*.— " The place where this was done is stiled " Sodom and Egypt, and the *great city* " *where our Lord was crucified;* which, if " literally understood, signifies Jerusalem, " but if mystically understood, ROME, or the " Roman empire."—And no one, I may add, will suppose it is perverting the prophetic emblem, if it be applied, solely, to Rome; especially, if it be recollected, that as Jerusalem was the head of the Jewish, so Rome professes to be the head of the Christian empire; and also, that the once crucifying of our Lord at Jerusalem, is but a faint emblem of the thousand crucifixions he has since undergone in the multiplied persecutions and tortures of the members of his mystical body; and, I may add, which he still undergoes in the daily offerings, the mystical services, the superstitious masses of the church of Rome.

Hear, also, to this point, the testimony of a late very respectable writer on the subject of prophecy.† " As to the great city, men-

---

NOTES.
* Burkit in loco. † Langdon in loco.

" tioned under the figurative names of So-
" dom and Egypt, and compared also to Je-
" salem, where our Lord was crucified, we
" shall find by following visions that Rome,
" with its empire, is meant. It is called So-
" dom, on account of the abominable crimes
" committed in it; Egypt, on account of
" abounding superstition and idolatry, and
" the cruel bondage in which it holds the
" people of God: And it is compared to
" Jerusalem, being said to be the city where
" our Lord was crucified; because while it
" pretended to be an holy city, it had killed
" the prophets and saints, and crucified Christ
" afresh in his members. Here it may be
" more especially observed, that as in the
" beginning of the chapter the temple is the
" emblem of the Christian church, that city,
" with its empire, in which the church is com-
" prehended, may very properly be compar-
" ed to Jerusalem, the city in which the Jew-
" ish temple stood: And as our Lord was
" crucified within the jurisdiction of the Ro-
" man empire, and by the Roman authori-
" ty, and the Papal empire has succeeded to
" the other, and claims an equal extent, there
" is a propriety in saying that our Lord was
" crucified in the great city Rome, consi-

"dered in connexion with the empire of which it is the capital."

Having laid this foundation as to the use and application of prophetic figures, to which much might be added, were it necessary, the way is plain to proceed with my subject, in an attempt to shew, that by BABYLON THE GREAT, whose fall is predicted in the text, is meant the present anti-christian power of Papal Rome.

This fact will, at once, appear most palpably evident, if, with attention, you are pleased to follow me in a consideration of the several articles of analogy, between ancient and modern Babylon, designed to justify the prophetic allusion.

1. Did Nebuchadnezzar, the king of Babylon, *set up an image*, and call upon the subjects of his empire to fall down and worship it, so hath the Nebuchadnezzar of the church of Rome, supported by the magi of his kingdom, set up, and continued to set up images innumerable, to which the homage of bowing and kneeling is continually paid in churches, in many public places, and even on the common country roads, by the subjects of this mystical empire, as is well known to those who have passed through this idolatrous country.

2. Did the decree of the king of Babylon enjoin homage to this image on pain of being cast *into the midst of a burning fiery furnace;* so doth the church of Rome enjoin homage to her idols on pain of exclusion from her communion, with the tortures of the inquisition in this world, and the pains of purgatory and damnation in the next.*

3. Did Nebuchadnezzar actually inflict, or attempt to inflict, the pains of the fiery furnace on some who refused to bow down to his image; so hath the church of Rome actually inflicted, on thousands of innocent Protestants, refusing to partake in her idolatries, all the tortures which imagination could invent.

Let the history of her persecutions, massacres, slaughters and burnings testify to this fact.†

T t

NOTES.

* The Author once had his own hat knocked off by the bayonet of a soldier, belonging to a party who escorted and protected a Bishop and his confederates, during a very thronged procession, at Nantes, because he would not do customary homage at the presence of the Host, which was carried along the streets, claiming religious homage, during the farcical exhibitions on the celebration of the Fête de Dieu.

† " Satan has opposed the Reformation with cruel *persecutions*. The persecutions with which the Protestants, in one kingdom and another, have been tormented, by the church of Rome,

4. Was ancient Babylon the seat and source of idolatry in the Pagan; so is Rome in the Christian world.

NOTE.

have been, in many respects, beyond any that were before. So that Antichrist has proved the greatest and most cruel enemy the church of Christ ever had; agreeable to the description given of the church of Rome. *And I saw the woman drunken with the blood of the saints, and with the blood of the martyrs of Jesus.—And in her was found the blood of prophets, and of saints, and of all them that were slain upon the earth.*

The heathen persecutions had been very dreadful; but now persecution, by the church of Rome, was improved, and studied, and cultivated as an art or science. Such methods of tormenting were found out, that were beyond the invention of former ages. And, that persecution might be managed more effectually, there were certain societies established in various parts of the Popish dominions, whose business it should be to study, improve, and practise persecution in its highest perfection, which are called the courts of inquisition.* A perusal of the histories of the Romish persecution, and their courts of inquisition, will give that idea, which a few words cannot express.

* These infernal tribunals were first erected in the twelfth century by the infamous Father Dominic, under the patronage of Pope Innocent III. in order more completely to extirpate the Waldenses, and other pretended heretics. It is difficult to conceive, that if God had delivered the world entirely into the Devil's hands, (as Satan once pretended) that his ingenuity and malice could have invented any thing more detestable and shocking. In fact, there is scarcely a method that could delay or pervert justice, but they have adopted it in their forms; nor does there seem a possible method of torture but they have invented and repeatedly exercised. The reader, whose nerves can bear such reiterated scenes of cruelty, may read Baker's History of the Inquisition—the History of the Inquisition at Goa, written by a Papist, and similar works. But to shew how far it is possible for human nature to go, let him read the following extract from a sermon preached at Evora, on occasion of one of the most horrid scenes the sun ever beheld, an *auto de fe*, when they burn or rather roast heretics (as

Did her kings rule over many kingdoms and provinces; fo this anti-chriftian idola-

NOTE.

they call them) alive, from a principle of religion. "Beloved Portuguefe," faid the inhuman wretch, "let us return thanks to Heaven, for his great goodnefs in giving us this holy tribunal (the Inquifition.) Had it not been for this tribunal our kingdom would have become a tree without flowers or fruits, fit only to be committed to the flames. What progrefs has herefy made, for want of an Inquifition, in England, France, Germany, and the Netherlands! It is evident, had it not been for fo great a bleffing, our country would have been like to thofe above-mentioned."

When the Reformation began, the beaft with feven heads and ten horns began to rage in a dreadful manner. After the Reformation, the church of Rome renewed its perfecution of the poor Waldenfes, and great multitudes of them were cruelly tortured and put to death. Soon after the Reformation, there were alfo terrible perfecutions in various parts of Germany, and efpecially in Bohemia, which lafted for thirty years together, in which fo much blood was fhed for the fake of religion, that a certain writer compares it to the plenty of waters of the great rivers of Germany. The countries of Poland, Lithuania, and Hungary were, in like manner, deluged with Proteftant blood.*

* "If Rome *Pagan* hath flain her thoufands of innocent Chriftians, Rome *Chriftian* hath flain her ten thoufands. For, not to mention other outrageous flaughters and barbarities, the croifades againft the Waldenfes and Albigenfes, the murders committed by the Duke of Alva in the Netherlands, the maffacres in France and Ireland, will probably amount to above ten times the number of all the Chriftians flain in all the ten perfecutions of the Roman emperors put together."

"By means of thefe and other cruel perfecutions, the Proteftant religion was in a great meafure fuppreffed in Bohemia, and the Palatinate, and Hungary, which before were Proteftant countries. Thus was fulfilled what was foretold of the little horn." *And of the ten horns that were in his head, and of the other which came up, and before whom three fell, even of that horn that had eyes, and a mouth that fpake great things, whofe look was more ftout than his fellows: I beheld and the fame horn made war with the*

trous harlot is said to *sit upon many waters; with whom the kings of the earth have commit-*

NOTE.

saints, and prevailed against them. And what was foretold of the beast having seven heads and ten horns. *And it was given unto him to make war with the saints, and to overcome them ; and power was given him over all kindreds, and tongues, and nations.*

Also Holland, and the other low countries, were, for many years, a scene of nothing but the most affecting and amazing cruelties, being deluged with the blood of Protestants, under the merciless hands of the Spaniards, to whom they were then in subjection.— But in this persecution the Devil in a great measure failed of his purpose, as it issued in a great part of the Netherlands casting off the Spanish yoke, and setting up a wealthy and powerful Protestant state, to the great defence of the Protestant cause ever since.

France also is another country which, since the Reformation, in some respects, perhaps, more than any other, has been a scene of dreadful cruelties suffered by the Protestants there. After many cruelties had been exercised towards the Protestants in that kingdom, there was begun a persecution of them in the year 1571, in the reign of Charles the IX. king of France.

It began with a cruel massacre, wherein seventy thousand Protestants were slain in a few days time, as the king boasted; and in all this persecution, he slew, as is supposed, three hundred thousand martyrs. And it is reckoned, that about this time, within thirty years, there were martyred in this kingdom, for the Protestant religion, thirty-nine princes, one hundred and forty-eight counts, two hundred and thirty-four barons, one hundred and forty-seven thousand five hundred and eighteen gentlemen, and seven hundred and sixty thousand of the common people.

The Parisian massacre was aggravated with several circumstances of wantonness and treachery; but we hope that the above numbers are exaggerated. Thuanus, their own historian, reckons thirty thousand lives destroyed in this slaughter; but Protestant authors seem to have reason for supposing them not less than one hundred thousand in the whole. But the most horrid circumstance in the history is, that when the news of this event reached Rome, Pope Gregory XIII. instituted the most solemn rejoicings, giving

ted fornication, and the inhabitants of the earth have been made drunk with the wine of her fornication.

NOTE.

thanks to Almighty God for this glorious victory!!!—An instance that has no parallel, even in hell.

But all these persecutions were, for exquisite cruelty, far exceeded by those which followed in the reign of Lewis XIV. which, indeed, are supposed to exceed all others that ever have been; and being long continued by reason of the long reign of that king, almost wholly extirpated the Protestant religion out of that kingdom, where had been before a multitude of famous Protestant churches all over the country.* Thus it was given to the beast to make war with the saints, and to overcome them.

* *The Persecution under Lewis XIV.*—This followed the revocation of the Edict of Nantes, A. D. 1685. The following extract is taken from a French work of reputation.

" The troopers, soldiers and dragoons went into the Protestants' houses, where they marred and defaced their household stuff, broke their looking-glasses, and other utensils and ornaments, let their wine run about their cellars, and threw about their corn, and spoiled it. And as to those things which they could not destroy in this manner, such as furniture of beds, linen, wearing apparel, plate, &c. they carried them to the market place, and sold them to the Jesuits and other Roman Catholics. By these means the Protestants in Montaubon alone were, in four or five days, stripped of above a million of money. But this was not the worst.

" They turned the dining-rooms of gentlemen into stables for their horses, and treated the owners of the houses where they quartered with the highest indignity and cruelty, lashing them about from one to another, day and night, without intermission, not suffering them to eat or drink; and when they began to sink under the fatigue and pains they had undergone, they laid them on a bed, and when they thought them somewhat recovered, made them rise, and repeated the same tortures. When they saw the blood and sweat run down their faces and other parts of their bodies, they sluiced them with water; and putting over their heads

5. Was ancient Babylon a scourge to the people of God, and did she bring them into

NOTE.

kettle-drums, turned upside down, they made a continual din upon them till those unhappy creatures lost their senses. When one party of these tormentors were weary they were relieved by another, who practised the same cruelties with fresh vigor.

At Negreplisse, a town near Montaubon, they hung up Isaac Favin, a Protestant citizen of that place, by his arm-pits, and tormented him a whole night by pinching and tearing off his flesh with pincers. They made a great fire round a boy about twelve years old, who, with hands and eyes lifted up to heaven, cried out—"My God, help me!"—And when they found the youth resolved to die rather than renounce his religion, they snatched him from the fire just as he was on the point of being burnt.

"In several places the soldiers applied red hot irons to the hands and feet of men, and the breasts of women. At Nantes they hung up several women and maids by their feet, and others by their arm-pits, and thus exposed them to public view stark-naked. They bound mothers that gave suck to posts, and let their sucking infants lie languishing in their sight for several days and nights, crying, mourning and gasping for life. Some they bound before a great fire, and, being half roasted, let them go—a punishment worse than death. Amidst a thousand hideous cries, and a thousand blasphemies, they hung up men and women by the hair, and some by their feet, on hooks in chimneys, and smoaked them with wisps of wet hay till they were suffocated. They tied some under the arms with ropes, and plunged them again and again into wells. They bound others like criminals, put them to the torture, and with a funnel filled them with wine, till the fumes of it took away their reason, when they made them say they consented to be Catholics. They stripped them naked, and, after a thousand indignities, stuck them with pins and needles from head to foot. They cut and slashed them with knives, and sometimes with red-hot pincers took hold of them by the nose and other parts of the body, and dragged them about the rooms till they made them promise to be Catholics, or till the cries of these miserable wretches, calling upon God for help, forced them to let them go. They beat them with staves, and thus bruised, and with broken bones,

a seventy years captivity? so this anti-christian power hath been a scourge to the true worshippers of God in modern times, and hath had a great part of the Christian church

NOTE.

dragged them to church, where their forced presence was taken for an abjuration. In some places they tied fathers and husbands to their bed-posts, and, before their eyes, ravaged their wives and daughters with impunity. They blew up men and women with bellows till they burst them. If any, to escape these barbarities, endeavoured to save themselves by flight, they pursued them into the fields and woods, where they shot them like wild beasts, and prohibited them from departing the kingdom, (a cruelty never practised by Nero or Dioclesian) upon pain of confiscation of effects, the gallies, the lash, and perpetual imprisonment; insomuch that the prisons of the sea-port towns were crammed with men, women and children, who endeavoured to save themselves by flight from this dreadful persecution. With these scenes of desolation and horror, the popish clergy feasted their eyes, and made only a matter of laughter and sport of them."

Other cruelties.—Beside the Protestant blood shed in these persecutions, Popery has to answer for the lives of millions of Jews, Mahometans, and barbarians. When the Moors conquered Spain in the eighth century, they allowed the Christians the free exercise of their religion. But in the fifteenth century, when the tables were turned, and Ferdinand subdued the Moriscoes, (the descendants of the above Moors) many hundred thousands of them were forced to be baptized, or burnt, massacred, or banished, and their children sold for slaves; besides an innumerable multitude of Jews, who shared the same cruelties, chiefly by means of the infernal Inquisition. A worse slaughter, if possible, was made among the natives of Spanish America, where fifteen millions are said to have been sacrificed to the genius of Popery in the course of about forty years. Well, therefore, might the inspired apostle say, that at mystic Babylon's destruction—*In her was found the blood of prophets, and of saints, and of all that were slain upon the earth!* Rev. xviii. 24.——[See Edwards's History of Redemption, with notes, page 452, 459, of the London, or new American edition.]

in more than Egyptian bondage for twelve hundred years.

During this bondage it is that the TWO WITNESSES—the *few* faithful, who, in every age, have testified to the truth; (as some have supposed) but if so, there may be also an allusion, and perhaps a primary one, to the TWO OLIVE TREES of the prophet's vision, *the anointed ones that stand by the Lord of the whole earth.*

The olive tree afforded light from its fatness, and nourishment from its fruit. Understanding, therefore, the purport of the TWO WITNESSES, as explained by the angel, to be the two OLIVE TREES, and the TWO CANDLESTICKS, *standing before the God of the earth,* I am rather inclined to think, that they have a more extensive, mystical, and important meaning than what they have been generally understood to imply. If the olive trees and candlesticks were an emblem of spiritual and divine communications during their standing in the Jewish, what should hinder the same application whilst they stand in the Christian church?

As the gifts and graces shed down upon the ministers of our blessed Lord, and upon his churches, after his ascension, were supposed to have been typified or prefigured by the anointing and common oil of the sanctuary; so the olive tree as giving light and heat, and, I may add, nourishment too, was found in the usage and appointment of heaven, no unbecoming representation or emblem of those spiritual communications which were then shed upon the true worshippers, and which will ever be continued as long as Christ is the vine, or true olive, and his people the needy branches.

May we not then suppose, that by these TWO OLIVE TREES and the TWO CANDLESTICKS, *standing before the God of the earth,* is meant the *sources* of divine and spiritual supplies to his church, the *medium* of communication, or methods of *outward* and *open exhibition;* or shall we say, that the emblem may partake a little of each, and stand a lively figure of them all?

If you ask how this interpretation can consist with the epithet, with their being called *witnesses,* it may be answered, they are justly and literally so to be stiled. Are not the word of God preached, and his ordinances administered, by his faithful ministers, properly to be stiled WITNESSES for God?—

And if you choose to retain the number *two*, may we not say the *spirit* and the *word*, with their usual and outward methods of administration, are signified; or say the word, and the ordinances of God in general, or the whole exhibition of the testimony of God, whether in things inward and spiritual, or in things outward and visible?

With this interpretation agrees well the idea of their prophesying *in sackcloth*; for no one can pretend, but the administration of the word and worship of God, in the Romish church, is so beclouded by ignorance, stiled darkness; by superstition and error, and by the ministry of a corrupt priesthood, as to lay just foundation to say, that the witnesses, with this interpretation, are emphatically prophesying in sackcloth.

With the same idea consists, very exactly, the *term* of time in which these witnesses are appointed to prophesy:—It is during the whole reign of Antichrist, the forty-two months, or twelve hundred and sixty years. *And I will give*, or appoint, *unto my two witnesses*, and *they shall prophesy a thousand two hundred and threescore days, clothed in sackcloth.*

With the same interpretation agrees the

declaration or expofition of the angel in the next verfe. *Thefe are the* TWO OLIVE TREES *and the* TWO CANDLESTICKS *ftanding before the God of the earth.* And, in fact, there feems nothing in the chapter but what may, with as great apparent truth, be reconciled to this interpretation, as to any other; and there are fome things in it which cannot, with eafe, be interpreted as applicable to the witneffes, in any other fenfe, underftood or explained.

And if any fhould be difpofed to believe, that the prefent reigning perfecuting infidel power, now waging war againft all revealed religion, in France, is likely to be the *death* of thefe fame witneffes, who, for a long time, have already been made to prophefy in fackcloth, perhaps the opinion may find fupport from the declaration of the angel: *And when they fhall have finifhed their teftimony, the beaft that afcendeth out of the bottomlefs pit, fhall make war againft them, and fhall overcome them, and kill them.* If this interpretation be true, the mourning witneffes are now fuffering death in thofe parts of myftical Babylon, where the exifting exterminating power has prevailed.

Did time allow, and was the prefent a

proper place in the order of my discourse, I might expound upon the whole chapter, and easily reconcile any expressions which, at first view, might appear intricate, or doubtful, to the spirit of this interpretation. Suffice it, for the present, to say, that with this interpretation agrees well the declaration made respecting the injury these witnesses are able to do their enemies. *And if any man will hurt them, fire proceedeth out of their mouth, and devoureth their enemies.* And of nothing short of the administration of Heaven can it be said: *These have power to shut heaven, that it rain not in the days of their prophecy.* And of nothing short of this can it be said—*They have power over waters to turn them to blood, and to smite the earth with all plagues as often as they will.* And very correspondent to the death of the witnesses, and to the lying of their dead bodies in the *street of the great city*, is the death, the broken and demolished state of external religion in those parts of Papal Rome, in which the present exterminating power hath prevailed. And equally correspondent is the declaration, that *they of the people, and tongues, and nations;* probably those nations and churches out of the communion of the church of Rome, *shall see their dead bodies three days and an half, and,* by a more lively administration of the word and ordinances of God, *shall not suffer their dead bodies to be put in graves.*

And over the death of these witnesses it is, that the men of this world *shall rejoice, and make merry, and shall send gifts one to another; because these two prophets tormented them that dwelt on the earth.*

To the resurrection and final exaltation of these witnesses well applies the verses succeeding. *And after three days and an half, the spirit of life from God entered into them, and they stood upon their feet, and great fear fell upon them that saw them. And they heard a great voice from heaven, saying unto them—Come up hither. And they ascended up to heaven in a cloud, and their enemies beheld them.* During these events it is said—*And the same hour was there an earthquake.* May it not mean the earthquake now *begun*—the present convulsions amongst the nations, (for so in prophetic stile the word signifies) which are to be succeeded by the opening of the temple of God in heaven. *And the temple of God was opened in heaven, and there was seen, in his temple, the ark of his testament; and there were lightnings, and voi-*

this was a member of the Christian church, and set by God in the most eminent station in his church, and was honoured above all other princes that ever had been in the world, as the great protector of his church, and her deliverer from the persecuting power of that cruel scarlet-coloured beast. Mr. Lowman himself styles him *a Christian Prince, and Protector of the Christian Religion*. God is very careful not to reckon his own people among the Gentiles, the visible subjects of Satan, Num. xxiii. 9. *The people shall not be reckoned among the nations.* God will not enroll them with them; if they happen to be among them, he will be careful to set a mark upon them, as a note of distinction, Rev. vii. 3, &c. when God is reckoning up his own people, he leaves out those that have been noted for idolatry. As among the tribes that were sealed, Rev. viii. those idolatrous tribes of Ephraim and Dan are left out, and in the genealogy of Christ, Matth. i. those princes that were chiefly noted for idolatry, are left out. Much more would God be careful not to reckon his own people, especially such Christian princes as have been the most eminent instruments of overthrowing idolatry, amongst idolaters, and as members and heads of that kingdom that is noted in scripture as the most notorious and infamous of all, for abominable idolatry, and opposition and cruelty to the true worshippers of God. And especially not to reckon them as properly belonging to one of those seven heads of this monarchy, of which very heads it is particularly noted that they had on them the names of BLASPHEMY, which Mr. Lowman himself supposes to signify idolatry. It was therefore worthy of God, agreeable to his manner, and what might well be expected, that when he was reckoning up the several successive heads of this beast, and Constantine and his successors came in the way, and there was occasion to mention them, to set a mark, or note of distinction on them, signifying that they did not properly belong to the beast, nor were to be reckoned as belonging to the heads, and therefore are to be skipped over in the reckoning, and Antichrist, though the eighth head of the Roman empire, is to be reckoned the seventh head of the beast. This appears to me abundantly the most just and natural interpretation of Rev. xvii. 10, 11. It is reasonable to suppose, that God would take care to make such a note in this prophetical description of this dreadful beast, and not, by any means to reckon Constantine as belonging properly to him.—If we reckon Constantine as a member of this beast having seven heads and ten horns, described chap. xvii. and as properly one of his heads, then he was also properly a member of the great red dragon with seven heads and ten horns that warred with the woman, chap. xii. For the seven heads and ten horns of that dragon, are plainly the same with the seven heads and ten horns of the beast. So that this makes Constantine a visible member of the devil; for we are told expressly of that dragon, ver 9. that he was *that old serpent, called the Devil and Satan.* And to suppose that Constantine is reckoned as belonging to one of the heads of that dragon, is to make these prophecies inconsistent with themselves. For here in this 12th chapter, we have represented a war between the dragon and the woman cloathed with the sun; which woman, as all agree, is the church; but Constantine, as all do also agree, belonged to the woman, was a member of the Christian church, and was on that side in the war against the dragon; yea, was the main instrument of that great victory that was obtained over the dragon there spoken of, ver. 9—12. What an inconfiſtency therefore is it, to ſuppoſe that he was at the ſame time a member and head of that very dragon, which fought with the woman, and yet which Conſtantine himſelf fought with, overcame, and glorioufly triumphed over! It is not therefore to be wondered at, that God was careful to diſtinguiſh Conſtantine from the proper heads of the beaſt; it would have been a wonder if he had not. God ſeems to have been careful to diſtinguiſh him, not only in his word, but in his providence, by ſo ordering it that this Chriſtian emperor ſhould be removed from Rome, the city that God had given up to be the ſeat of the power of the beaſt, and of its heads, and that he ſhould have the ſeat of his empire elſewhere.

Conſtantine was made the inſtrument of giving a mortal wound to the heathen Roman empire, and giving it a mortal wound in its head, viz. the heathen emperors that were then reigning, Maxentius and Licinius.— But more eminently was this glorious change in the empire owing to the power of God's word, the prevalence of the glorious goſpel, by which Conſtantine himſelf was converted, and ſo became the inſtrument of the overthrow of the heathen empire in the east and west. The change that was then bro't to pass, is represented as the destruction of the heathen empire, or the old heathen world, and therefore seems to be compared to that dissolution of heaven and earth that shall be at the day of judgment, Rev. vi. 12. to the end. And therefore well might the heathen empire, under the head which was then reigning, be represented as wounded to death, chap. xiii. 3. It is much more likely, that the wound the beast had by a sword, in his head, spoken of ver. 14. was the wound that the heathen empire had in its head, by that sword which we read of, chap. i. 16. and xix. 15. that proceeds out of the mouth of Christ, than the wound that was given to the Christian empire and emperor by the sword of the heathen Goths. It is most likely that this deadly wound was by that sword with which Michael made war with him, and overcame him, and cast him to the earth, chap. xii. 9. and that the deadly wound which was given him, was given him at that very time. It is most likely, that the sword that gave him this deadly wound, after which he strangely revived, as though he rose from the dead, was the same sword with that which is spoken of, as what shall at last utterly destroy him, so that he shall never rise more, chap. xix. 15, 19, 20, 21. This wounding of the head of the beast by the destruction of the heathen empire, and conversion of the emperor to the Christian truth, was a glorious event indeed of Divine Providence, worthy to be so much spoken of in prophecy. It is natural to suppose, that the mortal wounding of the head of that savage cruel beast, that is represented as constantly at war with the woman, and persecuting the church of Christ, should be some relief to the Christian church; but, on the contrary, that wounding to death, that Mr. Lowman speaks of, was the victory of the enemies of the Christian church over her, and the wound received from them.

It is said of that head of the empire that shall be next after the sixth head, and next before Antichrist, and that is not reckoned as properly one of the number of the heads of the beast, that *when it comes, it shall continue a short space*, chap. xvii. 10. By which we may understand, at least, that it shall be one of the shortest, in its continuance, of the successive heads. But the government seated at Ravenna, in the hands of the Goths, or of the deputies of the Greek emperors,

that thou shalt take up this proverb against the king of Babylon, and say—How hath the oppressor ceased! The golden city ceased!—The whole earth is at rest, and is quiet; they break forth into singing: Yea, the fir-trees rejoice at thee, and the cedars of Lebanon, saying—Since thou art laid down, no feller has come up against us. Hell from beneath is moved for thee, to meet thee at thy coming: it stirreth up the dead for thee.

Thy pomp is brought down to the grave, and the noise of thy viols; the worm is spread under thee, and the worms cover thee.

How art thou fallen from heaven, O Lucifer! Son of the Morning, how art thou cut down to the ground, which did weaken the nations!

They that see thee shall narrowly look upon thee and consider thee, saying—Is this the man that made the earth to tremble? that did shake kingdoms? that made the world as a wilderness? and destroyed the cities thereof? that opened not the house of the prisoners?

For I will arise up against them saith the Lord of Hosts, and cut off from Babylon the name and remnant, the son and nephew saith the Lord. I will also make it a possession for the bittern, and pools of water; and I will *sweep it with the besom of destruction saith the Lord of Hosts.*

Having thus taken but a very brief survey of the *joyful*, though *awful* expressions of exultation at the destruction of ancient Babylon, let us, for a moment, examine what there is, upon sacred record, to answer this emblem in respect to the downfall of mystical Babylon.—*And after these things I saw another angel come down from heaven, having great power; and the earth was lightened with his glory. And he cried mightily with a strong voice, saying, Babylon the great is fallen, is fallen, and is become the habitation of devils, and the hold of every foul spirit, and a cage of every unclean and hateful bird. For all nations have drunk of the wine of the wrath of her fornication, and the kings of the earth have committed fornication with her, and the merchants of the earth are waxed rich thro' the abundance of her delicacies. And I heard another voice from heaven, saying, Come out of her, my people, that ye be not partakers of her sins, and that ye receive not of her plagues: For her sins have reached unto heaven, and God hath remembered her iniquities. Reward her even as she rewarded you, and double unto her double, according to her works: in the cup which she hath filled, fill to her double. How much she hath glorified herself, and lived deliciously, so much torment and sorrow give her: for she saith in her heart, I sit a queen, and am no widow, and shall see no sorrow. Therefore shall her plagues come in one day, death, and mourning, and famine; and she shall be utterly burnt with fire: for strong is the Lord God who judgeth her. And the kings of the earth, who have committed fornication and lived deliciously with her, shall bewail her, and lament for her, when they shall see the smoke of her burning. Standing afar off for the fear of her torment, saying, Alas, alas! that great city Babylon, that mighty city! for in one hour is thy judgment come. And the merchants of the earth shall weep and mourn over her: for no man buyeth their merchandise any more: The merchandise of gold, and silver, and precious stones, and of pearls, and fine linen, and purple, and silk, and scarlet, and all thyme wood, and all manner vessels of ivory, and all manner vessels of most precious wood, and of brass, and iron, and marble, and cinnamon, and odours, and ointments, and frankincense, and wine, and oil, and fine flour, and wheat, and beasts, and sheep, and horses, and chariots, and slaves, and souls of men.—*

And the fruits that thy soul lusteth after are departed from thee, and all things which were dainty and goodly are departed from thee, and thou shalt find them no more at all. The merchants of these things, which were made rich by her, shall stand afar off, for the fear of her torment, weeping and wailing. And saying, Alas, alas! that great city, that was clothed in fine linen, and purple, and scarlet, and decked with gold, and precious stones, and pearls! For in one hour so great riches is come to nought. And every ship-master, and all the company in ships, and sailors, and as many as trade by sea, stood afar off, and cried, when they saw the smoke of her burning, saying—What city is like unto this great city! And they cast dust on their heads, and cried, weeping and wailing, saying, Alas, alas! that great city, wherein were made rich all that had ships in the sea by reason of her costliness! for in one hour she is made desolate. Rejoice over her, thou heaven, and ye holy apostles and prophets; for God hath avenged you on her. And a mighty angel took up a stone like a great milstone, and cast it into the sea, saying, Thus with violence shall that great city Babylon be thrown down, and shall be found no more at all. And the voice of harpers, and musicians, and of pipers, and trumpeters, shall be heard no more at all in thee; and no craftsman, of whatsoever craft he be, *shall be found any more in thee; and the sound of a milstone shall be heard no more at all in thee; and the light of a candle shall shine no more at all in thee; and the voice of the bridegroom and of the bride shall be heard no more at all in thee: for thy merchants were the great men of the earth; for by thy sorceries were all nations deceived. And in her was found the blood of prophets, and of saints, and of all that were slain upon the earth.*

"And after these things I heard a great
"voice of much people in heaven, saying,
"Alleluia! Salvation, and glory, and honor,
"and power, unto the Lord our God: For
"true and righteous are his judgments; for
"he hath judged the great whore, which did
"corrupt the earth with her fornication,
"and hath avenged the blood of his servants
"at her hand. And again they said, Alle-
"luia! And her smoke rose up for ever and
"ever. And the four and twenty elders, and
"the four beasts, fell down and worshipped
"God that sat on the throne saying, Amen;
"Alleluia!—And a voice came out of the
"throne, saying, Praise our God, all ye his

" servants, and ye that fear him, both small
" and great. And I heard as it were the voice
" of a great multitude, and as the voice of
" many waters, and as the voice of mighty
" thunderings, saying, Alleluia! for the Lord
" God omnipotent reigneth.

Did time allow, I might follow several other prophecies in their application to this same anti-christian church, and shew the evidence they all carry of a threatened overthrow; but I shall wave this for the present, expressing all necessary to be expressed in this place, in the words of an eminent English writer on this subject.*

" The prophecies of Daniel, St. Paul, and St. John, though *singly* of great weight, receive additional force if brought near and illustrated by each other. Having already examined them separately, and apart, let us now consider them together, and collect the evidence that arises when they are taken in one view, and form an entire and perfect whole.

From the most cursory view of the three predictions it is evident, that the same scheme

NOTE.
* See Hallifax's Sermons, page 328.

and conftitution of things, the fame events, perfons and times, the origin, continuance and deftruction of the fame tyrannical power, (which power, by Daniel, is noted by the appellation of the *little horn*, by St. Paul is denominated *the man of fin*, and by St. John is branded with the titles of the *beaft*, and the *falfe prophet:*) are *diftinctly* foretold in all.

If Daniel defcribes the kingdom in which the little horn was to arife, by fuch emblems as can belong to none but the Roman, the fame emblems, to pre-figure the kingdom of the beaft and the falfe prophet, are alfo employed by St. John, from whom we farther learn, that his appropriated place of refidence is the city of Rome.

If Daniel reftrains the fovereignty of this Roman power to the European or weftern part of the empire, after it was divided into ten fhares, the fame reftriction is intimated in one of the epiftles of St. Paul, and is more explicitly declared by the beloved difciple in the Apocalypfe. If Daniel reprefents the nature of this ufurped dominion as different from any other, St. Paul and St. John inftruct us, that this diverfity confifts in its being fpiritual, not a civil dominion, which is therefore to be fought for, *not* in the Heathen, but in *Chriſtian* Rome. If the inſtances in which this ſpiritual dominion is exerted, according to Daniel, be chiefly theſe—aſpiring to ſupreme and uncontroulable authority over the inhabitants of the earth—affecting divine titles and honors—enjoining the worſhip of dæmons and departed ſaints—prohibiting marriage—working falſe miracles—and perſecuting and killing thoſe who oppoſe its claims; the ſame particulars are related, and with new additions and explications in the writings of St. Paul and St. John. If the *duration* of this eccleſiaſtical polity be limited by Daniel to *a time,* and *times,* and *the dividing of time,* the ſame duration is expreſſed, and, in a variety of phraſes, by St. John, by whom the reign of the beaſt is fixed to a *time,* and *times,* and *half a time,* or to three years and an half, or forty-two months, or twelve hundred and ſixty days.

And laſtly, if the demolition of this extraordinary polity be denounced by the prophet of the Old Teſtament, the ſame intereſting event is promiſed by the two apoſtles of the New. Such a number of coincidencies, all ſo ſtrange and unuſual in their kinds, to be found in the compoſitions of three perfons, living in different, and one in a very remote period, cannot fairly be afcribed to any other caufe than to the impulfe of the *felf-fame fpirit,* who *taught them all things,* which it was neceffary fhould be communicated for the admonition of the church of Chrift, *upon whom the ends of the world* fhould *come.*

Now of the characters recorded in fcripture, as the undoubted marks of Antichrift, many, at leaft, have been fhewn to belong, exclufively, to the *tyranny* now exifting in Papal Rome. For, *firft* of all, this power is certainly a Roman one: *Secondly,* it is confined to the limits of the Latin, or weftern empire: *Thirdly,* it arofe among the ten kingdoms into which that empire was parted by the northern barbarians; *Fourthly,* its throne or feat is in the city of Rome: *Fifthly,* it is a Chriftian power; and, *fixthly,* it is difcriminated from all others, by being of the fpiritual or ecclefiaftic kind. Thefe are circumftances fo plainly realized in that part of Chriftendom which is fubject to the Roman Pontiff, that it is not poffible, by any art or fubtilty of our adverfaries, they can be evaded or denied."*

NOTE.

* See the eleventh of Bifhop Hurd's Sermons on the Prophe-

After such testimony and volumes to the same effect which might be produced, if necessary, you will not deem it harsh, uncharitable, or unfair, if I say, the object pointed at in these prophecies, must infallibly be the present *tyrannical*, though, blessed be God! the *tottering* church of Papal Rome. This is the haughty *Babylon*, and this is *the woman arrayed in purple and scarlet-colour, and decked with gold and precious stones, and pearls, having a golden cup in her hand, full of abominations, and filthiness of her fornication.* And this is the *woman*, upon whose *forehead was a name written*, MYSTERY, BABYLON THE GREAT, THE MOTHER OF HARLOTS, and ABOMINATIONS OF THE EARTH. And this is the woman that was seen *drunken with the blood of the saints, and with the blood of the martyrs of Jesus.* And this is the *woman* that is denominated by the *great city which reigneth over the kings of the earth.*

If, in this place, you think proper to ask any thing respecting the *rise, continuance,* and final destruction of this multi-formed

---
NOTE.
cies, where the prophetic characters of Antichrist, above described, are shewn, and in a very satisfactory way, to be, fairly, applicable to the church of Rome.

devouring monster, I answer, briefly, that according to the present most approved calculations we are authorized to say, that the *origin* of this anti-christian power was gradual, though its actual continuance is several times plainly expressed by the prophets to be *twelve hundred and sixty years.*

"Sometime between A. D. 500, and the end of the reign of the Goths, which was A. D. 553, when Narses took Rome and their dominions in Italy from them, and began the exarchate of Ravenna, the reckoning of twelve hundred and sixty years must begin. But Antichrist cannot be supposed to start up into view at once, in a sudden manner, as he will not fall without *many preparatory circumstances.* He became, by degrees, distinguishable, and doubtless his ruin will be brought on by several steps in Providence.

Therefore, if we begin at the earliest date, when we may suppose he first presented himself to view, the end of the period will bring us to the first steps towards his fall; but if we begin at the latest time, *twelve hundred and sixty years,* will bring us to the complete ruin of his power.

The first open breach between the western and eastern churches was, as we have said, about the year 500. To reckon twelve hundred and sixty years from that time brings us to A. D. 1760. And it is remarkable that from that very year, when the Jesuits had excited the resentments of the kings of Europe, which finally brought on the dissolution of that order, the power of the church of Rome has been very apparently declining, and several plain steps have been taken by the providence of God toward her utter destruction. Convents have been suppressed, and their revenues seized in kingdoms where superstition had long reigned without controul.

The infernal Courts of Inquisition have received severe checks, by which they are likely to be soon annihilated, in countries most noted for Romish bigotry.

Liberty of conscience has been given to Protestants in nations which had long been devoted to the papacy.

Roman Catholic princes begin to withhold from Rome the customary revenues. Even a late Pope, by his liberal writings, has lent his help to render Romish superstition ridiculous. And *appearances are still proceeding.*"*

NOTE.
* Langdon on Revelation, page 266—7

If, on the ground of the calculation juſt now mentioned, we proceed, the concluſion obviouſly is, that the deſtruction of Babylon is *very near at hand.* If to 1760, the date of the commencement of her fall, be added fifty years, the term in which ſhe is ſuppoſed to be falling, the ſum will be the period of her expected overthrow. And from appearances, now before us, we have good ground to conclude, that, if the decree of Heaven goes on for ſixteen years to come, until 1810, as it has for four years paſt, the denunciation for the deſtruction of Babylon will be fully accompliſhed.

As to times and ſeaſons, it is not for us exactly to know; and whatever miſtakes we make in our calculation of numbers, it does not however, at all alter the decree, or poſtpone the effect.

Hear the teſtimony of an eminent divine on this ſubject.*

" Whatever miſtakes the Jewiſh Rabbies
" might fall into in their interpretation of Da
" niel's ſeventy weeks, and in their attempts
" to fix the preciſe time of the Meſſiah's com-

NOTE.
* Doctor Bellamy's diſcourſe on the Millennium, publiſhed in 1758,—page 34 of this work.

"ing; and whatever miſtaken notions any of
them had about the nature of his kingdom,
as though it was to be of this world, and
he to appear in all earthly grandeur, and
although his coming, to ſome, might ſeem
to be ſo long delayed, that they began to
give up all hopes of it, and to contrive
ſome other meaning to the ancient prophecies, or even to call in queſtion the in-
ſpiration of the prophets; yet neither the
miſtakes of ſome, nor the *infidelity* of o-
thers, at all, altered the caſe. Days, and
months, and years haſtened along, and one
revolution, among the kingdoms of the
earth, followed upon another, till the *fulneſs of time* was come, till all things were
ripe, and *then*, behold, the Meſſiah was
born! Even ſo it ſhall be now.

"Whatever miſtakes Chriſtian Divines
may fall into, in their interpretation of ſix
hundred and ſixty-ſix, the number of the
beaſt, or in their endeavors to fix the preciſe time when the twelve hundred and
ſixty years of Antichriſt's reign ſhall begin
and end; or whatever wrong notions ſome
may have had, or may have about the nature of the Millennium, as though Chriſt

"was to reign, personally, on earth; and if
"some, mean while, begin to think that all
"things will go on as they have done, and to
"conclude, that the *expectation* of these glori-
"ous days which has prevailed in the Chris-
"tian church, from the beginning, is merely
"a groundless fancy; yet none of these things
"will at all alter the case. Days, and months,
"and years, will hasten along, and one revo-
"lution, among the kingdoms of the earth,
"follow upon another, until the *fulness of
"time* is come; till all things are ripe for
"the event; and then the ministers of Christ
"will accomplish, in *reality*, what St. John
"saw in his visions: *I saw an angel fly in the
"midst of heaven, having the everlasting gos-
"pel to preach unto them that dwell on the
"earth, and to every nation, and kindred, and
"tongue, and people.* And then shall it come
"to pass, that the veil of ignorance which
"hath so long spread over all nations *shall
"be destroyed*, and knowledge shall so great-
"ly increase, that it shall be as though *the
"light of the moon* were *as the light of the
"sun; and the light of the sun sevenfold*, un-
"til *the knowledge of the Lord cover the earth
"as the waters do the sea.* And then there
"*shall be nothing to hurt or offend in all God's*

" *holy mountain.* For Babylon fhall fall, Sa-
" tan be bound, and Chrift will reign, and
" truth and righteoufnefs univerfally prevail
" a *thoufand years.*"

Having, thus, confidered who it is over whofe deftruction all holy beings are called to rejoice, and faid fomething of the *origin, continuance,* and expected downfall of this power, I proceed,

II. To confider the *caufe* of this awful difafter.

Rejoice over her thou heaven, and ye holy apoftles and prophets; for God hath avenged you on her.

If we confine our refearches after the procuring caufe of this difafter to the appendages of Babylon, we fhall find it in *her own guilt.*

Permit me to point out her guilt as hinted at in the chapter from which my text is taken.

1. Babylon is charged with the extent of her idolatry.

The kings of the earth have committed fornication with her; that is, have been embraced by her idolatrous communion—united with her in a general apoftacy from God.

2. She is charged with a felfifh, mercena-

ry spirit in the concerns of her administration. *The merchants of the earth are waxed rich through the abundance of her delicacies.* " By the merchants understand all such as trade in Babylon's wares; her pleasing and costly wares of pardons, masses and indulgencies, by which so many are enriched; as well as those who trade in images, and in all the costly trappings of their idolatrous worship, and especially in the souls of men."

3. She is spoken of as *contaminating* and endangering those who tarried within her limits, exposing the people of God to be bewitched by her sorceries. *And I heard another voice from heaven, saying, Come out of her my people, that ye be not partakers of her sins, and that ye receive not of her plagues.*

My brethren, doth not this solemn decree, for the separation of God's people from the sins and abominations of Babylon, preach to us in these United States, even to us, who inhabit this asylum of the distressed, to beware of the habits, customs, influence and inchanting prerogatives of those who are fleeing before the vengeance of an incensed God? *Be not partakers of her sins, that ye receive not of her plagues.*

This caution is supported by the annunciation of the angel of God. *And there followed another angel, saying, Babylon is fallen, is fallen, that great city, because she made all nations drink of the wine of the wrath of her fornication. And the third angel followed them, saying with a loud voice, If any man worship the beast and his image, and receive his mark in his forehead, or in his hand, the same shall drink of the wine of the wrath of God, which is poured out without mixture into the cup of his indignation: and he shall be tormented with fire and brimstone in the presence of the holy angels, and in the presence of the Lamb.*

4. The guilt of Babylon is spoken of as sending forth a cry: *For her sins have reached unto heaven, and God hath remembered her iniquities.* Either a cry of the persecuted and suffering church, or a cry for vengeance. *And when he had opened the fifth seal, I saw under the altar the souls of them that were slain for the word of God, and for the testimony which they held. And they cried with a loud voice, saying, How long, holy and true, dost thou not judge and avenge our blood on them that dwell on the earth? And white robes were given unto every one of them; and it was said unto them, that they should rest yet for a little*

season, until their fellow-servants also, and their brethren, that should be killed as they were, should be fulfilled.

5. A *remembrance* of the persecuting spirit of this anti-christian power is spoken of as warranting a decree for vengeance from the Court of Heaven. *Reward her even as she rewarded you, and double unto her double, according to her work; in the cup which she hath filled, fill to her double.*

It is probable this injunction or command is given to the ministers—to the ministering angels of God's judgments, in behalf of his church; and though it doth not call for the peaceful followers of the Lamb to wage a carnal warfare with this intolerant power, yet it doubtless authorises our prayers that her destruction may be speedy and inevitable.

6. The last *inherent* cause of this awful calamity I shall mention, is found in the pride and haughtiness, luxury and voluptuousness of this self exalted anti-christian power.— *How much she hath glorified herself and lived deliciously, so much torment and sorrow give her. For she saith in her heart—I sit a queen, and am no widow, and shall see no sorrow. Therefore shall her plagues come in one*

day, death, and mourning, and famine; and she shall be utterly burned with fire: for strong is the Lord God who judgeth her.*

I am led to conclude this branch of my discourse, by adding, that the *final* cause of the destruction of Babylon is the *sentence* of God against her. This sentence is pronounced by an angel from the court, from the *tribunal* of heaven. *And he cried mightily with a strong voice, saying, Babylon the great is fallen, is fallen. And a mighty angel took up a stone like a great milstone, and cast it into the sea, saying, Thus with violence shall that great city Babylon be thrown down, and shall be found no more at all.* If you ask the reason of this judicial sentence from the tribunal of heaven, it is said—*For by thy sorceries were all nations deceived. And in her was found the blood of prophets, and of saints, and of all that were slain upon the earth.*

Having pointed out who it is over whose destruction holy angels and men are called upon to rejoice, and considered the *cause* of this awful catastrophe, my subject leads,

III. To consider the *means* by which this event shall be brought about.

And what *means*, my audience, should you suppose might be adequate to such a task?

to the task of overturning a power which hath subsisted more than twelve hundred years, supported by the kings of the earth, who drink of her cup, and delight in her sorceries—who have long since lent their aid for her support against the voice of reason—the demands of Heaven, and the cries of perishing thousands?—What power is equal to the task of accomplishing even the *decree of Heaven* against such might, such united force as Babylon is able to bring into the field? more especially, when you consider that for the terror of her enemies, and for the comfort of her friends, this intolerant power professes to have in possession the keys of heaven and of hell?

Retreat you will be ready to say from such a task! Let no one be so presumptuous as to provoke her to anger, as to stir up her fury!—Many have been devoured by this leviathan, by this multi-formed, insatiable monster; and God forbid that any more should be swallowed up, whilst they are able to make but a feeble, though honest attempt!

Our fears, my friends, are relieved whilst I read to you, from the inspiration of God, that the angel that pronounces the decree of destruction is commissioned from the Court of Heaven; has *great power, and that the earth is lightened with his glory.* And to support the executioner of the sentence it is added, *for strong is the Lord God who judgeth her.*

As then the decree hath its origin in heaven, and the promulgation of it is by a messenger from Heaven, we are authorised to look to Heaven for MEANS to accomplish what its decree hath ordained.

Did it please the Lord of Hosts, in ancient time, to promise deliverance to the Hebrews in Egyptian bondage; and did he not graciously provide the means of deliverance? —Was it in after times threatened against this rebellious people that, for their hypocrisy and sins, they should go into captivity; and did not a righteous God provide the means to execute the sentence?—Hear the appointment of heaven to this task. *O Assyrian! the rod of mine anger, and the staff in their hand is mine indignation! I will send him against an hypocritical nation, and against the people of my wrath will I give him a charge to take the spoil, and to take the prey, and to tread them down like the mire in the streets. Howbeit he meaneth not so, neither doth his* heart think so; but it is in his heart to destroy, and cut off nations not a few.

Wherefore it shall come to pass, that, when the Lord hath performed his whole work upon Mount Zion, and on Jerusalem, I will punish the fruit of the stout heart of the king of Assyria, and the glory of his high looks; for he saith, by the strength of my hand I have done it, and by my wisdom; for I am prudent: and I have removed the bounds of the people, and have robbed their treasures, and I have put down the inhabitants like a valiant man.

I cite this passage at length, not only that the sentiments under consideration may be supported, as to *means* of execution, appointed by the decree of Heaven; but to teach that means may be appointed, and may even execute the will of Heaven, and yet be themselves wholly ignorant of the God they are serving—be vastly sinful in what they do, and be, finally, sorely punished for the ungodly deed.

Again, did it please God to promise deliverance to the captive Jews from Babylon; and did he not gird his man for the purpose? *Thus saith the Lord to his anointed, to Cyrus, whose right hand I have holden, to subdue nations before him; and I will loose the loins of kings, to open before him the two-leaved gates, and the gates shall not be shut: I will go before thee, and make the crooked places straight: I will break in pieces the gates of brass, and cut in sunder the bars of iron. For Jacob my servant's sake, and Israel mine elect, I have even called thee by thy name: I have surnamed thee though thou hast not known me. I am the Lord, and there is none else, there is no God besides me: I girded thee, though thou hast not known me.*

These examples of means provided for the accomplishment of mercies promised, or for the execution of judgments denounced, in the wisdom of God, lay good foundation for us to proceed, and afford unerring direction to us in our enquiries after the means or methods which God will provide and use, for the execution of the awful sentence of which our subject treats.

Babylon is fallen, is fallen! But by what means is she to be brought down?

The state of this anti-christian church is spoken of under several figures or emblems, all of which are to have their end in some method suited to the destruction of the original figure.

If we ask after the destruction of this

church under the figure of Babylon, we shall find the means pre-figured under the pouring out of the sixth vial—the vial which all present expositors allow to be now running.

And the sixth angel poured out his vial upon the great river Euphrates; and the water thereof was dried up, that the way of the kings of the east might be prepared.

I need not detain you here to say that the river Euphrates signifies the wealth, the revenues, the strength and support of whatever kind, by which Papal Babylon hath, in time past, been upheld:—And if you wish to know whether this river hath been, or is now drying up, you may be informed by asking those who can tell to what end the revenues of the church of Rome have lately come. You may ask where are her privileges and prerogatives, her churches, her church-lands, her wonted revenues from princes and from subjects, especially, in respect to those parts of the empire on which the contents of this vial have already been poured?—You may ask, where is that faith, that *implicit* faith which was once put in her?—that domination which she maintained over the consciences of men?—Where are her idols—her masses—her superstitions

—her ministers?—As to her revenues, it will be answered, they have ceased;—as to faith, confidence and trust in this once reputed fountain of truth and infallibility, it will be said, it is departed; her subjects have thrown off the mask, and refuse to be hoodwinked any longer. As to her idols, so far as there was any value in them, they are now passing in coin; and as to her ministers, they are executed and dispersed. Even the college of Sorbonne* is obliged to yield up her magi, and give them, to her foes, a prey.

If you ask why the drying up of the river Euphrates is spoken of, *that the way of the kings of the east may be prepared?* I answer, in a word, that as ancient Euphrates was dried up, that the way of her enemies, who came from the east, might be prepared, in their approach to her destruction; so this mystical river is dried up, that the city itself may become an easy prey.

On this passage hear the language of a judicious divine.†

" In the drying up of the river Euphrates,

NOTES.
* A celebrated institution, or college, for the residence of doctors, professors, and students in divinity, at Paris, who suffered in the general calamity.
† Burkit in loco.

manifest allusion is had to the manner of old Babylon's destruction. The river Euphrates *ran through old Babylon,* and was a greater defence to it than its celebrated walls, which, for thickness and height, were the wonder of the world. Cyrus, " the leader of the Kings of the East," when he took Babylon, cut many ditches, and let the river Euphrates run out, and so he and his soldiers entered the city, and took it. As the drying up of Euphrates, *then,* was an immediate forerunner of the destruction of Babylon; in like manner, the drying up of Euphrates, signify it what it will, shall be the immediate forerunner of the destruction of anti-christian Babylon, whenever it shall be. The Romish Euphrates being dried up, the Romish Babylon will hasten, amain, towards its final ruin."

Whether the Euphrates of the Romish Babylon is not already so far dried up, as that the Kings of the East have made a breach upon her, let facts and daily intelligence determine.

What though you call the instruments of this successful attack upon Rome a lawless banditti—a race of infidels—men, who profess to " know no God but Liberty, and no

Gospel but their Constitution."—What then! are they not, in the hand of God, as well chosen instruments for the execution of threatened vengeance upon mystical Babylon, as the heathenish kings of the east were, for the same design, upon Babylon of the Chaldees?

Those who look through the great plan, viewing the purposes of Heaven upon a broad scale, believe and know that Kings and Captains, in all ages; nay, that even wicked men and devils, in the fullness of their rage, are yet under the divine controul; that the wrath of the whole, in the end, shall *praise him*, and the *remainder he is able to restrain*.

In running through with the destruction of Babylon, the prophet notices a movement of a very extraordinary nature; an exertion made to oppose the deluge which Almighty God is causing to overspread the anti-christian world. But, alas! a feeble exertion, and, in the end, does but expedite the overthrow denounced.

And I saw three unclean spirits, like frogs, come out of the mouth of the dragon, and out of the mouth of the beast, and out of the mouth of the false prophet. The apostle proceeds to interpret the objects presented. *For they are the spirits of devils, working miracles,*

which go forth unto the kings of the earth, and of the whole world, to gather them to the battle of that great day of God Almighty.

" In the foregoing verses," saith the author just now cited, " an account was given of the
" subject upon which the *sixth* vial was pour-
" ed out, namely, upon the river Euphrates.
" Here we have an effect that followed there-
" upon; a warlike expedition, or gathering
" to battle. Where, note 1. The principal
" commanders, in this battle, the Dragon,
" the Beast, and the False Prophet.

" 2. The instruments employed and made
" use of by them who are said to be, for their
" nature, *spirits;* for their quality, *unclean;*
" for their number, *three;* for their *similitude*
" and resemblance *like frogs;* namely, with
" respect to their corrupt origin, and their
" numbers—they swarm and croak in all
" places, and live both in the water and up-
" on the earth:—by all which, many inter-
" preters understand emissaries, missionaries,
" negociators, solicitors and legates, sent
" forth, and employed by Antichrist for the
" support and strengthening of him and his
" kingdom, by soliciting the kings of the
" earth to join together in battle against his
" enemies."

We need no testimony to support the opinion that the nuncios, legates, bishops and monks of the church of Rome have been industriously, and, speaking after the manner of men, but too succesfully employed in ranging the present combination of kings against the progress of the divine decree.—But *Babylon is fallen, is fallen* in the councils of heaven, and no popish emissaries shall prevail to parry the fatal blow. True, they have boasted their art and success in parrying the arguments, and the appeals of Protestants in time past, but they cannot parry the judgments of God.

And he gathered them together into a place, called in the Hebrew tongue Armageddon.

" He, that is Almighty God, by his per-
" missive providence, suffered the kings of
" the earth to hearken to Antichrist's mission-
" aries, and to assemble and gather together,
" as Jabin and Sisera gathered together a-
" gainst Israel to their own destruction: And
" whereas the place of their gathering to-
" gether and destruction is called ARMAGED-
" DON, that is so named from the event of
" the battle, signifying such a place where
" the enemies of the Lord shall be destroy-
" ed."

If any are disposed to enquire after this place of destruction, let them peruse the accounts of the many bloody battles which have been fought since resistance has been made to the purposes of heaven in the *existing* decree, and anticipate the destruction yet to follow.—One hundred and fifty, if not two hundred thousand, are supposed to have perished in all the conflicts, battles, sieges, assassinations and executions which have taken place since the present vial has begun to run. Witness, especially, the late very serious rencounters between the forces of France and the allied armies, in and about the Austrian Netherlands, as well as upon all their frontiers, and we may add also the massacres of internal commotion.—Must not such torrents of blood be placed to the account of the *battle of the great day of God Almighty?*

If this anti-christian power, for her apostacy from God, and for her idolatry, be figured forth to us under the degrading and abominable idea of a prostitute, her destruction is said to come from the hatred of the ten kings or kingdoms heretofore in her idolatrous communion.

And the ten horns which thou sawest are ten kings, which have received no kingdom as yet;

but receive power as kings one hour, or at the same time, *with the beast. These have one mind, and shall give their power and strength unto the beast.*

But, in the day of God's wrath, whilst the *sixth* vial continues to deliver its mysterious, but avenging contents, *the ten kings shall hate the whore, and shall make her desolate and naked, and shall eat her flesh, and burn her with fire.*

If it please God to set forth this antichristian power under the denomination of a beast, his destruction, with his adherents, is threatened by an angel of God, not only as to this life, but as to the life to come.

And the third angel followed them, saying with a loud voice, If any man worship the beast, and his image, and receive his mark in his forehead, or in his hand, the same shall drink of the wine of the wrath of God, which is poured out without mixture into the cup of his indignation: and he shall be tormented with fire and brimstone in the presence of the holy angels, and in the presence of the Lamb.

If it please God to speak of this idolatrous and intolerant power under the character of the *man of sin, whose coming is after the working of Satan, with all power, and signs, and lying wonders;* his destruction is denounced as being brought about by the vindictive justice of God:—*Whom the Lord shall consume with the spirit of his mouth, and shall destroy with the brightness of his coming.*

If this power is represented as interwoven with the civil power of the *fourth* great kingdom of the world; if the civil and ecclesiastical power of Rome forms *the iron and the clay,* well may its destruction be predicted by the rolling of the stone (cut out, not with human hands, but by the providence of God,) against the legs, or rather the feet and toes of this kingdom, which is founded of iron and clay—partly *strong* and partly *weak*—partly *true* and partly *false:* well, I say, may destruction come from the stone prepared of God with this design. *Thou sawest,* saith Daniel to Nebuchadnezzar, *till that a stone was cut out without hands, which smote the image upon his feet that were of iron and clay, and brake them to pieces: And the stone that smote the image became a great mountain, and filled the whole earth.*

Can I better set before you the interpretation of this portion of prophecy, than in the words of Bishop Newton, supported by the celebrated Mr. Mede?* "As the fourth kingdom, or the Roman empire, was reprefented in a twofold ſtate; firſt, ſtrong and flouriſhing, *with legs of iron*, and then weakened and divided, with *feet and toes, part of iron and part of clay;* ſo this *fifth* kingdom, or the kingdom of Chriſt, is deſcribed likewife in *two* ſtates, which Mr. Mede rightly diſtinguiſheth by the names of *regnum lapidis*, the kingdom of the ſtone, and *regnum montis*, the kingdom of the mountain; the *firſt*, when the *ſtone was cut out of the mountain without hands;* the *ſecond*, when it became itſelf *a mountain, and filled the whole earth.*

"*The ſtone was cut out of the mountain without hands.* The kingdom of Chriſt was firſt ſet up while the Roman empire was in its full ſtrength, with *legs of iron*. The Roman empire was afterwards divided into ten leſſer kingdoms, the remains of which are ſubſiſting at preſent. The image is ſtill ſtanding upon his *feet and toes of iron and clay.* The kingdom of Chriſt is yet *a ſtone of ſtumbling, and a rock of offence.* But the ſtone will, *one day*, ſmite the image upon the feet

NOTE.
* Newton on the Prophecies, vol. ii. page 244.

and toes, and destroy it utterly, and will it-self *become a great mountain, and fill the whole earth:* or, in other words, *the kingdoms of this world shall become the kingdoms of our Lord and of his Christ,* and he *shall reign for ever and ever.*

" We have, therefore seen the kingdom of the *stone*, but we have *not yet seen* the KINGDOM OF THE MOUNTAIN. Some parts of this prophecy still remain to be fulfilled; but the exact completion of the other parts will not suffer us to doubt of the accomplishment of the rest also, in due season."

And what period of time, my brethren, hath ever looked so likely to be introductory to the regnum montis, to the kingdom of the mountain, as the present? Is not the *stone* now rolling against the feet and toes of the mighty image? And when it shall have split in sunder the heterogeneous and unnatural mixture, of which the empire of Rome is now composed; when the civil and ecclesiastical authority (which hath so long composed what, in the dignity and pride of anti-christian glory, hath been stiled THE HOLY ROMAN EMPIRE,) shall be separated or dissolved, there will be good ground to believe, that the empire of Jesus Christ—the regnum montis, will begin.

The rolling of the stone, then, and the increase of it to the size of a mountain, may justly be placed to the account of *means* ordained of God for the destruction of mystical Babylon—the empire of the church of Rome.

And if it may not be presuming too far, I would venture to assert, that appearances are not only now favoring the introduction of the REGNUM MONTIS, but that it has already begun, and is considerably advanced in its progress. But,

How shall the *little stone* become a mountain, and how shall it destroy this mighty image, this anti-christian colossus, which hath stood so many a storm?

Must it not *acquire a power—gain a momentum* equal to the task?

Must there not be some power applied beside reason and argument; the force of which this power hath found means so long to withstand?—Undoubtedly, you will say, there must be such a power—but where is it to be found, and from what quarter must it come?

Behold, my brethren, behold in the scenes now passing in the drama of Europe—another Assyrian and his host!—another *ax* in the hand of *him that heweth therewith,* and another *saw* in the hand of *him that shaketh it!*—

In the same group behold another Cyrus, *whose right hand* the Lord hath *holden to subdue nations before him*—before whom the Lord *loosened the loins of kings*, and opened before him the *two-leaved gates.* Before whom the Lord went to *make crooked places straight;* to break in pieces *the gates of brass,* and *cut in sunder the bars of iron:*—Whom the Lord *surnamed,* and whom he *girded* with power, though the Assyrian *knew him not.*

If this language seem too mysterious to any, let them receive a familiar stile, and behold the regnum montis, the kingdom of the mountain, begun on the Fourth of July, 1776, when the *birth* of the MAN-CHILD— the hero of civil and religious liberty took place in these United States. Let them read the predictions of heaven respecting the increase of his dominion—that he was *to rule all nations with a rod of iron;* that is, bring them into complete and absolute subjection; and that the young hero might be equal to this mighty conquest, he is supported by an omnipotent arm; he is *caught up unto God, and to his throne.* Behold, then, this hero of America wielding the standard of civil and religious liberty over thefe United States! —Follow him, in his ftrides, acrofs the Atlantic!—See him, with his fpear already in the heart of the beaft!—See tyranny, civil and ecclefiaftical, bleeding at every pore!—See the votaries of the tyrants; of the beafts; of the falfe prophets, and ferpents of the earth, ranged in battle array, to withftand the progrefs and dominion of him, who hath commiffion to break down the ufurpations of tyranny—to let the *prifoner out of the prifon-houfe;* and to fet the vaffal in bondage free from his chains—to level the mountains—to raife the valleys, and to prepare an high way for the Lord!

Againft all oppofition to the execution of this decree, the Lord, from the heavens, will laugh. *He that fitteth in the heavens fhall laugh, the Lord fhall have them in derifion.—Thou fhalt break them with a rod of iron; thou fhalt dafh them in pieces like a potter's veffel. Be wife now, therefore, O ye kings, be inftructed ye judges of the earth.*

It feems no unnatural conclufion from ancient prophecy, and from prefent appearances, that in order to ufher in the dominion of our glorious Immanuel, as predicted to take place, and ufually called the *latter-day-glory*, TWO GREAT REVOLUTIONS are to take place; the *firſt* outward and political; the *ſecond* inward and ſpiritual.—The *firſt* is now taking place; its happy effects we, in this country, already enjoy; and O that the Lord would gracioufly put it into the hearts of his miniſters and churches, nay, of all now under the dominion of civil and religious liberty, to begin the *ſecond* revolution, that which is *inward* and *ſpiritual*, even the *revolution* of the heart. Come forth then, may we not pray, all ye votaries of truth! ye advocates for the ſpiritual empire of the LATTER DAY, come forth!—

Let the ſtandard of truth and of duty, the ſtandard of allegiance to God, through faith in his beloved Son, be ſet up! Let us preach, let us pray, let us fight, manfully, the warfare of faith—not doubting, but in God's own time, the glorious things, of which the prophets have ſpoken, ſhall be fulfilled!

Behold the *firſt* revolution, (through the agency of the hero of America) in this country, already begun, nay, already accompliſhed!—why not then NOW begin the ſecond?

What encouragement is there to proceed, whilſt we ſee ſome of the laſt events taking place, under the sixth vial, which are to precede the glory of the latter day, to be *ushered* in immediately on the pouring out of the seventh!

I have now gone through with a consideration of the *means* appointed of God for the overthrow of mystical Babylon. These means, I make no doubt, you will believe fully adequate to the execution of the decree. It now only remains that I consider,

Lastly, The foundation which the execution of this decree lays for universal joy.

Rejoice over her thou heaven, and ye holy apostles and prophets; for God hath avenged you on her.

If there was no other cause of rejoicing on this mighty occasion, but the invitation of heaven to the general concert, sufficient cause might be found for the emotion the event demands.

But we are not called to rejoice without sufficient light afforded, to guide us in this rational and Christian exercise.

1. There is cause of universal joy on this occasion, because by the destruction of mystical Babylon, the great Michael of the church hath gained a very important victory over the principalities and powers of hell. The

placing of one, bearing *horns like a lamb,* and speaking with the mouth *of a dragon,* in highest authority in the church of Christ, is allowed, on all hands, to be a master-piece among all the devices of Satan; the highest, the most crafty and successful effort which the wicked one hath ever played off against the interests of Christ in any age of the world. —Well then may the detection and overthrow of Satan, in this scheme of ruling the church, in the garb of an angel of light, demand the liveliest acclamations of general joy.

2. A participation in this general anthem of praise, at the downfall of Babylon, is demanded, as matter of exultation on the part of the holy prophets, apostles and martyrs, whose blood she had formerly shed. *Rejoice over her thou heaven, and ye holy apostles and prophets; for God hath avenged you on her.*

And in her was found the blood of prophets, and of saints, and of all that were slain upon the earth.

3. There is cause of joy, at this event, on the part of the church, as in her advancings to her promised perfection and glory, she shall not be obstructed by the persecutions, massacres, inquisitions, tortures, and thunders of this apostate church of Rome.

4. On the part of all who have received, and now maintain the teftimony of God, as recorded in his holy word, there is caufe of joy, that the fulfilment of the many prophecies refpecting *Antichrift*, the *man of fin*, &c. are fulfilled, and thereby an accumulation of evidence is obtained of the authenticity of the fcriptures, as being in deed and in truth the LIVELY ORACLES OF GOD.

5. There is caufe of joy, in this folemn and affecting event, becaufe it is one of the *laft* things to take place, before it fhall be proclaimed—*The kingdoms of this world are become the kingdoms of our Lord and of his Chrift, and he fhall reign for ever and ever.*

And I heard a loud voice faying in heaven, Now is come falvation, and ftrength, and the kingdom of our God, and the power of his Chrift; for the accufer of our brethren is caft out, which accufed them before God day and night.

This fubject being a leading object, in this work, you will permit me to prefent, in a very brief manner, the feveral denunciations of wrath againft myftical Babylon, and fhew the acclamations of joy that immediately follow, on account of the important and interefting events which follow.

Is the anti-chriftian power of Rome fet

forth by the *iron and clay* of the great image? and is it to be dashed in pieces by the stone cut out without hands? immediately it is predicted, that the stone that smote the image became a *great mountain and filled the whole earth.*

Is this intolerant power represented by the *horn which came up* among the ten horns;—by the horn which *had eyes like the eyes of a man, and a mouth speaking great things.* I *beheld, then,* saith the prophet, *because of the great words which the horn spake: I beheld even till the beast was slain, and his body destroyed, and given to the burning flame. I saw in the night visions, and behold, one like the Son of Man came in the clouds of heaven, and came to the Ancient of Days, and they brought him near before him. And there was given him dominion, and glory, and a kingdom, that all people, and nations, and languages should serve him. His dominion is an everlasting dominion, which shall not pass away, and his kingdom that which shall not be destroyed.*

Is this power spoken of as to rise, after the *falling away,* in the character of the MAN OF SIN—*the son of perdition, who opposeth and exalteth himself above all that is called God, or worshipped; so that he as God, sitteth in the temple of God, shewing himself that he is God—it is the same whom the Lord shall consume with the spirit of his mouth, and shall destroy with the* BRIGHTNESS OF HIS COMING.

And after the destruction of Babylon, as recorded in this nineteenth chapter, *I heard,* saith the apostle, *a great voice of much people in heaven, saying, Alleluia: Salvation, and glory, and honor, and power, unto the Lord our God: for true and righteous are his judgments; for he hath judged the great whore, which did corrupt the earth with her fornication, and hath avenged the blood of his servants at her hand.*

In the conclusion of the whole scene of distress, of which the nineteenth chapter of this book is a lively picture, the twentieth chapter begins with the introduction of the Millennial-day.

And I saw an angel come down from heaven, having the key of the bottomless pit, and a great chain in his hand. And he laid hold on the dragon, that old serpent, which is the Devil, and Satan, and bound him a THOUSAND YEARS.

After such descriptions of success, and joy to follow, in favor of the church of Christ, after the downfall of Babylon, you will not wonder that the church should be called, nor that she should be disposed to rejoice at the overthrow.

I have now gone through with the doctrinal part of my discourse: I have considered *who it is*, over whose destruction holy beings are called upon to rejoice—the *cause* of this disaster—the *means* employed to bring it about, and the foundation it lays for universal joy.

If, after such lengthy illustrations, any reflexions might be admitted, may they not, briefly, in view of the objects of this work, be such as follow?

1. If the general scope of our subject is allowed to be consonant to the word of God, and be truly applicable to those objects towards which it has been directed; no one can be at a loss for a key to the providence of God in the national, civil, and ecclesiastical convulsions which are now shaking, to the foundation, some of the most potent powers in Europe.

Is not the day of the divine vengeance come?—Are not the vials of the divine indignation now pouring out?—Is not Babylon, like a millstone, sinking into the sea?— Is not this the time of the falling of the stars

—the dethroning, in church and state, of those who, by their iniquities and tyrannies, have out-run the compassion of their God? *And the stars of heaven fell unto the earth, even as a fig-tree casteth her untimely figs, when she is shaken of a mighty wind.*

Is not this the time of the rise of the beast from the bottomless pit, who shall make war against the witnesses, and shall overcome them, and kill them?

Is not the time now introducing, in which it shall be said by the angel—*Thrust in thy sickle, and reap; for the time is come for thee to reap; for the harvest of the earth is ripe?*

And the angel thrust in his sickle into the earth, and gathered the vine of the earth, and cast it into the great wine-press of the wrath of God.

And have we not cause to fear, that after the finishing of the present sixth vial, which dries up the mystical Euphrates, the order will be issued to pour out the seventh into the air—as some suppose, upon all the subjects of the Prince of the Power of the Air, throughout the world? *And the seventh angel poured out his vial into the air; and there came a great voice out of the temple of heaven, from the throne, saying.—It is done. And there were voices, and thunders, and lightnings; and there was a great earthquake, such as was not since men were upon the earth, so mighty an earthquake, and so great.*

And do we not begin to see the characters and proceedings opening to view, which fulfil the prophetic declaration, immediately on the fall of Babylon?—*And is become the habitation of devils, and the hold of every foul spirit, and a cage of every unclean and hateful bird?*

Is not the time now come, in which, from the many slaughters which are continually taking place, the scene may be supposed to be begun, in view of which saith St. John, *And I saw an angel standing in the sun; and he cried with a loud voice, saying to all the fowls that fly in the midst of heaven, Come and gather yourselves together unto the supper of the great God; that ye may eat the flesh of kings, and the flesh of captains, and the flesh of mighty men, and the flesh of horses, and of them that sit on them, and the flesh of all men, both free and bond, both small and great.*

To what height of distress the world may yet, in judgment for their disobedience to God, be allowed to come, God only knows:

But in view of the awful, judicial prospect, well may we cry out, *O Lord rebuke me not in thine anger, neither chasten me in thy hot displeasure!* Cover us, O thou gracious and compassionate Redeemer, by the broad hand of thy protecting providence, until the indignation be over-past!

But from these solemn scenes we are all, but especially as many as have good hope in God, allowed to turn off our eye, whilst, on equally sure ground, we are called to contemplate *the blessedness which shall speedily follow.*—To support your confidence on this subject, I need but refer you to the general annunciation of praise from the choirs of heaven, which our subject hath noted, as immediately to follow the destruction of the enemies of God, and of his people. *We give thee thanks, O Lord God Almighty, which art, and wast, and art to come, because thou hast taken to thee thy great power, and hast reigned!—*

2. In view of our subject may we not reflect, that, however the doctrine of the Millennium—the doctrine of the thousand years of prosperity, promised to the church of Christ, may have been neglected, decried or misunderstood, yet it is a doctrine plainly contain-

ed, and solidly established in the word of God —and as such is entitled to the credit, the study and embrace of all who believe the scriptures to be the unchanging oracles of God.

3. If this doctrine be true, we justly conclude, that those ministers of Christ, who, in the several ages of the church, have been pursuing and enquiring after the glorious Millennial-day, have not been pursuing a shadow, nor following a phantom.

4. If they are to be justified in their researches, and if, whilst under the clouds of antiquity, they rejoiced in view of the distant, yet assuredly approaching scene, how much more may we be justified in such pursuit, and in increasing joy, whilst the "reddening streaks of the morning betoken to the weary traveller, that the day is at hand?"

5. If the great Michael of the church intends to usher in his glorious dominion by the previous accomplishing of TWO GREAT REVOLUTIONS—the *first* outward and political—the *second* inward and spiritual; and if he hath already advanced so far in the majesty of his power, as to have completed the *first* revolution in this country, through the instrumentality of the sons of men, how

necessary and proper, that the *second* should now be undertaken, and carried on through the instrumentality of the sons of God?

Can we, who are ministers of Christ—can the churches of our Lord, throughout this our delightful land—can we unitedly or severally be willing to suffer, that the civil and military exertions of our country should contribute more to the prosperity of the Zion of God, than the sons of Zion themselves?— Can we be willing that, with the prowess and dignity of men, these should so worthily and valiantly have discharged the duties allotted them, whilst we, loitering upon our posts, refuse to hear the voice of our illustrious Leader, in his word and providence, commanding us to imitate his example, and to press forward to exertion, to victory, and to renown?

For a moment let us cast our eye upon the vision of St. John respecting this matter. *And I saw heaven opened*—that is, the ordinances of heaven, or the scenes displayed in the church of Christ, by the ministers and churches of Christ, which, in the language of prophecy, signify heaven; as a people of a contrary spirit and character are set forth by the *earth*, or nations of the earth:

And behold a white horse, and he that sat upon him was called Faithful and True; and in righteousness he doth judge and make war. And the armies which were in heaven, that is, in the church militant, and, it may be, triumphant, *followed him upon white horses— emblems of valor, of victory, and of triumph —cloathed in fine linen, white and clean.— And out of his mouth goeth a sharp sword, that with it he should smite the nations; and he shall rule them with a rod of iron: and he treadeth the wine-press of the fierceness and wrath of Almighty God. And he hath on his vesture and on his thigh a name written,* KING OF KINGS, AND LORD OF LORDS.*

If, my Christian Brethren, we profess to belong to the armies of the living God—to be in the train of the great Michael of the church, why not press on?—Why not keep close to our Leader, that we may be within the hearing of his orders—may imitate his example—may perform exploits before him —may prove ourselves worthy to hold rank in such an heavenly train?

But *how*, in what manner follow on, you

NOTE.

* For an exposition of this passage, see Lowman, Burkit, or Langdon in loco.

may be ready to say?—Must we take arms? —Must we go to war?—Must we commence hostilities against the empires, the kings, the tyrants, the civil and ecclesiastical establishments of the world?—Yes, my brethren, this is our duty, and here is our employment: But always remember, with our valiant fileleader, that, in the accomplishment of this second revolution, *the weapons of our warfare are not carnal, but mighty, through God, to the pulling down of strong holds; casting down imaginations, and every high thing that exalteth itself against the knowledge of God, and bringing into captivity every thought into the obedience of Christ.*

Such, my brethren, are our weapons, and such is our warfare. Happy for the true servants of *Christ*, that, as yet, they are not called, in this present conflict, to engage in the bloody contests of ungodly men—not to welter in the scenes of war, where the battle of the warrior is, and garments rolled in blood. It may be in the accomplishment of the *first* great political revolution, something like this may be necessary; but, in this land, at present, we have little to do, but with an armour of truth, of righteousness, and of peace.

But if, in the general conflict, it should

happen that the once vanquished Lion—the political and, I may add too, the Protestant Dragon, should return to persecute the woman which brought forth the MAN-CHILD—the warrior of the world—the pionier of the church; we need not a spirit of prophecy to say, that the jaws of this insatiable leviathan shall again be broken, in a manner answerable to the spirit—to the redoubled fury and reiterated strokes of those who, under God, at first gave the promised hero of civil and religious liberty birth.

If any should ask on what authority we ground an allusion to the Protestant persecuting power under the idea or figure of a dragon—I answer, That the chapter from whence this language is taken is of a very extensive and momentous signification.

It truly is enveloped in some degree of mystery, as it was undoubtedly designed to be, especially, under the characters of the *woman*—the *eagle's wings*—the *wilderness*—the *man-child*, and the *dragon*, who seeks to devour the struggler as soon as he shall be born.

But as a key to this chapter, I would humbly, and in the fear of God, presume to say, that, under the character of the woman and her sorrows, we have exhibited the state and strugglings of the true church of Christ, in every age of the world, in which she hath, or may be called to suffer, from the Christian æra until the consummation of all things. That under the general figure of the dragon we have exhibited the most considerable enemies and persecutors of the church of Christ in every age; Satan himself, that old serpent, the Devil, being the prime instrument, and first mover of the whole. That by the wilderness, we are to understand a state of spiritual dearth and barrenness, or those leaves, shades, and darkening boughs of superstition, which have been as the shades of a wilderness to hinder the spiritual growth; or, lastly, a wilderness in the literal and common acceptation of the word. And, by the general figure of a MAN-CHILD, you are to understand the particular and several deliances, which the church of Christ, in any, and in every age of the world, hath enjoyed, from its first institution until the present moment. And, by the two wings of the great eagle, may we not understand the special providence and agency of Almighty God in these several very interesting events?

In this sense, denoting the power of God in conquering the enemies of his people, and in securing them under the banner of his own protection—the phrase is used in Exodus xix. 4. *Ye have seen what I did unto the Egyptians, and how I bare you on* EAGLE'S WINGS, *and brought you unto myself.* And after a long course of protection afforded to the people of God, through the wilderness of Sinai, and their settlement in the promised land, it is again said, Deut. xxxii. 9—12. *For the Lord's portion is his people; Jacob is the lot of his inheritance. He found him in a desert land, and in the waste howling wilderness: he led him about, he instructed him, he kept him as the apple of his eye. As an eagle stirreth up her nest, fluttereth over her young, spreadeth abroad her wings, taketh them, beareth them on her wings; so the Lord alone did lead him, and there was no strange god with him.*

Under the same idea of the divine agency and protection afforded, saith the Psalmist—*Because thou hast been my help, therefore, in the shadow of thy wings, will I rejoice.*

This foundation being laid as a key to the chapter, may we not proceed, and say, that the woman denotes the state of the church in its firſt inſtitution? *And there appeared a great wonder in heaven, a woman cloathed with the ſun;* it may be with the veſtments of the ſun of righteouſneſs; *and the moon under her feet;* the earth and other ſublunary things in their proper place; *and upon her head a crown of twelve ſtars;* guided and governed by the unadulterated doctrines of the twelve apoſtles. In this character, the church of Chriſt at firſt ſtood forth; but ſo ſoon was the truth beclouded—her privileges reſtrained, and her members perſecuted, that ſhe, ſtruggling for civil and religious liberty, is denominated as *being with child,* as *travailing in birth, and pained to be delivered.* The character of a woman the church is ſuppoſed to take, as denoting her delicacy—her fruitfulneſs, and her need of protection.

But under the laſhes of paganiſm and heatheniſh tyranny, ſhe was obliged to groan out the ten perſecutions, until, in the perſon of Conſtantine the Great, the firſt Chriſtian emperor, ſhe brought forth her firſt-born, and lived, for a while, under the happy dominion of civil and religious liberty.

And who would have thought that, in proceſs of time, proſperity would have produced such pride, dominion and tyranny in spiritual, and in earthly things; even in those who have but just now emerged from a suffering and persecuted state?

But, alas! behold the Pagan Dragon restored to life, in the papal, anti-christian image! And under this papal, persecuting power behold the series of heathenish persecution again renewed!

How did the woman again labor to be delivered, and what were the effects of her labor, under papal tyranny, but the glorious reformation which took place in the sixteenth century, under the preaching of Wickliff, John Huss, and Jerom; and afterwards carried on by Luther, Calvin, and others?

And shall it, may it now be said, that the spirit of protestantism—the hero of deliverance from the thraldom of Popery, ever become so degenerated as, in the smallest degree, to act over the part of its Papal and Pagan predecessors? Let the persecutions of civil and ecclesiastical power, under Mary, James, Laud, and others, whilst they struggled for uncontrouled dominion in church and state, " in things civil and ecclesiastical," answer to this point!

The sufferings of the Protestants, under

this new-formed intolerant power, do well answer to the character of the church—of the woman in her suffering and persecuted state.

But, behold! how soon does the persecuted woman receive an answer to her solemn appeals, and reiterated cries? See, on the wings of a bounteous providence, how she is wafted across the Atlantic, and settled in these peaceful American abodes!—Happy, that as the time of general redemption comes, her enemies are held in partial restraint.— Here she is pursued and persecuted only in outward and civil things; though what designs might have been formed against her religious freedom we cannot say.

In a word, behold the hero of civil and religious liberty born in these western climes! And see him already on his way back to demolish the proud and haughty establishments of civil and ecclesiastical tyranny, which have in these several forms, persecuted his mother, whilst she labored to give him birth!

And is it too much to suppose, that, in his progress back, he will demolish all that is contrary to the spirit of the truth—to the intent and design of that power, under whose auspices he now proceeds, conquering and to conquer; whether such counterfeits of truth be found in Protestant, in Papal, or in Pagan Rome? Especially, whilst you read, that this hero is to *rule all nations with a rod of iron, and is caught up to God and to his throne?*—If you request any further illustrations to authenticate this interpretation, attend to the declaration, that when the Dragon, in his multi-formed character, was cast out, was conquered, disappointed, or disgraced, he persecuted the woman that bro't forth the man-child. And thus, my audience did the Pagan Dragon, in the person and persecutions of Julian the Apostate; and thus did the Papal Dragon, in all the persecutions, thunders, and councils, by which he hath vexed and destroyed the Protestants; and thus has the Protestant Dragon done, not only in heavy persecutions for conscience sake, but, especially, in the flood of troops, armies and fleets—Britons and Irish, Brunswickers and Waldeckers, Hessians and Anspachers, which this red dragon vomited forth for the destruction of the woman in the American wilderness, during the late unprovoked and cruel war; and thus is this Protestant Dragon, even now, but too ready to express of his persecuting temper, in opening upon these defenceless states the Algerine Corsairs—in committing depredations upon our commerce, and in letting loose, or in countenancing their savage allies, in making war upon our western frontiers. But we believe in God, our hope and confidence is in him, and to his protecting power and providence do we, therefore, humbly appeal.

You will not now doubt of the propriety of the allusion, just now hinted at, respecting the persecuting power of the Protestant Dragon—nor at all deny the propriety of our holding ourselves in lively and animated readiness to break the jaws of this leviathan, as God may give us power, should he attempt again to break our peace.

And if any should be disposed to ask what has become of the eagle, on whose wings the persecuted woman was born into the American wilderness, may it not be answered, that she hath taken her station upon the broad seal of the United States; and from thence has perched upon the pediment of the first government-house, dedicated to the dominion of civil and religious liberty, where she is still to be seen, an emblem of the protection of Providence towards our present government, and towards this our happy land.

If any should be disposed, further, to ask whether the dragon of the regions below, even that old serpent called the Devil, and Satan, is to be seen in any other form than as animating the dragons—the combinations of civil and ecclesiastical power, in the many external injuries they have wrought against the church of God on the earth? I answer, yes, in every age of the church, whether her external state has been peaceful or troublesome: The errors in doctrine—the breaches upon the purity of Christian practice—the scisms, divisions and discords in churches—the prejudice, hatred and malice which have, at times, prevailed in the church, have been, for the most part, but the ebullitions of Satan, the great dragon of dragons, who continually goeth about, as a roaring lion, seeking whom he may devour; and hapless state the church, too frequently, has been in, that even within her own bosom, the Devil himself should find so many willing instruments of his pleasure, agents of his infernal craft. Look abroad upon our churches, and behold the dearth of religion—the want of unity, animation and zeal amongst both ministers and people; and pray, oh fervently pray, that when, as at the present time, the enemy shall come in like a flood, the spirit of the Lord, in his word, in his ministers and churches, may lift up a standard against him.

But returning to the important subject of the *second* great revolution, after which it is our duty constantly to labor, may we not add, in view of the example of our late political struggle—

If, then, noble exertions for the first revolution have been made by our brethren, guided by heaven in the field, and in the cabinet; are not we now, as Christians, and as ministers, to be guided?—Is it not full time, that we should be led, by the zeal of their noble example, whilst we fight the battles of the Lord of Hosts, in our closets and in our families—in our churches and in our pulpits?

Pursuing this object, let us reason the point, for a moment, with yonder infidel—Let us ask what more evidence he needs of the truth of the scriptures, than to see the events, long since predicted, daily fulfilling before his eyes?—Let us ask him to read a page or two in a late publication, on the subject of prophecy, as the testimony of Jesus.*

NOTE.
* See Hinsdale's Disco. A. P. vol. iv. page 128.

• "Where are now those renounced cities, Nineveh, Babylon and Tyre, whose desolation was so often denounced by the prophets?—What is now the condition of Jerusalem and Judea?—Are they not *trodden down of the Gentiles*, and likely to be still trodden down, until *the times that the Gentiles shall be fulfilled?* How remarkably do the actions and state of the Turks, who have so long trodden them down, agree to what was predicted of them? *He shall come with horsemen, and many ships, and shall overflow and pass over.* He shall enter into the glorious land, and many countries shall be overthrown. Do you not find it even so? And that he hath stretched out his hand over the land of Egypt, with the *Lybian at his steps*, whilst *the Arabians still escape out of his hand.*

Hath not the state of Egypt, for many past ages, been just as was foretold? *a base, and the basest of kingdoms,* without a ruler of her own, and *wasted by strangers?*

Observe the *fourth* kingdom of Daniel's vision broken into ten. Behold that wonderful power, *diverse from the first*, which hath arisen up among them, with a *look more stout than his fellows*, and a *mouth speaking great things*, even great words against the

MOST HIGH: that power which weareth out the faints of the MOST HIGH, and changeth times and laws. Behold him *cafting down the truth to the ground; forbidding to marry*, and commanding to *abftain from meats:* Yea, behold him *fitting in the temple,* in the church *of God, and fhewing himfelf* that he is God, whofe coming is with *figns and lying wonders.* And remember that the feat of this horrid tyrannical power is *that great city which ftandeth on feven mountains,* and which, in the days of the prophecy, *reigned over all the kings of the earth.*—In fine,

" You fee the church of God fubfifting, at this day, in the world—the fame church which, before Chrift, was continued in the feed of Abraham, and which, at and after his coming, took that new form which Daniel faw under the name of the KINGDOM OF HEAVEN; and hath ever fince fubfifted among the Gentiles. You know the prefervation and final prevalence of this fociety, together with the hoftile attempts, and final ruin of all her enemies, have been predicted by all the prophets from Mofes to St. John.

" Now, when ye fee this very church prefent in exiftence and enlargement, after all the attempts which have been made, in all manner of ways, and through a long succession of ages, for her destruction; and notwithstanding she has all the seeds of desolation in herself, has often been extremely feeble, and in the hand of her enemies, and at the point of death: When you see this, you behold an event, which, though perfectly corresponding to hundreds of scripture-prophecies and promises, is yet UNPARALLELED IN THE HISTORY OF THE WORLD. Suffer me to repeat, IT IS UNPARALLELED IN THE HISTORY OF THE WORLD. The most unlikely event, when it was foretold, ever to have existed, and which indeed never could have existed, but by the marvellous providence of God, defeating the influence of natural causes, that he might fulfil the designs of his mercy—that he might *confirm the words of his servants, and perform the counsel of his messengers;* and, at the same time, that he might *frustrate the tokens of the liars, and make diviners mad,* and close the mouth of infidels in *perpetual silence.*

" Thus is the spirit of prophecy the testimony of Jehovah to the sacred scriptures as his OWN ORACLES, and to Jesus as the Christ, and of consequence to the Christian Religion AS DIVINE."

And where shall the ministers of Christ next turn their attention, in order successfully to carry on the purposes of this second, this inward and spiritual revolution of the heart?

Unless the great Michael of the church should aid, our hopes of success would be lost; but so long as we have his promise—*Lo, I am with you always, even to the end of the world*—we are encouraged to go on.

Let us, then, make our addresses to men of understanding—to men of sound judgment, and rectitude of heart, and solicit the force of their interest and example.

Let us even attempt to touch the ambition of the ambitious, by pointing them to the robes of distinction, and inconceivable marks of favor in the regions of glory, which await the man whom the king delights to honor.

Let us assail the castle of the miser, and tell him, that in the regions of glory are rivers of treasure, floods of salvation, a thousand fold more regaling to the appetites of the soul, than earthly substance can be to the body.

Let us guide the wandering views of the man of business, by setting before him the necessity of seeking *first the kingdom of God and his righteousness, that all these things* may be added.

May we not arouse the attention of the stupid, the obstinate, and sensual, by painting to them, in lively colours, the danger to which they are exposed, as well as the baseness of *earthly* and *sensual* gratifications, in comparison with those which are intellectual and heavenly?

May we not solicit the aid of the improved, the elevated, and the polite, by assuring them that a field of improvement, prospects of elevation, and the most finished examples of heavenly grace, are all presented to their embrace, in the pursuit of the rewards promised by our exalted king?

And, last of all, may we not, with high prospects of success, humbly suggest, that by the example and influence of the female world, even of the most delicate and refined, much might be done to further the purposes of heaven?—If any of our fair audience should say, " We have not yet learned the paths of piety ourselves: we are, alas! but too far from hope of setting good example to others, or of aiding the interests of virtue, by the feeble efforts of what, at best, can be only ſtiled the improvements of nature, deſtitute of the refinements of heavenly grace:"—Let us pray them to lend their hand to ſome guardian angel, who may lead them, perhaps, abroad to view the wondrous traces of wiſdom, and of power, in all creation's handy works; and when, from the oracles of truth, they become farther convinced of the being of a God—of his equitable, holy, juſt and good laws—of their own imperfections of heart and life—of their final accountableneſs at the bar of an impartial judge; they may be willing to follow their heavenly guide into the retirements of ſecret devotion, and there unboſom the ſoul to God, imploring the pardon and ablution of ſin, through the blood of the Lamb. What though a tear of contrition find its way, evincing the deep woundings of the heart, purſued by an upbraiding conſcience, for time and talents miſimproved—for neglect of God, the univerſal Creator—for neglect of the overtures of proffered mercy—for the grievings of the holy ſpirit of God, occaſioned by the pride of the heart, refuſing to bow to the ſceptre of ſovereign grace? What though, from cauſes like theſe, a tear of contrition might fall, and the boſom heave in sighs of penitence and prayer? If pardon for the soul, and acceptance with God should be the happy fruit, and a life of unexampled piety the permanent effects—how interesting the change—how promising the prospect!

With support of numbers, and example of graces such as these, with what success might the advocates of truth plead the cause of heaven, and how soon might we expect that in the place of unbelief, stupor, insensibility and hardness of heart; we should discover the seeds of the happy wished-for revolution already to be sown, and the effects to appear in full and abundant sheaves of heavenly grace!

But—whither do I run, leading my audience—fathers and brethren, it may be, into paths less promising than those in which they have been accustomed, successfully to tread!—I pause, then; nay, I draw to a conclusion by saying, in the words of a respected father in the church of God, on the subject of Ministerial Character and Duty,*—" It requires no small attention and labor to seek out fit and acceptable words, as the preacher expresses it, to stir up the attention of the

NOTE.
* Witherspoon, vol. i. A. P. page 19.

inconsiderate—to awaken, secure, and convince obstinate sinners—to unmask the covered hearts of hypocrites—to set right the erring, and encourage the fearful."

Notwithstanding this, may we not all, animated by the prospects of promised aid, go forth manfully, to fight the battles of the Lord—to play the man for God, and for the cities of our God; knowing that in our faithful exertions the name of the Lord is honored, though Israel be not gathered.

Finally, my brethren, " Have we seen the scriptures sealed by past events; let it exalt our faith into a full assurance, that all the prophecies which remain, and especially those which speak of JESUS' FUTURE GLORY, shall receive, in due time, their perfect accomplishment.

" This GRAND ÆRA is approaching with a speed rapid as the flight of time. The night is far spent, the day is at hand. In this prospect, with what ardour should we pray—THY KINGDOM COME;"* and in the fervency of our united devotions, may we

NOTE.
* Hinsdale, A. P. vol. iv. p. 133, 134.

not add—*thy will be done on earth, as it is done in heaven;* for *thine*, gracious God! *is the kingdom,* and thine is *the power,* and thine ſhall be the *glory,* world without end. AMEN.

END OF THE FIRST VOLUME.

PART I.

A Discourse by the Reverend Dr. Bellamy, founded on Revelation xx. 1, 2, 3. *And I saw an angel come down from heaven, having the key of the bottomless pit,* &c.

PAGE.
9. The Scriptures, by their Promises and Prophecies of good Things to come, are well calculated to keep alive the Faith of God's People in the Day of Trial.
21. A Summary of Promises respecting the Increase of the Redeemer's Kingdom.
23. When shall these Things be?
25. From the Faithfulness of God we have no Cause to daubt the Fulfilment of his gracious Promises to his People.
34. Human Mistakes, as to Time, no Bar in the Way of the final Event.
36. Because Christ once stiled his People a little Flock, it is no Sign they will always appear so.
42. Seventeen Thousand may be saved to one Soul finally lost.
44. God knows best when to bring these Things to pass.
45. A Veteran in the Service of God, animating the Followers of the Lamb.
48. Christ loves to have his Ministers and People faithful.
49. As David gathered Materials for the Temple, to be built in Solomon's Day, so we are to do our Endeavor to favor the great Building of God.

PART II.

A Treatise by the late learned and highly esteemed President Edwards, entitled, " An Humble Attempt to promote explicit Agreement and visible Union of God's People in extraordinary Prayer, for the Revival of Religion, and the Advancement of Christ's Kingdom on Earth, pursuant to Scripture-promises and Prophecies concerning the last Time"—founded on Zechariah viii. 20, 21, 22. *Thus saith the Lord of Hosts, It shall yet come to pass, that there shall come people, and the inhabitants of many cities:— And the inhabitants of one city shall go to another, saying, Let us go speedily to pray before the Lord, and to seek the Lord of Hosts:*

CONTENTS.

I will go also. Yea, many people and strong nations shall come to seek the Lord of Hosts in Jerusalem, and to pray before the Lord.

PAGE.
63. Text is opened, and Union in Prayer recommended.
81. An Account of the Concert for Prayer.
90. A Memorial from Scotland.

Motives to a Compliance with what is proposed in the Memorial.

97. The Latter-Day Glory not yet accomplished.
115. The great Glory of the latter Day.
122. The Holy Spirit the Sum of Christ's Purchase.
127. The latter Day, eminently the Day of Salvation.
130. How the Creation travaileth in Pain for that Day.
136. Scripture Precepts, Encouragements and Examples of Prayer for Christ's Kingdom.
156. Dispensations of Providence at this Day, present with many Motives to Prayer for it.
171. The Beauty and good Tendency of uniting in such Prayer.
176. The particular and great Encouragement in the Word of God to express Agreement in Prayer.

Objections answered.

179. No Superstition in the Case.
185. The Concert not whimsical.
198. The Concert not Pharisaical.
201. The slaying of the Witnesses considered.
237. The Fall of Antichrist approaching.
241. The Time not known beforehand.
246. The Time not at a very great Distance.
266. His Fall will be gradual.
276. Good reason to hope that that Work of God's Spirit will soon begin, which will, in its Progress, overthrow Antichrist and Satan's Kingdom on Earth.
Ibid. The sixth Vial probably now in fulfilling.
296. Antichrist's Ruin speedily follows it.
304. However if otherwise, yet our Prayer will not be in vain.
305. Such an Agreement in Prayer no new Thing.
The Duty of agreeing to pray no new Duty.
The like practised in 1712, with the wonderful Consequence.
311. The Conclusion.

CONTENTS.

PART III.

A Discourse by the Reverend Mr. Austin, entitled—The Downfall of MYSTICAL BABYLON; or, a Key to the Providence of God in the political Operations of 1793-4—founded on Revelation xviii. 20. *Rejoice over her thou heaven, and ye holy apostles and prophets; for God hath avenged you on her.*

PAGE.
328. All Holy Beings are called upon to rejoice in the Calamities which God brings on his and their Enemies.
330. Plan of the Discourse.
331. Prophetic Figures point us to Papal Rome, as the Object of the divine Decree.
336. A Parallel run between ancient Heathenish, and modern Antichristian Rome.
337. Sketch of the awful Persecutions of Papal Rome, in a note.
344. The two Witnesses.
350. The present is the Time of the slaying of the Witnesses, and affords a Key to the Cause of the present Dearth of Religion in many Parts of the Christian Church.
361. The Prophecies of Daniel, of St. Paul, and of St. John respecting Babylon brought to a Point.
365. Of the Rise, Continuance, and probable Destruction of this anti-christian Power.
371. Causes of this Disaster.
375. Means by which it shall be brought about.
388. The little Stone smiting the Image, and becoming itself a great Mountain.
393. Two great Revolutions to usher in the Latter-Day Glory; *outward* and *political*—*inward* and *spiritual*.
395. The foundation of universal Joy in the Prospect.
401. The Time of the Falling of the Stars of Heaven is come.
403. The Doctrine of the Millennium is true.
405. Duty of Ministers and Churches.
408. The Protestant Dragon.
413. The Hero of America on his Way to demolish the Usurpations of Protestant, Papal and Pagan Rome.
415. The Eagle and her Station.
416. The Dragon of Dragons, and his efforts against the Church of God.
417. Address to an Infidel.
421. ——— to Men of understanding.

421. Address to the Ambitious.
———— to the Miser.
———— to the Man of Business.
422. ———— to the Stupid and Obstinate.
———— to the Elevated and Polite.
Hopes from the Example and Influence of the Fair.
423. The Fair Penitent led by a Guardian Angel to the Throne of Grace.

ERRATUM.—Page 344, line 5, after the word *supposed*, add, *have prophesied in sackcloth.*

THE subscribing EDITOR to the AMERICAN PREACHER presents his most affectionate and Christian regards to all his Fathers and Brethren in the Ministry; and, especially, to those who have aided in contributing Materials for the Execution of the Plan of that Work thus far; and is happy in being able to assure them, that their Labors have been, to such a degree, acceptable to the Public, that scarcely a Copy of the three First Volumes is to be found for Sale; and repeated applications are made to the Printer for further supplies. The Fourth Volume is now circulating, and promises fair to secure, and to increase the Reputation of this, generally, interesting Work.

As the present is a Day full of great Events, and a general attention to the dictates of Prophecy seems to be gone forth, it is proposed, that a Volume of Discourses, on the Subject of Prophecy, with particular application to Predictions now fulfilling, or yet to be fulfilled, shall be prepared, and issued, perhaps, at the close of the present Year.

Any of our Christian Brethren, who would contribute to the Execution of such a Plan, might be instrumental in reviving the Cause of Truth—in animating their Brethren, and of comforting the Church of God; and would receive the most grateful Acknowledgments from the Friends and Promoters of the proposed Volume.

Shortly will be put to Press a Volume of Discourses, preached on occasion of the late Visitation of the City of Philadelphia by the Yellow Fever, entitled, "A Comment on the Providence of God, in the late Visitation of the City of Philadelphia, by the Yellow Fever: or, Instructive Lessons to the People of the United States, on the Subject of that solemn Event, comprised, in a Number of Discourses, preached by several Ministers of Christ, on that Occasion, who are willing to leave this Testimony as a Memorial of the tragical Scene which gave it Birth."

Any of our Christian Ministers, who are willing to aid in the furtherance of either of the foregoing Designs, may be assured that their Contributions will meet a most friendly welcome, and be duly noticed in View of forwarding the Design for which they may be sent.

ELIZABETH TOWN, *May* 1, 1794.

www.ingramcontent.com/pod-product-compliance
Lightning Source LLC
Chambersburg PA
CBHW051738300426
44115CB00007B/618